CYBERSPACES OF EVERYDAY LIFE

ELECTRONIC MEDIATIONS

Katherine Hayles, Mark Poster, and Samuel Weber, series editors

ELECTRONIC MEDIATIONS   VOLUME 19

CYBERSPACES
OF EVERYDAY LIFE

MARK NUNES

UNIVERSITY OF MINNESOTA PRESS

MINNEAPOLIS • LONDON

Earlier versions of the material in this book were originally published in the following essays. "Baudrillard in Cyberspace: Internet, Virtuality, and Postmodernity," *Style* 29 (1995): 314–27; reprinted with permission. "Distributed Terror and the Ordering of Networked Social Space," *M/C Journal: A Journal of Media and Culture* 7.6 (2005); http://journal.mediaculture.org.au; reprinted with permission. "Ephemeral Cities: Postmodern Urbanism and the Production of Online Space," in *Virtual Globalization: Virtual Spaces/Tourist Spaces,* edited by David Holmes (London: Routledge, 2001), 57–75; reprinted with permission from Taylor and Francis Group. "Virtual Topographies: Smooth and Striated Cyberspace," in *Cyberspace Textuality: Computer Technology and Literary Theory,* edited by Marie-Laure Ryan (Bloomington and Indianapolis: Indiana University Press, 1999), 61–77; reprinted with permission. "What Space Is Cyberspace? The Internet and Virtuality," in *Virtual Politics: Identity and Community in Cyberspace,* edited by David Holmes (London: Sage, 1997), 163–78; copyright 1997 Mark Nunes; reprinted by permission of Sage Publications Ltd.

Excerpt from "Slip" by Maegan "la Mala" Ortiz; copyright 2002; reprinted by permission of the author. For complete poem see http://mamitamala.blogspot.com/2005_02_01_mamitamala_archive.html.

Published by the University of Minnesota Press
111 Third Avenue South, Suite 290, Minneapolis, MN 55401-2520
http://www.upress.umn.edu

LIBRARY OF CONGRESS CATALOGING-IN-PUBLICATION DATA
Nunes, Mark, 1965–
Cyberspaces of everyday life / Mark Nunes.
p. cm. — (Electronic mediations ; v. 19)
Includes bibliographical references and index.
ISBN-13: 978-0-8166-4791-0 (hc : alk. paper)   ISBN-10: 0-8166-4791-7 (hc : alk. paper)
ISBN-13: 978-0-8166-4792-7 (pb : alk. paper)   ISBN-10: 0-8166-4792-5 (pb : alk. paper)
1. Telematics.   2. Cyberspace.   3. Social networks.   I. Title.
TK5105.6.N86   2006
303.48'34—dc22   2006018870

Printed in the United States of America on acid-free paper
The University of Minnesota is an equal-opportunity educator and employer.

12 11 10 09 08 07 06   10 9 8 7 6 5 4 3 2 1

To my father, who brought a computer
home twenty-five years ago,
and to my mother, who finally
has an email address.

CONTENTS

ACKNOWLEDGMENTS

THIS BOOK is the result of more than a decade of work and play on computer networks. As a formal project, it began as a dissertation through Emory University's Graduate Institute of the Liberal Arts, under the care and guidance of Cindy Patton, John Johnston, and Allen Tullos. I owe a debt of gratitude to each of my readers for their challenging feedback and engaged support. I also owe thanks to the University of Virginia's Institute for Advanced Technology in the Humanities and, in particular, former director John Unsworth for giving me the resources to experiment with online scholarly forms. I would also like to thank the PMC-MOO diaspora, especially Shawn Wilbur and Heather Wagner, for their hours of online exchange. My former institution, Georgia Perimeter College, consistently supported my research, providing me with time and resources to develop my ideas and bring them to a wider audience.

A number of individuals helped to shape this project into its current form. Ken Hillis at the University of North Carolina, Chapel Hill, provided valuable and insightful commentary on early drafts. At the University of Minnesota Press, Doug Armato, as well as series editors Mark Poster, Kate Hayles, and Sam Weber, offered support and guidance of the project from its inception. Gretchen Asmussen and Laura Westlund answered a number of technical questions along the way and helped make my first book a straightforward task. I owe thanks as well to Jeni Henrickson and Mike Stoffel for their care and attention in preparing the final manuscript.

Above all else, I thank my wife, Marti Bailey Nunes, and my children, Matthew, Joshua, and Hayleigh, who tolerated long nights, lost weekends, and numerous other disruptions to our everyday life during the past ten years.

INTRODUCTION

NETWORKS, SPACE, AND EVERYDAY LIFE

I N A SINGLE GENERATION, network technology has radically altered everyday life in the developed world. The proof is the degree to which networks now pass unnoticed in daily life. Cyberspace, once a reference in a subgenre of science fiction, now marks a set of relations to computer-mediated communication (CMC) covering a range of everyday functions. More accurately, perhaps, we might say that the network itself defines and delimits "the everyday." While theorists once hypothesized the significance of an emerging world of "virtual sex" and online infidelity, mainstream media outlets now advertise digital dating services that promise to connect users with their ideal partners. While few of us have taken part in fully immersive virtual reality conferencing, email increasingly functions as the dominant mode of exchange, both in the workplace and in private life, at the same time that "anti-spamming" and "anti-phishing" laws have become a legislative priority. And in the most recent U.S. election, the Internet, rather than functioning merely as a point of rhetoric in the presidential debates, served instead as a dynamic arena for grassroots communication, fund-raising, mudslinging, and conspiracy building.

For the generation of students entering college in fall 2006, network connections have been as common a feature of their education as library cards. There is nothing futuristic about the Internet for these students. Rather, it marks a rather mundane feature of daily life. Increasingly, colleges are moving institutional functions to the Web, some (my own, for example) no longer printing a paper copy of the schedule of classes. Students registering for classes must interact with the catalog electronically, registering via networks from any computer running a Web browser. As a result, students are now introduced to networks *before* their first day of class, marking this mode of exchange as a precursor to any other definition of social space through the institutional structure of the college. Likewise, corporations increasingly expect a degree of network literacy that, if lacking, marks a kind of severe deficiency. Few sectors, from retail to manufacturing to professional, do not structure daily activities around network exchanges. Today, Internet access has penetrated everyday life in America and elsewhere around a networked globe. While we have hardly reached universal access—and "the Web" is hardly worldwide—Web-site addresses have become as common as trademark logos in the commercial world, and email has far surpassed the U.S. Postal Service in number of daily correspondences. To speak of CMC as a distinct facet of everyday life has become to some degree redundant to the extent that networks now penetrate the spaces of everyday life at a fundamental level.

Prior to 1990, the Internet served primarily as an email and file transfer system for academics and researchers across the United States. By the middle of the decade, the fabric of this medium had undergone two significant changes: commercial use, once forbidden across the U.S.-based backbone, had begun to outpace academic use; and with the growing popularity of the World Wide Web (WWW), a graphical, "point-and-click" interface became the dominant cybernetic vehicle for navigating Internet sites. The Internet maintained a phenomenal growth rate throughout the 1990s, from around 300,000 "host sites" at the start of the decade to more than 72 million by January 2000 (Internet Systems Consortium, "Internet Domain Survey, Jul 2004").[1] But this material expansion alone cannot account for the increasing presence of networked computers in elementary and secondary schools in the United States, or the appearance of Internet kiosks and electronic coffee shops worldwide.

Nor can it account for the explosive growth in capital investment in Internet companies, and, more generally, e-commerce, during 1998 and 1999.[2] While the "bubble" burst in March 2000, and along with it much of the media euphoria proclaiming the revolutionary (or catastrophic) potential of the Internet, the forms, structures, and practices of contemporary culture of the current decade continue to suggest an increasingly altered terrain of everyday life in a network society.

The sorts of human-computer interactions (HCI) that have become increasingly common in developed countries worldwide have made networked computers nearly ubiquitous. Consider, for example, the following scenarios:

An American college student sits in a computer lab learning a spreadsheet application. His accounting professor is giving a demonstration on cutting and pasting functions. The student opens up a separate window running a telnet application, which allows him to log into a multi-user gaming site—not unlike an elaborate set of chat rooms. He runs into an acquaintance of his, who lives in France, and the two have a casual conversation in real time.

An expectant mother receives a lab result that indicates an elevated hormone level. Her OB informs her that she has a statistically increased chance of complications in pregnancy or at birth. At home that night, she visits a commercial Web site targeted at parents and parents-to-be. She reads up on her test and what the results mean. She follows a link to a bulletin board where dozens of women have posted their own experiences with the unreliability of hormone-level tests.

A sales representative at an international convention in London is expecting a crucial piece of email from her director. Around the corner from her hotel, she notices a sandwich and coffee shop with a public computer terminal. She deposits a £1 coin in the slot and buys twenty minutes of Internet time. Using a Web-based interface, she accesses her email. After catching up on her correspondences, she uses her remaining minutes to read the headlines of an online version of her hometown newspaper.

None of these instances of CMC seems far-fetched, and, while hardly describing the daily experience of every individual in a developed country, such experiences with CMC and HCI suggest the emergence of networked structures within the spaces and places of everyday life. In each instance, the user interacts with networked technology as a medium rather than as a computational device. Indeed, it would seem that this past decade's fascination with information technology has grown from the power of the computer to function as a communication medium and social environment rather than from its capacity as a processor.[3] Note that in each of the examples above, CMC and HCI involve a form of spatiality of "sites," "addresses," and "rooms"; unlike the spatial language invoked in "surfing" television channels or "skipping up and down" the radio dial, where movement involves the user's operational relation to the device itself, CMC employs a language of entry and travel that positions the user *within* the medium, such that the user and not the device becomes operationalized. The ubiquity of the computer as a site of network interface foregrounds the degree to which "the network" now serves as an organizing concept for the spaces of everyday life. This sense of space is an integral part of the growing presence of the Internet in the daily lives of individuals around the developed world, and it parallels a shift in our understanding of computers as media rather than as computational tools.

There is something compelling in this description of CMC in terms of space. As the word "medium" implies, the computer increasingly serves as an environment for its users, not as an implement. Certainly, one could argue that the conflation of space and communication devices has a history that recedes back perhaps as far as the history of empires, roads, and delivery routes. But unlike earlier media, CMC "overcomes" space; the user experiences the medium itself as a spatial network—that is, as a space of interconnections. Perhaps we might date the beginning of this sense of space back to the telegraph operators of the nineteenth century, the first to experience the mediated presence of electronic communication that would become increasingly common in the twentieth century.[4] Electronic media of the last 150 years provided an experience of "bridging" or "connecting" remote locations, or it created a sense of community among a mass audience of (supposedly) like-minded individuals. Certainly the spatiality of CMC, captured in the popular and scholarly use of the term "cyberspace," takes part in this history, but at the same time, the experience of the medium as an environment became markedly more compelling—and more problematic—with the growing popularity of the computer as a communication device. In part, this shift emerges to the degree that the hand becomes involved in communication, in concert with both the eye and the ear. Movement is no longer limited to an initiating act (setting a dial), but instead *enacts* the user's relation to the medium itself.

In this sense, then, perhaps the first account of cyberspace appears in Vannevar Bush's 1945 description of the information user seated in the midst of a "memex" device, tracing paths of information from one record to the next. As an actual technical feat, Douglas Engelbart's development of "bitmapping" in the late 1960s provides another critical moment in HCI that placed the user *within* an information space.[5] With the inception of graphical user interfaces (GUIs), the space of the screen became an environment that the user could navigate by way of a mouse: a McLuhanite extension of the hand "into" the medium itself. Likewise, Ted Nelson's contemporaneous description of a hypertextual "docuverse" of information suggested the computer's potential to create an informational *environment:* a spatialized network of interconnected nodes traversed by a user. This history of HCI is, in some measure, a history of this spatializing impulse that places the user in a cybernetic zone of interaction, "steering" through a network of links. And with as many as 200 million users in the United States, and a billion worldwide, this experience of CMC in spatial terms has become an increasingly familiar feature of everyday life.[6]

As the commercial and public use of the Internet grew exponentially in the 1990s, the term "cyberspace" began to occur with greater frequency and encompassed a greater range of meanings as shorthand for the neither-here-nor-there experience of place produced during online interactions. True, the word "cyberspace" first appeared in the 1980s science-fiction work of William Gibson, most notably his 1984 novel *Neuromancer;* but it was not until the 1990s that it became a powerful cultural trope—first in America and then spreading virally elsewhere. And perhaps the First Conference on Cyberspace, held in 1990, and the proceedings that appeared the following year as *Cyberspace: First Steps,* should serve as the events that heralded the "dawn of cyberspace." This collection of speculative and technical essays took seriously the potential for computers and networks to generate robust information spaces, and, for many CMC theorists to follow, it served as a touchstone text in discussions of cyberspace. In a similar fashion, Pavel Curtis's LambdaMOO, brought online to the public in January 1991, provided an early articulation of cyberspace that shaped much of the discussion of the spatiality of CMC in the first half of the 1990s. While MUDs (Multi-User Dungeons or Dimensions) and MOOs (MUD, Object-Oriented) are today hardly the mainstream phenomena of MTV's chat rooms, these text-based environments attracted a number of critical inquiries in the 1990s precisely for the reason that they consciously emulated (albeit in words) immersive worlds. This concept of cyberspace as an immersive, virtual world would inform much of the popular and academic discussion of the potentials of CMC for the first half of the 1990s.

With the rise of the WWW and first-generation graphical browsers, networked communication figured even more prominently as an "environment" in which CMC would, quite literally, *take place*. By the mid-1990s, Web addresses and sites—*places* to visit—had begun to figure as an important part of corporate marketing.[7] At the same time that a growing awareness of AOL's chat rooms, Internet-based IRCs, and various other modes of real-time CMC created a sense of cyberspace as an immersive, communicative environment (popularized in films such as Irwin Winkler's 1995 thriller *The Net*), the exponential growth of the WWW, in size and in popular uptake, suggested the arrival of a new, digital frontier, an ever-expanding hypertextual terrain navigated by and staked out for the interactive user.[8] As such, cyberspace of the mid-1990s offered the exhilarating and foreboding image of a mediated social space that was no longer geographically determined and that placed "the world" at the user's fingertips, just a point-and-click away. The possibility of remote doctor consultations (or even surgical procedures), real-time professional conferences, and electronic "town hall" meetings created a vision of cyberspace as the conquest of geography by networked technology. It is in this environment that the White House's 1994 "Agenda for Action" could promise "the best schools, teachers, and courses . . . available without regard to geography, distances, resources, or disability. . . .The vast resources of art, literature, and science . . . available everywhere." A decade later, many of those euphoric predictions seem distant. At the same time, however, a significant portion of everyday life for a growing number of individuals involves a form of networked social space, articulated through a zone of interaction marked by a human-computer interface. Chat rooms have proliferated, not so much as replacements for civic space but as sites of media fusions, such as CNN's "The Spin Room"[9] and MTV's "Total Request Live," in which media figures and pundits interact with "viewers," who are engaged in their own Web-based forum simultaneous to the show. For a growing number of users, Web pages increasingly function as both public archives (a place for accessing tax forms, gathering product information, etc.) and private ledgers (the site for transferring funds, paying bills, etc.). And as scenes of media production, the Web increasingly blurs the lines between "objective" journalism and personal weblog, expert opinion and firsthand experience. Without question, cyberspace has become a matter of everyday life in what we might tentatively call a network society,[10] but in articulations that bear little resemblance to the euphoric dreams and dystopic nightmares of the preceding decade.

Getting Personal(ized)

This volume, *Cyberspaces of Everyday Life*, takes part in a "second generation" of books on the social, political, and cultural impact of CMC. It attempts to theorize cyberspace as lived space, both as it emerged in the 1990s and in its current articulations. As such, one cannot avoid a certain degree of abstraction in an attempt to construct a theoretically coherent understanding of the forms, structures, and practices of CMC. At the same time, however, it would seem somewhat disingenuous not to acknowledge that the "one" who cannot avoid this abstracting tendency is also a user of CMC, situated in very specific social, cultural, and experiential contexts: to acknowledge, in other words, that the "one" is *me*. A gesture toward the personal seems particularly justified in an account of cyberspace to the extent that the dominant formations of CMC as social space foreground a personalized (and privatized, in Williams's sense) experience of the medium. From the user's desktop (with its "My Documents" folder) to the cookie-driven Web page that customizes its content and appearance to match a user's profile, *preferences* increasingly function as a code-level determinant of both the user interface and the universe of information in which it interacts. Cyberspace, as such, is always *my* cyberspace (although I may not recognize it as such). The autoethnographic, the anecdotal, and the personal comment provide a critical intervention of its own sort, one that can counteract an all too common tendency in theory to misrecognize a blindness to situatedness as a form of "objectivity" or neutrality.[11]

For me, cyberspace "began" back in 1993, when I found myself logging onto a "PC-clone" computer in the Humanities Department workroom of DeKalb College, nestled between a Scantron machine for reading multiple-choice tests and a photocopier prone to paper jams. Using a telnet application to connect remotely to a computer in North Carolina, I was attempting to log onto an interactive database called PMC-MOO—my first encounter (to keep up with the autoethnographic theme) with *being online* in a "text-based virtual reality." *Wired* had just published its third issue, in which it ran a piece on MUDs titled "The Dragon Ate My Homework," with a sidebar mentioning PMC-MOO. I was intrigued. At that point, the workroom housed the only computer in the Humanities Department with an Internet connection. Most of us had desktop computers capable of running word processing software, but few of us had any need or interest in regular use of email. Within my department, long before the rise of online education or "humanities computing," I was somewhat of a rare breed in my familiarity with the interface. Computers had been in my life from a rather young age, dating back to 1977, when I had access to a ticker-tape DEC computer donated to my middle school by the Digital Equipment Corporation, headquartered just a few miles down the road. My family purchased a home computer in 1979—an Apple II+ with a cassette recorder attachment for saving programs (back when computers ran programs instead of *applications*). I learned the basics of BASIC, for the most part writing simple games. In my affluent, suburban high school, we had a well-equipped computer lab consisting of a dozen or so dumb terminals connected to a networked PDP-11. I had my first access to the Internet through that computer, but with no one to email, and with no need for transferring files, the network meant very little to me.

I had some interaction with computers during the 1980s: my first social exchanges using email; telnetting to the University of California, Berkeley, to play *Adventure*; writing freelance articles for a Unix trade magazine. For the most part, these moments stood at the periphery of my daily life. But by the early 1990s that relationship began to change, and change in a manner that would call increasing attention to the position of the network in spaces of everyday life. When I began to log onto PMC-MOO, I wasn't exactly sure what I was experiencing. It was clear to me, though, that the medium, while paralleling many features of the telephone, radio, or television, engaged me in a set of relations that did not easily reduce to the experience of any precursor medium. I found myself thinking more and more critically about my interactions with(in) the medium, eventually drafting a piece titled "Baudrillard in Cyberspace." In that piece, I argued that in real-time environments such as MUDs and MOOs, CMC allows for the production of a "hyperreal"[12] simulation of a comprehensive and comprehendible world, a model of the Enlightenment project that surpasses the real. Since the hyperreal only answers to its own system of logic, resistance could only take the form of a seduction that leads that system to its fatal ends: an "ironic revenge" that short-circuits its metaphysics of the code.[13] I argued that cyberspace contains the potential for this sort of short circuit of modernity's construction of the subject, community, and identity. The piece appeared simultaneously in print through the journal *Style* and online on my newly created Web page. Much as my encounters within PMC-MOO helped to formulate my early ideas about virtual worlds, my first experience with Web publication had a significant influence on my developing sense of the viral nature of hypertextuality. The range and number of linkages that developed in a matter of months—and developed without any further action on my part—suggested a mode of dissemination that was of a different order from paper publication. I began thinking about how institutional structures of the academy, from the undergraduate classroom to the tenure review board, were increasingly implicated in—and articulated by—a spatiality of the network. I became interested in trying to understand how it is that networks function in contemporary society, and how it is that networks structure everyday life.

My ideas about the spaces of CMC have altered somewhat since first writing "Baudrillard in Cyberspace," but in many ways this current volume marks a culminating moment in what has been nearly a decade of trying to come to terms with articulations of "the network" in everyday life. To some degree, I spend fewer hours today engaged in online exchanges than I once did. At the same time, the network has become all the more integrated into my daily life. The interface, as that zone of personalized and privatized interaction with global networks, now travels with me all the more easily through wireless laptops and Web-ready cell phones. The hallucinatory quality of cyberspace may have worn off, but in its very banality, the degree to which the spatiality of the network penetrates daily life suggests a significant shift in social space. To some degree, then, the chapters of this book map a critical trajectory that is also a personal trajectory. In its more theoretical and abstracted engagements, I am attempting to provide a framework for understanding how it is that we might make sense of CMC in terms that address its *place* in everyday life. In doing so, I am specifically attempting to theorize both "media" and "space" in a manner that is to some degree abstracted from everyday experience of these terms. But in order to achieve this, I increasingly found myself turning toward my own relation to CMC, either explicitly, through first-person address and anecdotal account, or implicitly, through my choice of Web sites reflecting major life events (www.babycenter.com) or the idiosyncrasies of personal history (www.concordjournal.com). This book maps that process in a way that, rather than detracting from the theoretical material, speaks to a very specific form of critical engagement.

Notes toward a Spatial Analysis of CMC

When friends and colleagues ask me about my work, I typically respond by saying that I write about "cyberspace," hoping that the term holds enough cultural capital to suggest the general field of my research. When pushed, I try to explain that I am interested in theorizing how network technology produces social space. To this statement, I typically get the response: "Space? Well, of course, there's no real space there, is there?" The response is quite understandable, given that our everyday understanding of space treats "space itself" as an emptiness awaiting objects. But as I will elaborate in the first chapter, in order to begin discussing cyberspace as space, it is essential that we become willing to rethink the nature of space, or rather, *denature* our dominant assumptions about space. It is easy enough to get the "average" Internet user to understand cyberspace as a metaphor. One might even be willing to admit to an understanding of cyberspace as a *mental space* of ideas. But *real* space, our everyday experience tells us, defines itself through a world of objects—by giving place to objects. Yet, at the same time, our everyday experience of spatiality admits to a sense of space in which bodily dispositions and daily social practices determine one's own relation to space itself. Not only am I situated *in space;* I *situate* space through my *lived incorporations and articulations of space.* Our own understanding of social space is predicated upon *relation,* enacted in material form, conceptual structure, and lived practice. But rather than treating *social* space as a special case of a more general ontological category, I would argue that the relational processes that take part in the production of social space are likewise implicated in all modes of spatiality. "Cyberspace," therefore, brings to the foreground both our assumptions about the nature of space and the ways in which our everyday experiences of space undermine these same assumptions.

In developing my critical vocabulary to analyze space, I owe a great deal to the work of Henri Lefebvre, and in particular to his book *The Production of Space,* which became a cornerstone of sorts for a variety of postmodern studies in the 1990s.[14] Rather than presenting a synopsis of the argument I develop in chapter 1, it is worth acknowledging in this introduction the degree to which Lefebvre's work marks a shift in critical theory, particularly in France. Starting with Henri Bergson, much of twentieth-century continental philosophy focused on temporality as an active, vital domain, treating space as inert, inactive, and critically uninteresting. While Bergson began the century by turning philosophy away from a spatial logic and toward a sense of temporality, Lefebvre's work returns us to a critique of the assumptions of Cartesian and Kantian space, with the intention of rescuing space as a critical field of study. Lefebvre marks a decisive break from Bergson in French thought by refusing to treat space as passive and inactive. In contrast to Bergson, Lefebvre's entire analysis of space demands an understanding of space as a dynamic process involving material forms, conceptual structures, and lived practice. Lefebvre sees two traditions of thought that have dominated modernity's understanding of space. In an empiricist tradition, space functions as a container for *res extensa:* bodies and objects. In a mentalist/idealist tradition, space is "in mind," a conceptual structuring of *res cogitans:* signs and discourse. In contrast to either tradition, Lefebvre argues that space is neither solely a conceptual structuring, nor is it an a priori emptiness that simply awaits the arrival of objects. For Lefebvre, one can understand space only in terms of a dialectical relation between differing modes of spatial production. More specifically, he maintains that space is produced by and productive of a dynamic interplay of material, conceptual, and experiential processes. Lefebvre's analysis allows for a critical approach to metaphorical and material space that recognizes the complex relation between the two. But even this account of space is incomplete, as it loses sight of the everydayness of space—its lived component. In this regard, his spatial analysis is neither materialist nor idealist, claiming a dialectical relation between the material and conceptual that is also inseparable from an account of lived spatial practice. As such, Lefebvre's spatial analysis provides an important critical foundation for a spatial analysis of "cyberspace," in which the relation between materiality and metaphoricity is particularly problematic.

All of Lefebvre's critical theory rests upon the assertion that space is a social product. As such, Lefebvre sets up a domain for spatial analysis that clearly breaks with Cartesian and Kantian traditions. With Descartes, space as *res extensa* remains separate and untouched by *res cogitans.* This dualism establishes a radical separation between a mental, living realm of being and a mechanistic, material realm of space. Likewise, Kant treats space as a priori to phenomena: a container for the contained. This Cartesian-Kantian tradition provides an ontological foundation for a "scientific" view of space that remains dominant into the twentieth century.[15] Bergson's critique of spatial reasoning is specifically a critique of Cartesian-Kantian space as applied to a domain of vitality, defined as (and in effect limited to) an experience of *durée.* But in the same way that Bergson "rescues" time from space through phenomenology, Lefebvre attempts to rescue space from modernity through dialectics, placing it once again in a domain of vital, dynamic relations. As Edward Soja notes in his critique of modern geography, the Cartesian-Kantian tradition "treat[s] space as the domain of the dead, the fixed, the undialectical, the immobile—a world of passivity and measurement rather than action and meaning" (37). By breaking with a Cartesian and Kantian logic of space, Lefebvre opens the door for an analysis of space as a dynamic process.

To apply Lefebvre to CMC would mean to acknowledge that any spatial analysis of cyberspace must be able to account for a dynamic relation of material form, conceptual representation, and dispositional practice that produces networked social space. While the "metonymic error" of materialism treats space as a self-evident material presence, the "metaphoric error" of idealism treats space strictly as a semiotic field (Lefebvre, *The Production of Space* 98). In contrast, Lefebvre calls attention to the necessary relation between representation and materiality in social space, as enacted by the "users" who inhabit and embody this space.[16] This emphasis on the lived anchors Lefebvre's spatial analysis by continually forcing an examination of the produced-and-producing relation between material and conceptual processes. A spatial analysis of CMC must acknowledge that cyberspace involves a range of material processes that include, in part, its spread as a network of unequal development; the screen, keyboard, and mouse of the computer itself; the presence of these interface devices at home, in public institutions, and out on the street. Cyberspace also involves processes of representation such as its image in the media as marketplace, agora, frontier, and public sphere; the use of spatial language (locatives, place-names, "sites," etc.) on the Web; its function as a networked, signifying system for a "global society." Finally, cyberspace also involves a range of experiential processes that embody this space, including a restructuring of the "workday" through email memos, intranets, telecommuting, and outsourcing; media consumption—and production—in a hypertextual environment; access to global networks and databases for financial, commercial, and civic transactions; a redefinition of social contact as interaction and transmission. We cannot treat cyberspace merely as a metaphor, nor can we reduce it to a material production that, in Lefebvre's words "propounds and presupposes" its spatial practice (*The Production of Space* 38). Instead we find ourselves mapping a complex interrelation of metaphor, materiality, and "everyday life." In the attempt to create online democratic forums and electronic auction houses, home-page free-speech platforms and Listserv confessionals, the metaphorical writing of space involves itself in an intricate interplay with both the material and the lived. An analysis of these "virtual topographies" reveals something richer than a metaphorics of space; it suggests instead the lived practices that embody these representations and material relations.

We should be wary of falling into a false choice between what Lefebvre calls the illusion of transparency and the realistic illusion (*The Production of Space* 27–30): on one hand, the idealist wants to map a perfect correspondence between mental and material structures; on the other, the materialist imagines a "true" space uncorrupted by representations. Instead we find an interaction between the two: an interaction that is *enacted in practice*. Thus, Lefebvre's spatial analysis breaks us from the habits of abstraction and forces us to think about space in these dynamic terms. Certainly cyberspace has all the potential to become the mentalist abstraction ne plus ultra. Likewise, in the "space of flows" (to use Manuel Castells's term) set up by a global network capitalism, one can imagine a cyberspace void of lived experience, defined only in terms of a material network and a ceaseless flow of business-to-business transactions. But any spatial analysis of the dynamics of cyberspace must also address the lived practices of a growing number of individuals who count electronic correspondence, browsing and searching for information, ludic acts of real-time games and MP3 file exchanges, etc., as part of the banalities of everyday life. Whatever politics of cyberspace we are to locate, it will have to take into account the kinds of material, conceptual, and experiential processes that are caught up in the production of social space in a "network society." Are we engaged in the production of new spaces and new social relations, or merely simulating social structures in a hyperreal form? How does our experience of the global and the local, the public and the private, alter in a network society? What is the significance of outsourcing and "virtual classrooms" in the production of social space? These sorts of questions provide a context for an analysis of cyberspace that would have been equally crucial for Lefebvre: the context of everyday life. Space is not a thing, Lefebvre insists, but a social process. Likewise, we find that cyberspace is not where we go with network technology, but how we live it. And indeed, we are already living it.

Living Cyberspace

In attempting a spatial analysis of CMC, in part I am attempting to map a sense of the lived onto the Internet. A strictly materialist rendering of space would force us to understand the experience of being online as profoundly aspatial, or conversely, limited to the material interface of the computer itself. In pursuing a spatial analysis, however, I am suggesting that there is a basis for understanding space itself as experiential, and the networks of space as lived experience. In discussing the "everyday," I am well aware that I am writing within a genealogy of sorts that owes much, once again, to the work of Henri Lefebvre. Lefebvre's work on the everyday attempted to locate the quotidian within a theoretical framework (Marxist or post-Marxist) that resisted the scale necessary to embrace lived experience. Art, philosophy, and literature of the twentieth century, he claimed, attempted to erase everyday experience as such. The goal of a "critique of everyday life" would be to liberate the possibilities for social and cultural forms that elude the dominant structures of society—possibilities already at root in the practices of daily life. Toward the conclusion of the first volume of *Critique of Everyday Life,* Lefebvre describes the "programme" for such a critique as:

(a) [...] A methodical confrontation of so-called "modern" life on the one hand, with the past, and on the other—and above all—with *the possible*

(b) [...] A criticism of the trivial by the exceptional—*but at the same time* criticism of the exceptional by the trivial, of the "elite" by the mass—of festival, dreams, art and poetry, by reality

(c) [...] A confrontation of effective human reality with its "expression": moral doctrines, psychology, philosophy, religion, literature

(d) [A study of] the relations between groups and individuals in everyday life [that] interact in a manner which in part escapes the specialized sciences (1.251–52)

Much of what Lefebvre set out both in his later urban studies and in his more generalized program of spatial analysis calls upon a similar critical methodology: to enunciate terms of the possible within the structures of everyday life, specifically marked by those moments that fall beyond the rationalizing impulses of the social sciences or urban planning.

In a recent article, Mark Poster presents an analysis of Lefebvre's use of "everyday life," with specific interest in its usefulness as a critical intervention in the context of a contemporary life saturated by CMC and other media. In his analysis, he notes the degree to which the everyday stands for Lefebvre as a kind of "residual" to the dominant structures of society, culture, and politics ("Everyday (Virtual) Life" 746). Yet, in Lefebvre's faith in the everyday as a locus of a totalizing "humanity," Poster finds a critical shortcoming that fails to acknowledge the constructedness and situatedness of subject-positions (746–48). He concludes that any "theory of the quotidian" must provide for a critical account of "the specific cultural mechanisms through which the subject is constituted, and by which the subject constitutes the world" (748). I would agree with much of Poster's critique of Lefebvre, in particular his understanding of the everyday as a residual to dominant social structures and cultural narratives. In my own account of the everyday, I am particularly interested in how Lefebvre's spatial analysis frames this term as a process of practice—as the lived articulations that *give body* to space. Rather than falling into an easy humanism, I am apt to think of the everyday specifically in terms of embodied spaces—as the dispositional practices that provide a lived experience of both the material forms and the conceptual structures involved in the production of space. Donna Haraway's discussion of situatedness, Pierre Bourdieu's analysis of habitus, and Judith Butler's use of performative materialization become, in the context of this book, critical interventions in a spatial analysis of everyday life in a network society. As a residual, then, the everyday maps both the dominant articulations of social space (a passivity, in Lefebvre's terms), as well as a form of abjectness in the face of the dominant processes that aim to shape and regulate lived articulations of social space. In analyzing the spaces of everyday life, I am attempting to address how dispositional practices serve as situated sites for the production of cyberspace.

Overview

In attempting to address how network structures take part in spaces of everyday life, I am particularly interested in understanding what is often treated as inconsequential or "trivial"—double clicks and key strokes—as measures of an embodiment of social space. I am also concerned with the ways in which large challenges to ontological categories of social space—the public and the private, the global and the local—are played out not in theoretical accounts, but in lived, daily experience.

In the first chapter, "The Problem of Cyberspace," I attempt to sketch out the emerging field of scholarship that has addressed the spatiality of CMC. I identify a tendency in CMC scholarship to perpetuate a form of dualism that separates cyberspace from real space, treating it as a conceptual structure. In doing so, such criticism has failed to address the problem of space raised by cyberspace—namely, the difficulty one has in *locating* space itself. The chapter assesses the difficulties posed by this dualist approach and attempts to reassert the inseparability of materiality and conceptual structure in both the spaces of communication and the spaces of everyday life. It builds upon this critique and asserts a theoretical framework through which to consider the reality of cyberspace as lived space. By drawing on a view of space as relational and dynamic, rather than as abstract and passive, I attempt to rethink space as an event produced by material, conceptual, and experiential processes. An examination of conceptual structures, material forms, and lived practices reveals that cyberspace is indeed enacted in heterogeneous and heteromorphic spaces of everyday life. Furthermore, a critical analysis of these processes reveals the productive relation of each in the other. In other words, one cannot reduce a discussion of the production of social space to a privileged analysis of any one material, conceptual, or experiential process. Finally, this examination suggests that these heteromorphic virtual topographies do not coordinate into any overall system, but rather interpenetrate each other, producing "spaces in conflict."

The remaining three chapters apply this theoretical construct to specific articulations of social space in a network society. Chapter 2, "Virtual Worlds and Situated Spaces," examines how Web pages construct sites that enact spaces of control for their users and, in doing so, take part in a history of conceiving of the world as a comprehensive, comprehendible whole. In addition to these monadic "virtual worlds," one can also find spaces that situate everyday life in spaces that open up to aberrant lines of thought and highly situated accounts of what it means to "be" online. As such, these interpenetrating articulations of cyberspace suggest altered relations between the "global" and the "local" in a network society. Chapter 3, "Email, the Letter, and the Post," provides a comparative media analysis of the rise of the British postal system in the seventeenth century and the growth of email as a common medium of exchange. It examines how these media take part in the production of social space that is never limited to the "confines" of the medium itself. In the same way that the medium of postal exchange maps the shifting social spaces of the seventeenth and eighteenth centuries, the rise and spread of email as a dominant medium suggests an altered relation between the public and the private in a contemporary networked world. Chapter 4, "Student Bodies," addresses corporeality and the spaces of everyday life enacted through CMC in the university, through both distance education and computer-aided instruction. It examines the social capital associated with the dominant cybernetic model for point-and-click learning while drawing upon Bourdieu's concept of habitus, to discuss how we might better understand online learning as an event involving bodily and discursive dispositions. The afterword, "Digital Dis-strophe," addresses how the twin events of March 2000 (the "bubble burst") and September 11, 2001, affected the relation of networked social space to the spaces of everyday life. In short, I maintain that while much of the hype surrounding "cyberspace" has faded, the network structures of CMC are all the more dominant in the production of social space. And as distributed networks become a common feature of everyday life, so too do systems of distributed control.

The Internet has by no means left the scene of cultural experience. But undoubtedly we are now experiencing a second generation of critical analysis and popular account of CMC, in which the prophecies of the 1990s are being replaced by a banality of the network. But I would argue that to some degree, the more invisible the technology, the more it has become a matter of everyday life. By the everyday, I do not mean to foreground a specific understanding of "human experience," or for that matter to emphasize "the human" in a way that is unproblematic. By the everyday, however, I hope to emphasize that "theory" has its mappings in the dispositional practices of lived experience, as the lived embodiment of culture.

THE PROBLEM OF CYBERSPACE

MUCH OF THE WORK I have done on CMC over the last decade has been driven by an attempt to ask, in various ways, a single question: Where does cyberspace take place?[1] When I first began asking a version of this question back in the mid-1990s, the terms of debate were notably different, obsessed as we were then with the promises and threats posed by telepresence and virtual worlds. Today, some ten years later and well beyond the end of the "cyberspace decade,"[2] the question may seem a bit anachronistic. Few theorists or media critics today are willing to embrace the sort of rhetoric that seemed coin of the realm in the 1990s—claims that, for better or for worse, networked computers were creating a *new world of information space,* distinct from the everyday spaces and places of brick-and-mortar and flesh-and-blood. Yet, while the rhetoric may have cooled, reference to the Internet in spatial terms—as cyberspace or some other *place*—still occurs frequently on television and in print. This sense of space is also still mapped by the verbs of displacement—browsing, cruising, going—that have become common parlance for our human-computer interactions, along with our use of locatives

1

and the spatial-geographic language of sites, addresses, and links that describe the material, conceptual, and experiential arrangements of the World Wide Web and other instances of networked communication. At the same time, it is easy to discount the *reality* of this sense of space, and thus to dispel the illusion of cyberspace. After all, I can tap on my computer screen and remind myself that I have not *really* gone anywhere. Ten years later, I still sit, somewhat uncomfortably, approximately eighteen inches from a monitor, hands in relaxed claws, typing on a keyboard. This easy dismissal, however, does not really account for the difficulty one has in acknowledging the sense of space produced by and producing the medium and environment of CMC: the fact that when I refer to cyberspace, I can assume that my reader knows what I am talking about, though not, perhaps, to what I am referring. The degree to which the question "Where does cyberspace take place?" still poses a problematic of sorts—a tangle of material, conceptual, and experiential involvements and conflicts—suggests that it is a question still very much worth asking.

The *problem of space* posed by CMC is as much epistemological and ontological as it is phenomenological, asserting itself at a nexus of language and materiality, conceptual structure and corporeal experience. Spatiality—an experience of space as mapped by these interacting processes—marks a problematic that resists either an easy affirmation or a simplistic dismissal of the "reality" of cyberspace. What exactly do we mean by "space" in everyday life? What is the referent for this space called cyberspace? Does it make sense to speak of a space of computer-mediated communication, and if so, what "sense" of space do we map by using this term?

(Dis)locating Cyberspace

The question "Where does cyberspace *take place?*" forces us to address our own assumptions about the everyday experience of space on and off the 'Net. In its simplest form, the problematic of space posed by the question sets up a binary of sorts: cyberspace *must* "take place" either *somewhere* or *nowhere*. Any easy dismissal of the spatiality of CMC hinges upon the claim that cyberspace "takes place" nowhere, and that all references to a space of CMC are merely metaphorical—an artifact of language use. Cyberspace, in this reading, would only take place in language, never in *real space*. But where, for example, do real-time online interactions, such as those established in an environment like LambdaMOO, *take place?* MOOs and MUDs provide a compelling sense of place by encouraging users to experience a sense of telepresence. Players in a MOO meet in rooms and have conversations, but these events literally take place neither *here* (at the computer screen) nor *there* (at some other location), but rather within the medium itself. Paradoxically, the firsthand experience of what Baudrillard might call the "ecstasy of communication" in a MOO is hardly noticeable and ultimately quite ordinary, since this highly mediated form of interaction simulates unmediated communication. "Where are you in real life?" is a fairly common question in a MOO, but I would argue that the text-generated "worlds" of CMC work against this sort of interaction, encouraging players to communicate with each other according to a rhetoric of proximity, not distance. One does not "go" somewhere when picking up the telephone. But when the computer couples with these same telephone lines, suddenly spatial and kinetic metaphors begin to proliferate. Users experience *location* in two zones of interaction: one situated physically in front of a keyboard (in real life); the other, equally as compelling, situated "within" the medium.

A similar doubled sense of place occurs on the Web, experienced as a *dislocation* of the user from a "here" of one page to a "there" at a distance—thus all the hype in the mid-1990s over "cruising the information superhighway" or "surfing the 'Net." With corporations inviting potential customers to "visit us at www.___.com," the Web now serves as a "place" for marketing and commerce. Yet it is not merely the fact that CMC can substitute for geographic displacement (I "go" to Amazon.com and buy a book, rather than going to the nearest bookstore) that creates this sense of dislocation. It is the fact that from the perspective of the user, the interface defines point-and-click control as a mode of mapping, the browser screen a constantly changing indicator denoting "you are here." The potential to shift that mediated sense of presence from one Web site to another in effect defines cyberspace as an "area" of virtual experience, linking one's current location with previous sites, as well as a virtuality of possible "next" sites.[3] This sense of control, connecting what is currently on the user's screen with the potential "directions" he or she could travel (forward, back), understands presence in relation to a metaphorical mobility at the user's command, yet always structured by the "here" of the interface itself. At no point does this cybernetic *movement* challenge a "reality" of space defined beyond language and delimited by material forms.

Clearly any account of cyberspace will have to acknowledge the doubled nature of this relation between spatiality and presence. From an experiential level, users obviously distinguish between a "here" of physical presence and a "here" of telepresence. As Michael Holmes's discourse analysis of online environment suggests, real-time CMC users mark *two* deictic centers in their "speech": one indicating physical location; the other marking a shared location "in" virtual space, a "shared formulation of the network itself as a space for references to conversational copresence" (215). Likewise, much as place deictics mark a sense of copresence or *coplacement* for users of real-time CMC distinct from physical location, the ability to alter an information landscape through a point-and-click interface marks a sense of deictic *displacement* by the user from one site to another, at the user's command. The problem of cyberspace, however, relates specifically to how we understand the *real situation of the user* in relation to CMC, given this doubling. If we are willing to acknowledge the "hereness" of cyberspace only as *mere* metaphor, we do so by likewise limiting the *real space* of CMC to the material relation of user to keyboard. The "space" of cyberspace, in other words, remains firmly within scare quotes. Cyberspace marks a problematic to the extent that this doubling begins to blur—thus much of the (apocalyptic) media criticism in the 1990s bemoaned the increasing slippage between "real" and "metaphorical" space through CMC. Such an approach does indeed attempt to resolve the problem of cyberspace, but it does so within a framework that places language and "space itself" on opposite sides of an unbridgeable ontological and epistemological divide.

Yet, even if we were to declare that cyberspace *takes place* only in language, we must still be able to account for the specific context of language use that would make the "placeness" of CMC culturally legible in everyday life. Why, for example, does this deictic split occur when this communicative event is mediated via the computer, rather than, say, through the telephone? In this regard, cyberspace holds something in common with "TV land," to the extent that the placeness of cyberspace is both marked by and exceeds the material location of the medium interface. While the telephone gives each user its own "here," television suggests a shared "here" of a dispersed mass audience, an intersubjective third space or "nonspace" by way of mediation (Morse 99–116). In the 1950s, "TV land" occurred in common parlance to refer to the space that viewers inhabit in relation to the screen. "Hello out there in TV land" suggests a space of negotiation between the media outlet and the recipient at home. TV land is, in effect, the living rooms of middle-class America in the 1950s, tuned to Milton Berle and the Texaco Star Theater. In a similar gesture, cyberspace marks a negotiation of space between the (virtual middle-class) computer user and the information presented on the screen, be that a Web page, a chat room, or an email. The direction of the two metaphors, however, is different. In cyberspace, the user enters into this space as a locus of engagement. TV land as an imaginary or metaphorical space maintains an unbridgeable displacement from the real position of the viewer in his or her living room—and to breech that distance is to inhabit the extra-rationalist world of children, fools, and psychotics.[4] In contrast, cyberspace places one "within" this metaphorical space. And in fact, by way of CMC, TV land can now articulate a space in which events on screen very often involve and engage the audience through email "call-ins" and real-time chat rooms running in tandem with live, televised broadcasts. While prior media may have appeared as "doors" or "windows" onto other worlds, with cyberspace those worlds become navigable terrain, explored in explicitly spatial terms.[5] In other words, the "here" of cyberspace, while doubled, denotes a sense of place that straddles the language/materiality divide: a "hyperpotential"[6] *hereness* that coincides with a material presence (my body, here at the keyboard), yet at the same time displaces that presence "into" networks of exchange.

To speak of cyberspace as merely an artifact of language does not really account for this novel relation to space, as both material form and conceptual structure, mapped by the everyday use of network technology. In part the problem of cyberspace is compounded by a more general problem of metaphor and its relation to "the real." How we are to address a question such as "Where does cyberspace take place?" depends upon how we understand this gap between the "metaphorical space" of media(tion) and the "real space" of physical situatedness and geographic distance.[7] The problem of cyberspace arises to the degree that the sense of each space begins to overlap. To treat cyberspace as metaphorical is certainly not to argue that metaphors, or, more generally, language, are without impact on everyday life.[8] The question, rather, concerns the degree to which we understand the impact of language as distinct from the material forms that are thought to occupy space qua space—and thus how firmly we are to set that ontological divide between materiality and language. When we speak of the Internet as an information superhighway, for example, or some other metaphor involving speed and mobility, we need to consider how a common metaphor for the mobile privatization[9] of life in developed nations also involves itself in the production of *real space*, as marked by the forms and practices of everyday life in a network society. Cyberspace may well take place in language, but does not language itself take place *somewhere*?

The problem of cyberspace occurs precisely at this presumed line between language and materiality, a line that ultimately treats the computer screen as a kind of border or boundary between two senses of space. If "real" space can only define physical situatedness of objects, then the only "real" space of CMC exists at the level of the materiality of the medium itself, in the form of servers, terminals, and a network of wires and towers. This is what Lance Strate calls the "physical space" of cyberspace, distinct from (and secondary to in many ways) "conceptual" and "perceptual" space.[10] Cyberspace, as an expression or transmission of this material system, as *communication,* maintains the status of a message—a symbolic exchange. Its space is always *other than* the space of material forms. The problem of cyberspace, however, arises at the collapse of this distinction between medium and message, between materiality, metaphor, and conceptual structure, forcing us to reconsider our assumptions about the space in which metaphor, symbol, and concept "take place." How we understand the space of language, then, will have a significant impact on how we attempt to locate cyberspace as lived space.

Cyberspace and the Message/Medium Dualism

In much of our everyday language use, the medium of a message is treated, as Lakoff notes, as a conduit: thoughts are "carried" through language by way of writing or speech.[11] This "conduit fallacy" of communication gives rise to a concern over the degree of transparency of the medium conveying the message. Here the dream emerges of a purely transparent medium in which thoughts express themselves perfectly in the mystic's "language of the angels" (Ryan par. 8) or Leibniz's divine language of numbers (Baudrillard, *Simulations* 103). In this framework, the message is taken to be aspatial and immaterial, whereas the medium—be it embodied speech, material graphemes, or CRT pixels—takes place in the material world of spatial extension, at best neutral, and at worst corruptive. It is the apparent "immateriality" of digital transmission that allows CMC to perpetuate a message/medium dualism that demotes materiality and "real space" to the irrelevance of computer screens and keyboards, while treating cyberspace as a mental realm of pure communication. The doubled "hereness" of CMC speaks to this dualist doubling of presence, one situated by physical location, and the other coupled to a locus of communication understood as immaterial. As such, the question "Where does cyberspace take place?" speaks to a context well beyond that of CMC—a context involving entrenched cultural assumptions about the relation of language and materiality to presence.

As Derrida suggests, the presumed immateriality of an immediate, transparent mode of communication ("speech") is constructed upon a dualism opposed against the materiality of the graphical mark. The immateriality of the message, this dualism maintains, *precedes* the medium, which occupies space as a simulacrum of presence articulated in material form. The "space of writing" functions as a space *other than* the here-and-now of presence, a space that displaces presence from an absent point of origin to a present point of arrival (Derrida, *Dissemination* 109). Given this *fort:da* of writing and communication, the dream of a pure medium attempts to rescue writing from its fallen status in western metaphysics as a second-order simulation of presence. To the degree to which writing can erase its marks, and thus appear as an immaterial presence in every sense of the word, the medium can pull off this dissimulation. As Mark Poster notes in his discussion of Derrida and electronic writing:

> Plato distrusted writing to the extent that he aimed to define truth as a mental experience in which an ideal reality corresponded perfectly to its mental representation. . . . In its distance from that mental experience, writing is in opposition to speech and is haunted by a certain distance from it. Writing is thus burdened by the "disgrace" of being a mere copy of a mental reality. (*The Mode of Information* 102)[12]

With the presumed immediacy and transparency of electronic writing, however, that distance—both between thought and mark and between dispatch and arrival—appears to shrink. CMC becomes a kind of hyper-writing in the sense that the erasure of marks is "complete." In its presumed immateriality, the symbolic exchanges of electronic writing present an apotheosis of logocentrism.[13] Whereas Derrida describes a history of writing as a material presence that supplants the more present and immediate spoken word, one would be led to believe that CMC holds the potential to allow writing and speech to merge[14] in a transparent language, in which thoughts communicate "perfectly." In effect, the "space of writing" in CMC undermines the distinction between simulation and dissimulation. For this reason, popular accounts of interactions in cyberspace can simultaneously suggest the dangers of virtual impostors and the intimacies of a digital "language of the heart." No longer a counterfeit or a reproduction, writing achieves its transcendence on the Internet: as third-order simulation of "direct" speech.

In this regard, CMC presents a curious context for mediated communica-

tion. On one hand, the material mediation of interlocutors reinforces the illusion of the conduit fallacy of language, or what Katherine Hayles discusses
as the "information/matter duality" of cybernetic communication (13). At the
same time, however, the experience of telepresence reinforces the illusion of a
disembodied embodiment via language itself. Certainly much of the early theorizing on CMC did indeed perpetuate this corporeal/noncorporeal divide,
marking off cyberspace as a strictly mental realm, and thus taking part in a cybernetic lineage that dematerializes and disembodies information, presented
most often in the 1990s as some form of "agora of ideas" in which the idiosyncrasies of flesh apparently no longer matter.[15] As Michelle Kendrick notes, this
fundamentally dualist approach denigrates *res extensa* in the name of cogito,
treating CMC as "the triumph of the algorithmic mind over a physical body
that refuses to be fully computed" (145). Or, put more euphorically and succinctly by Internet pundit John Perry Barlow, "Nothing could be more disembodied than cyberspace. It's like having your everything amputated" (quoted
in Kelly 185).[16] Far from unique, this representation of space presents itself
throughout modernity in what Lefebvre calls the "anaphorization" of abstract
space, where one "transforms the body by transporting it outside itself and
into the ideal-visual realm" (*The Production of Space* 309). In this reading, cyberspace functions as an idealist space that understands being-in-the-world as
a mental rather than a physical event. And certainly the most euphoric procla-
mations of cyberspace tended to adopt this vision, describing the Internet as a
realm of pure thought, unmediated by one's material place in the world.

The vision of CMC as a retooling of Marshall McLuhan's electronic noosphere provides just such a rendering of cyberspace, to the extent that it maps
a digital "global village" that transcends the spatial and temporal constraints
of the physical globe.[17] For this reason, the earliest popular accounts of virtual
communities placed cyberspace in a transcendent relation to geographic space,
such as Howard Rheingold's account of electronic *agorae*[18] or Pierre Levy's
"collective intelligence."[19] Liberated from the determinations of material form,
cyberspace figures as a fluid space of poiesis and play.[20] This radical dislocation of the presumed imaginary space of CMC from the spaces of everyday life
is described as producing a kind of "playground" for exploring possible selves
and possible worlds.[21] Such a vision of cyberspace, however, still leaves unre-
solved the terms that define the *real situation of the user* (thus the concern over
the *reality* of the Internet's "imagined communities," grounded in symbolic
exchange rather than material location[22]). The problem of cyberspace occurs

across this gap separating the materiality of bodies and the construction of selves and societies mediated by technology, what Allucquere Stone describes as "the crosscurrents of fiction and physicality" (180). Such accounts also give rise to a vision of cyberspace as a Baudrillardian nightmare of virtual worlds in which the "map precedes the territory" and "the real" loses its power as referent. The more robust the illusion, the greater the promises—and dangers—of collapsing the distance between the space of the imaginary and the space of the real, creating a "shadow world [taking] up no space. . . . [in which] every day, millions of individuals are coming home from work or school, booting up their computers, and, in effect, disappearing into other realities" (Slouka 43). While "TV land," one could argue, functions in a very similar capacity as an imagined community of middle-class American viewers, the *hallucinatory* quality of cyberspace implies a potentially dangerous blurring of the imaginary and the real. The result is, in Baudrillard's words, a "satellization" of the real, a "bubble world" of symbolic exchange without referent, or rather, a referent without a grounding in the actuality of material form.

Of course, much of this understanding of cyberspace returns to William Gibson's own definition of the term in *Neuromancer,* describing it as a "consensual hallucination" occurring at the social level (51). As the term "hallucination" implies, cyberspace, while imaginary, superimposes itself onto the real, becoming a space of real actions and interactions. The fears and potentials of cyberspace are measured by the degree to which these two spaces interact with one another. And while, ten years later, some of the shrillest arguments against cyberspace as an end of the real seem decidedly dated, it is worth noting that the concerns expressed in the digital jeremiads of the 1990s focused very much on the *problematic* of cyberspace as a site where language and materiality intersect. How are we to make sense of the relation between a sense of presence as corporeal location and a sense of presence mediated through networks of symbolic exchange?

In much of the theoretical and popular discussion of virtual worlds and telepresence in the second half of the 1990s, Julian Dibbell's account of a "rape in cyberspace" often served as a touchstone for the reality of text-based actions in CMC, in part because it called attention to this sense of the real as both mediated and immediate experience. According to Dibbell, through the use of the object-oriented programming language that underlies the structure of LambdaMOO, a character was able to make it appear that several female characters were being sexually and physically assaulted in a public space. One of the most striking features of Dibbell's account of the societal upheaval that ensued in the MOO, as players held a town forum to discuss the assault and assess the punishment, is the blurring of language and action that provides the operative assumptions of real-time exchanges. As one LambdaMOO player noted, "In MOO, the body is the mind," intimating that the immateriality of cyberspace is at the same time described and acted upon as a space in which embodied events do indeed *take place* (quoted in Dibbell 40). More precisely, it would seem that while speech and writing converge in the dream of an idealist space of transparent communication, virtual worlds operate as spaces of everyday life by articulating a fundamental assumption about the "nature" of networked social space: that *to type is to do.* As Stephen O'Leary notes in his study of Wiccan and pagan rituals in a chat room on AOL, all actions are in effect incantations; when someone declares "I light the candle," this "virtual candle" is lit (797–99). The problem of space presents itself at this moment when we can no longer maintain the ontological gap between materiality and language, when language finds its place in the world of embodied experience and the computer screen no longer serves as a boundary between real space and cyberspace.

But just as I can tap on my computer screen and remind myself that I haven't *really* cruised or surfed anywhere, certainly I am aware that I haven't *really* lit a candle. The real, in other words, still rests comfortably in a world of objects, with cyberspace denoting a world of *mental* acts. To return to our forced binary: if cyberspace takes place *somewhere,* then it certainly doesn't take place *here,* stated with all the certainty of Samuel Johnson's refute of Bishop Berkeley. Much of the early criticism of cybertheory attempted to dispel the illusion of cyberspace in this sort of fashion.[23] As indicated by the frequent use of "RL" to distinguish "real life" from online interactions, such accounts maintain that cyberspace does indeed *take place,* but does so by situating the user in an immaterial realm of symbolic exchange. Of course, CMC is no more immaterial than speech. In the same manner that speech is embodied as a speaker, so too does the material context of all communication call upon a space in which it takes place. Cyberspace as a space of symbolic exchange plays into a mentalist conception of disembodied space to the extent that one is willing to treat language itself as transparent, disembodied, and purely symbolic. The problem of space, however, forces us to acknowledge that language, and more generally communication, is a materiality as much as it is a conceptual, symbolic system, based very much in situated moments of exchange. The incantations of lighting virtual candles—or the realities of cyber-rape—only make sense within specific material arrangements, marked by the presence of multiple users at multiple computers, linked via networks in real-time exchange. The space of language and the space of cyberspace coincide to the extent that communication takes place as both a materiality and a symbolic exchange. While the "electronic word" may *transmit* as an immaterial exchange, it *takes place* within a context of situated materialities and practices.

The problem of cyberspace is marked by our difficulty in reducing space to either materiality or metaphor. By casting the spatiality of CMC as a world of pure symbolic exchange, distinct from the "real" world of materiality and presence, and thereby creating a binary opposition between the real world on one side of the screen and an imaginary world beyond, this understanding of cyberspace dislocates the spaces of communication from the spaces of everyday life. But perhaps this distinction is not so cut-and-dried. Certainly the space we are calling cyberspace neither begins nor ends at the computer screen.

The Event of Cyberspace: Virtual Topographies

A message-medium dualism suggests a version of Lakoff's conduit fallacy, treating the medium—be that spoken word, written text, or glowing pixel—as either vessel or vehicle for a message or thought. Such an approach to communication has a two-fold effect: it dematerializes the message such that the context of "delivery" becomes irrelevant to the message itself; and it treats materiality itself as suspect, capable of corrupting the purity of the message. In cyberspace, this conduit fallacy gives rise to some interesting situations. On one hand, it provides for the illusion of the Internet as a more "pure" form of communication: stripped of the "noise" of bodies, we are given an agora of the mind (and the heart) in which to show our "real" selves. Yet it likewise provides the basis for a fear of the counterfeit: anyone can claim to be anything. Both instances serve as sides of the same coin to the extent that the medium is treated as either a pure or a corruptive *channel for transmission.*[24] Thus, as in the case of LamdaMOO's "rape in cyberspace," the telepresence of CMC blurs simulation and dissimulation to the extent that we are willing to fall victim to one form or other of a conduit fallacy of language.

If, however, we are willing to consider medium and message as inseparable—not as a binary pair but rather as co-involved processes—then we are no longer thinking in terms of language as vessel or vehicle. We are also left with a

very different understanding of space and cyberspace, to the extent that materiality and semiotic structure are wedded together in an altered understanding
of situatedness. Ken Hillis makes a similar point in his discussion of the experience of users in virtual environments (VEs). Using James Carey's distinction
between communication as transmission and communication as ritual, Hillis
notes that the "ritual space" of telepresence occurs very much "within" a relational space, even though communication occurs "across" the medium (61–
64). Virtual reality, he argues, enacts communication as both a conduit transmission and a ritual event, such that "the act of transmission itself becomes an
ersatz place and constitutes a ritual act or performance" (63). Communication
takes place as a set of relations, one that *involves itself* in the medium. Following along a similar line of argument, I would suggest that cyberspace is enacted
and articulated in the relational interactions of individuals involved in CMC,
and mapped as a nexus of material and semiotic processes. The problem of
space posed by cyberspace foregrounds the degree to which the spaces of everyday life in a network society are produced by a dynamic relation of material and semiotic processes—an *event* articulated in specific contexts and delimited as a virtuality, that is, as a field of possibles. While cybernetics tends to
dematerialize communication through a message/medium dualism, this more
event-based approach would, in effect, *materialize* the context that is often obscured in accounts of cyberspace as mere metaphor or "pure" imaginary/men-
talist realm. It would call attention to the relational processes that allow the
event of cyberspace to take place—and make place—through material form,
semiotic structure, and lived practice.

If we begin to think of the spatiality of CMC in dynamic, relational terms,
we can now also begin to understand how (cyber)space is produced as a situated communicative event. As is clearest in instances such as the LambdaMOO
cyber-rape or an online ritual, the compelling claims to both a sense of space
and deictic presence involve a form of mediated performative speech act—
when the CMC user is "*doing* something rather than simply *saying* something"
with words (Austin, "Performative Utterances" 235). Performatives can never
occur only in language, but in a language context. As an *act*, they are *relational*
to the extent that they are subject to a situation; for the utterance to accomplish the act, it must take part within a given set of circumstances (Austin, *How
to Do Things with Words* 8). Thus, in Austin's famous discussion of marriage
vows, "I now pronounce you man and wife" only serves as a performative in
a given speech situation; or as Lyotard notes, the declaration of "The college

is now in session" has more to do with the situation of the speaker and audience than with the words per se (*The Postmodern Condition* 9–10). Likewise, the communicative event of "I light the candle" only functions as a performative within a very specific arrangement of speaker and audience, via networked computers. In this regard, Austin's discussion of illocutionary force provides an important corrective to the tendency to dematerialize CMC, and hence to treat cyberspace as something other than real space.[25] In Austin's account of speech acts, the performative occurs as the *expression* of illocutionary force within a given speech situation. Given the relation between act and situation, the success or failure of a performative speech act will depend on the relation between utterance and context. In order for a speech act to "go off," it must call upon an acknowledged set of conventions and be executed according to those conventions and by the conventionally prescribed individuals (*How to Do Things with Words* 14–15). Otherwise, these "unhappy" performatives "misfire": they do not occur per se.[26] Thus, the performative is only understood within "the total speech act in the total speech situation" (*How to Do Things with Words* 52). In discussions of disembodied virtual worlds or of the transparency of real-time exchanges that communicate (simulate/dissimulate) presence, then, we would want to consider the performative context that provides such events with illocutionary force. This is not to fall into the trap of believing that one could fully account for or calculate the "total speech act in the total speech situation" (although this might well be the cybernetician's dream).[27] It acknowledges, however, that whatever sense of space we refer to in the name of cyberspace, we are calling upon a specific performative (social) context involving both language and material form. Such a reading would have to recognize that the "space" of CMC is not metaphorical or mental but is rather the space of communication itself. This view situates language within a social context while at the same time providing for an understanding of the spatiality of CMC as both a symbolic and a material event. No longer a mere conduit, the medium *situates* the event of communication.

Of all the readings of Austin and speech act theory that have developed, Gilles Deleuze and Félix Guattari's appropriation provides a particularly useful rendering of this relation between language, embodiment, and space. Unlike traditional communication theories (and in contrast to the conduit fallacy of language), Deleuze and Guattari argue that language "is not the communication of information but something quite different: the transmission of order-words" (79).[28] As utterances, these order-words *discipline* language, and in doing so, they enact changes in social relations. Deleuze and Guattari position order-words along two axes, one that establishes a relation between bodies and utterances, and one that registers their power to discipline language. Order-words exist as a group of utterances (a "collective assemblage of enunciation") but at the same time they mark the material relations of power that form a given society (a "machinic assemblage of bodies") (88). This axis of bodies/enunciation defines for Deleuze and Guattari a relation between language and the world that refuses to reduce to a purely semiotic system, precisely because the performative act is immanent to the utterance itself (80–81). At the same time, order-words register along an axis of discipline (territorialization) and indiscipline (deterritorialization) in language (88). Language functions as a performative transmission of orderings (what Austin might call conventions); as such, the illocutionary force of order-words delimits the conditions of possibility for language, and not the other way around. These variable enunciations, given force by a pragmatic context, order and determine subjectivities and relations; it is thus always a matter of the "pragmatic implications" of these utterances, not merely their "signification" (Deleuze and Guattari 83). They serve as expressions of possible (and variable) relations within a given pragmatic context.[29]

To some degree, then, these two axes (bodies/enunciation and discipline/indiscipline) serve as the equivalent of Austin's "total speech act within the total speech situation." While orthogonal measures, each axis implicates the other in the power of the order-word within a given context. The de/reterritorializing power of language can only occur because order-words also function along an axis of illocutionary force. Likewise, the immanent power of the utterance on a "machinic assemblage of bodies" can only occur given the order-word's ability to discipline language's indisciplines. While the first axis (the relation between body and utterance) conditions the second, this second axis reveals the power of order-words both to repress and to liberate the "indisciplines" of speech.[30] In this Deleuzian revision of Austin's speech act theory, the "total speech act in the total speech situation" now involves a consideration not only of what conventional illocutionary forces *actually* exist as a "major" language, but also what *potentials* for variation exist within this configuration of utterances and bodies—a "minor" language. One finds the resistances of the minor not in opposition to order-words, but as a part of the "collective assemblage of enunciation" that the major attempts to determine (Deleuze and Guattari 106). To make language "stammer" involves a move from the actual to the virtual, from a territorialization of the order-word to an exploration of its deterritorializing effects (Deleuze and Guattari 98).

Speech act theory—particularly the version presented by Deleuze and Guattari—allows us to avoid the dualism of message and medium that has given rise to accounts of cyberspace as an immaterial agora of ideas, and to do so in a way that acknowledges space itself in dynamic, relational terms. Cyberspace in effect maps an event that involves both material form and conceptual structure. In doing so, it articulates actual lived space from the virtualities of possible use. Such an approach also calls upon us to understand the spatiality of CMC not merely as an arrangement of material effects, but, rather, as the interaction of these material forms with both the semiotic regimes of signification and the lived use of daily practice. One cannot help but *materialize* cyberspace to the extent that for any spatial metaphor for CMC to carry force, it must map a relational context between the symbolic and the material that would make such a performance possible, as well as the disciplining of language and relations enacted by such utterances. In other words, the "hereness" of CMC is at once an enunciative and corporeal event that determines multiple sets of relations between users, networks, and information. In this sense, the map *does* precede the world, or, more accurately, the map enunciates and thereby disciplines a world of material and symbolic relations.[31] Thus, the context of communication both obeys parameters of social space and maps potentialities of space and spatial relations.

As an event, what appears as metaphorical is perhaps best described as an articulation of cyberspace that enacts a set of real material and experiential relations, and does so within conditions of possibility that allow these relational processes to *go off* or *take place*. As early as 1995, with Microsoft's "Where Do You Want to Go Today?" ad campaign, one could find examples of CMC enacted as a space of efficiency and control, made possible via global networks, the daily practice of email, and an imagined community of geographically distributed users. A television commercial shows a female executive, "Jane on the plane," *cruising* from site to site via global information networks in the same way that her plane travels from point A to point B. Cyberspace here duplicates, yet with more efficiency and with greater control, a world of international markets, highways and airline routes, and global circulations: an information *superhighway* where the concepts of speed, freedom, and knowledge coalesce in a network of determinate, navigable sites and point-to-point contact.[32] As a performative event, use of the Internet in this capacity enacts a space of point-to-point contact, quite literally ordering a set of material and semiotic relations. Likewise, one can map articulations of cyberspace that resist, disperse, and contradict this sense of CMC as a space of control. Often these relations appear as "threats" to the ideological blanket of late capitalism or as representations of "inappropriate" contact: pornography before the eyes of children and bomb recipes in the hands of terrorists. Even in the banality of a cliché, such as "surfing the 'Net," one can identify alternate articulations of cyberspace. In contrast to Microsoft's "Jane on the plane" point-to-point spatiality, "surfing" suggests a less controlled or directed form of navigation. Part of the same 1995 "Where Do You Want to Go Today?" campaign, for example, presented a Microsoft Encarta television commercial in which a man researching hang gliding soon finds himself gathering information on birds and other "winged things," then drifting off on the winds of a monsoon to India and to the Himalayas. Both the "Jane on the plane" commercial and the Microsoft Encarta commercial ask the viewer to conceive of CMC in spatial terms, asking "Where do you want to go today?" at the end of the spot, but the space that the Encarta user traverses is significantly different from the space portrayed in the "Jane on the plane" ad. The Encarta commercial enacts a space that is planar and fluid, whereas in the "Jane" commercial, cyberspace is a highway of sorts connecting terminal points in a simulated world. The differences in spatiality are not merely conflicts in metaphor or differing accounts of an imaginary domain; rather, as an event, each articulates a specific set of relations among material forms (personal computers, phone lines, digital backbones), conceptual structures (cruising, surfing), and lived use (Web browsing in its multiple contexts), producing distinct, interpenetrating spaces of CMC.

In this context, a spatial analysis of CMC must acknowledge the performative aspect of this articulation—a mapping in the Deleuzian sense of calling forth the actual from the virtuality of collective assemblages of bodies and enunciations (Deleuze and Guattari 12–15). Space does not exist a priori to these relations, but rather is enacted in the dynamic relation of material and semiotic processes. In this regard, one might best describe the lived practice of cyberspace as *topographies* of CMC: performative speech acts that simultaneously map and create a territory (J. Miller 4–5).[33] These topographies are always, in effect, virtual to the extent that they provide conditions of possibility for an arrangement of materiality and semiotic structure through the (re)orderings of lived practice. If we are to understand cyberspace as lived space, we need to be able to address not only "where" it takes place, but how it is articulated in its varying forms. On one hand, at the level of the everyday experience of CMC—that is, as an enacted virtual topography—we can map cyberspace as a network-grid of point-to-point navigation inside a coordinate system. To draw on the language of Deleuze and Guattari, this virtual topography articulates a "striated space" where "lines and trajectories tend to be subordinated to points: one goes from one point to another" (478). Note that the "agora of ideas" is also very much a network of exchanges, a marketplace articulated as a striated space of circulations and flow.[34] In contrast to what Deleuze and Guattari describe as a striated space of circulations and control, enactions of cyberspace that foreground wandering actualize a "smooth space" of dissemination and drift, in which "the points are subordinated to the trajectory" (Deleuze and Guattari 478). These two functions, "allocation" and "distribution," serve as the dominant organizational principle that differentiates smooth and striated space.[35] A striated "highway" topography determines cyberspace as a cybernetic system of regulated connections between determined points on dedicated lines; conversely, a smooth topography articulates a "rhizomatic" cyberspace of fluid transit and continual passage.[36] These spaces are real to the degree that a "cybernetic" or "rhizomatic" representation of space can *discipline the virtual* as performative conditions of possibility, thereby delimiting actual space, as articulated in material form and lived practice.

It should be no surprise that these topographies not only present conflicting concepts of cyberspace, as "felicitous" performative speech acts they actualize antagonistic practices of CMC as spaces of everyday life. From within a striated topography, nomad/smooth space appears as a dangerous zone in need of containment. Much of the concern over pornography and gambling on the Internet draws on similar language to associate "uncontrolled" and "unregulated" with "dangerous" and "immoral." In the mid-1990s, for example, Gary Bauer of the Family Research Council evoked images of a perilously "open" cyberspace when calling for legislation that would "eliminate 'cyberspace' as a safe haven for pornographers. . . . by criminalizing 'free' obscenity on the Internet" ("Vote S. 652"). More recently, the Defense Advanced Research Projects Agency (DARPA) Total Information Awareness project attempted to utilize cybernetic principles of pattern recognition to "connect the dots" of terrorism "hidden" within the overwhelming entropy of distributed networks.[37] Conversely, within smooth topographies, striation appears as a resistance to the "natural" openness of smooth space. In this fluid topography, CMC is about the *flow* of information and ideas; regulation and striation amount to a strangulation of that flow and a death of the medium. Smooth topographies enact spaces that deterritorialize practice, whereas striated topographies "capture" these fluid flows into operational modes within a reterritorialized space of circulations.[38]

Of these two conflicting articulations, clearly the dominant topography of CMC attempts to enact a set of relations driven by what Lyotard calls the postmodern "logic of maximum performance": at all costs, communicate efficiently (*The Postmodern Condition* xxiv). Under this performativity principle, legitimation becomes a matter of establishing "the best possible input/output equation" (46). Advertisements for faster connections and more accurate search engines describe an Internet driven more and more by this performance logic. But the potential for a wide array of contacts, for the dissemination of information, and for the cross-pollination of social groupings suggests that other modes of experiencing the Internet are quite prevalent. Thus, corporations worry about work hours lost to games and "net-surfing," and, in college computer classrooms, students drift off from their assignments in multiple directions. Consider, for example, the case of Kurt Vonnegut's 1997 MIT commencement address, widely circulated on the Internet, copied and forwarded literally around the world. Unfortunately, Vonnegut had nothing to do with MIT's commencement that year, nor was the circulated speech his work. It was, in fact, a column written by Mary Schmich for the *Chicago Tribune*. Neither she nor Vonnegut had any idea how the mix-up occurred, or how the original column began its viral spread. While clearly an example of the power of the Internet to disseminate material and proliferate contact, the networks of postings mapped out by the comings and goings of this column hardly suggest the triumph of efficiency in a space of rational exchange. In contrast to this image, Schmich offhandedly suggests the phrase "lawless swamp" to describe cyberspace: a space of confusions, ambiguous margins, and muddled navigations. Again, the conflict between spaces of control and the "lawless swamp" of distributed flows does not reduce to a mere conflict in spatial metaphors; rather, it suggests a conflict in articulations of CMC, mapped as spaces of everyday life.

If we are to continue to understand cyberspace as a situated, performative event that places the material and the symbolic into a relation of lived practice, we will have to acknowledge the existence of multiple articulations of cyberspace in the everyday life experience of CMC. More generally, we will have to acknowledge that *space itself* mediates between heteromorphic virtual mappings and actual articulations. Cyberspace, rather than existing on one side of the computer screen (the symbolic realm of the message) or the other (the materiality of the medium), becomes an articulation of a networked space that is enacted in material form, conceptual structure, and lived practice throughout everyday life in a network society. Consider, for example, the multiple forms, structures, and practices involved in the conditions of possibility for a point-and-click spatiality of hypertextual links. As a "thing," hypertext appears as a multilinear, interconnecting lattice (like Foucault's "skein")[39], mapping multiple routes of passage—what Jay Bolter calls a topographic "writing space": "not the writing of a place, but rather the writing with places, spatially realized topics" (25). But hypertext is not inherently a drifting docuverse (to use Ted Nelson's term), nor does every hypertext application of necessity map a space of wanderings. Rather, these virtualities become actual to the degree that they articulate spatial relations of everyday life. One could just as easily identify in the hypertextuality of the WWW a space of circulation and control, navigated by efficient search engines and XML codings and targeted toward the "stickiest," highest-volume sites on the Web. The relation between the virtual and the actual, then, is not ontological (what cyberspace *is* or *is not*), but rather enactive (the event that *determines* and *articulates* cyberspace in its lived moment).

The difficulty we have in addressing the spatiality of CMC forces us to acknowledge that the reality of cyberspace cannot be limited to an immateriality of symbolic exchanges, fictive realms, or conceptual structures. As an event, cyberspace is produced by these varying mappings of practice, creating and revealing spaces of everyday life. As felicitous performatives, virtual topographies describe *maps of potential* that become actualized in lived practice. Cyberspace calls upon us to consider how space presents itself in a dynamic, relational form—an event involving materiality as well as semiotic structure and mapped by lived use. Users *enact* these topographies, and in doing so, articulate real spaces of everyday life.

Cyberspace/Social Space: Beyond the Box

An analysis of the spaces of CMC as virtual topographies implies an understanding of space as explicitly dynamic to the extent that assemblages of bodies and enunciations *enact* space, rather than merely occupy space. Such an approach to cyberspace sidesteps a message/medium dualism by asserting what Henri Lefebvre describes as the *truth of space:* that all space is social space, articulated at a nexus where concept, form, and practice intersect (*The Production of Space* 398–99). The message/medium dualism fails to treat cyberspace as a real space because it does not map distance between objects—defined as *res extensa;* it only draws upon space as metaphor, as image, or as idea. *Real* space, we seem to assume, must describe an arrangement of objects, a "state of affairs," or an abstract emptiness awaiting objects to hold in some relation. Given the dynamic, relational quality of virtual topographies, clearly a concept of space as an abstract container is inadequate to a discussion of the spaces of CMC.

Obviously the claim that abstract space is a limiting concept of space does not originate within the present argument, nor does it restrict itself to the concerns of media theory. Rather, one could argue that much of twentieth-century scientific and philosophical thought has involved a coming to terms with the Enlightenment's limiting notions of space. For our present discussion, however, it is worth noting that following on the euphoric heights of the Cyberspace Decade, a second generation of writing on CMC has taken up the problem of cyberspace within a larger analysis of a *history of space.* Such a project is certainly at the heart of Lefebvre's spatial analysis, to which I will shortly return in greater detail. For Lefebvre, space is a relation that is materially produced by an interplay of concept and practice but that is at the same time inseparable from this process of production. In language very similar to that Leibniz uses in his discussion of relational space, Lefebvre defines social space as "not a thing but rather a set of relations between things (objects and products)" (*The Production of Space* 83). Such an understanding of space provides a framework for understanding how performative events involving assemblages of bodies and enunciations do not merely occupy space, but rather enact it through virtual and actual relations.

This approach to space is in many ways a revitalization of a Leibnizian relational space that has informed a number of recent attempts to come to terms with the spatiality of CMC. For example, Margaret Wertheim suggests that the resonance of cyberspace in popular culture provides the most recent challenge in a century-long critique of Newtonian abstract space, conceived of as homogenous, absolute, and inert. In her exploration of the "cybernautic imagination," she notes the tendency in popular accounts of CMC to treat this realm as a space "beyond" the material—a spirit space (21–22). While she ultimately rejects this tendency to treat cyberspace as a digital "New Jerusalem," she finds significance in its challenge to a concept of space defined as an infinite container for material objects. Drawing heavily on Max Jammer's *Concepts of Space,* Wertheim points to the shift that occurs in Western thought starting with the perspectival drawing of the Renaissance and culminating in Newtonian physics, in which "empty space" became an ontological reality, thus breaking from Aristotle's understanding of a voidless space of places.[40] In the medieval world, heaven and earth were distinct spaces that did not need to obey the same principles of reality. With the rise of an absolute space that is conceived of as empty, inactive, and homogenous, heaven and earth collapse into one space (Wertheim 150–51). This notion of space as container can be found in glimpses of ancient thought, but it becomes a dominant concept with the rise of Enlightenment science and Cartesian logic. For over three hundred years, space had been treated as an absolute: homogenous, abstract, and distinct from the objects that find their place within it. From the late seventeenth century onward, "real" space has been defined as a state of affairs among objects in an infinite void. The problem of space arises to the extent that the spatiality of CMC supercedes this definition of *real* space as *abstract* space.

As Jammer and others have noted, Newton functioned as a key figure in solidifying this notion of abstract space in modern Western thought. In his debate with Leibniz, Newton argued that space is, as God, infinite; in contrast, Leibniz maintained a relational definition of space. This homogeneity of space served in part as a point of logical and theological critique for Leibniz, carried out in a series of letters with Newtonian advocate Samuel Clarke: if space were infinite and absolute, then God would have to be located *in* space—or be contiguous with space itself. While Newton's solution to this dilemma is to speak of space as God's sensorium, Leibniz's solution is to define space separate from the sphere of God and relative to the situation of "Co-existing Things" (quoted in Jammer 117). As Jammer notes, Leibniz's space connects with a pre-Aristotelian tradition in which space is defined in terms of forces between objects, not as a container: "a network of relations among coexisting things" (50). Unlike Newton's absolute space, Leibniz's relational space depends upon the specificity of particular dynamic interactions—an eventlike structure—to express a particular form. For Leibniz, "Men come to form to themselves the Notion of Space" through the dynamic changes in the "Relation of Situation" between "Co-existing Things" (quoted in Jammer 117). Space, for Leibniz, depends upon the relative relation of objects but also involves a cognitive structuring of past, present, and possible situations, which Leibniz likens to an individual's relation to a genealogical tree (Jammer 117–18). Thus, while accounting for actual situations of objects, it also accounts for a virtual structure as well.

While the theological concern is of little relevance to the present discussion, the distinction between Newton's absolute space and Leibniz's relational space has considerable significance to how we are to speak of the reality of cyberspace. Newton won out for some three centuries; it is not until the challenges of the non-Euclidean spaces of Riemann, the nonrectifiable curves of Koch, and the relativistic physics of Einstein surface that absolute space loses its absolute status. On the scale of everyday life, however, common Western understandings of space still tend to assume an abstract, homogenous space not too different from Newton's absolute space. We tend to see space as an emptiness awaiting objects.[41] But as Wertheim suggests, cyberspace presents a challenge of sorts to absolute space, a challenge that is becoming increasingly familiar to users of Web pages, email, and synchronous communication. Yet the experience of CMC in spatial terms indicates not only that cyberspace has the status of lived space, but also that the definition of space as an abstract container or an "infinite box"[42] is itself an inadequate concept for describing the spaces of everyday life, on or off the 'Net. For Jammer, Leibniz presents an interesting moment in Western thought in that he foreshadows the attack on Newtonian space by Einstein in the early twentieth century. For Wertheim, Leibniz has a similar import in understanding the relational nature of cyberspace as a "network of relationships" (299). Yet while Wertheim makes this point, she still divides cyberspace off from the space of bodies and material relations. She writes: "The fact that we now live with two very different kinds of space—physical space and cyberspace—might also help us to have a more pluralistic attitude toward space in general" (307). In contrast, I would suggest that physical space and cyberspace alike are produced at a nexus of material and semiotic relations. The problematic of cyberspace suggests a contemporary cultural difficulty in coming to terms with a relational understanding of space at the very moment when it is becoming an increasingly dominant mode as a concept of space. Taken as an "infinite box," space stands as an a priori emptiness, distinct from the objects located in it. In treating space as an event structure, however, we are forced to consider how the relation of these objects produces space itself. While involving the materiality of objects, the event of space is also produced by conceptual structures and lived use. Such an approach may at first glance appear overly dependent upon a social constructionist line of argument: physics would certainly argue that space exists with or without a human concept of space. But the argument I am making—that space itself is relational and dynamic—is only dependent upon the idea that the *use* of space is inseparable from the processes that give rise to space as material form and conceptual structure.[43] The processes that give rise to the event of space involve both conceptual structures and material forms in such a way that each is inextricably involved in the production of the other, as enacted in the lived experience of everyday life.

If we were to allow space a relational component—a dynamics in place of a static, a priori emptiness—we could begin to make sense of cyberspace as a real space of lived experience. Those theorists who have attempted to take cyberspace seriously have in effect suggested this sort of approach by calling attention to how cyberspace presents itself as a *social space,* with significant cultural implications. Such accounts emphasize that cyberspace—and in fact, space itself—is a product of dynamic interactions, the emergent result of the relation between symbolic exchanges, material forms, and lived experience. For example, in *Digital Sensations,* Ken Hillis draws upon a history of space similar to what Jammer describes, and he concludes that our current conceptions of space, specifically as informed by virtual environments, very much present a blending of experientially-centered Leibnizian relational space and a calculationally-abstracted Newtonian absolute space.[44] In creating virtual reality systems, designers in effect set up a backdrop of space that is both an abstract Cartesian grid and a Newtonian "container" for objects. At the same time, the subject plugged into such systems interacts with a space that is relational—literally produced by the situation of the user's body. In this account, the distinction between physical space and cyberspace is less clear precisely because the lived experience of relational space involves itself in both material and conceptual processes. Hillis's overarching concern, as well as his use of Leibniz, hold relevance for us here, namely: "how an experience of space—influenced by spatial concepts conceived within cultural contexts and social relations—in itself influences what it is to communicate" (77). Hillis's analysis of relational space within a discussion of mediated environments provides an important foundation for rethinking space at an ontological, epistemological, and phenomenological level. Drawing on Carey's distinction between ritual communication and transmissive communication, Hillis notes that much of communications technology is "designed to send messages *across* an empty space that is conflated with distance as an impediment to be overcome" (63). In contrast, ritual communication occurs *within* space, not *across* space (64).

This combining of the absolute, abstract, and relational through virtual technology results in a cultural context that is at once highly resonant yet also disruptive to dominant dualist assumptions of space as a container of objects. To think spaces of CMC, then, one must acknowledge that a message/mind–medium/materiality dualism does not account for space as an experience and the relation of that experience to both concepts of space and material processes involved in the articulation and accretion of space.

Hillis's analysis of the complexities of space provides an important context for understanding the problem of space posed by cyberspace—that space is a product of these material, conceptual, and experiential relations, not merely the field in which they occur. Rather than dividing off the mental/conceptual from the material/spatial, a relational account of space allows us to understand space as an event involving conceptual structures, material expressions, and lived experience, both actual and virtual. Such an approach to space also preserves Leibniz himself from what David Harvey calls the "Leibnizian conceit": since I am a monad that "internalize[s] everything there is, then all I need to understand the universe is to contemplate my own inner self" (*Justice, Nature, and the Geography of Difference* 70).[45] The processes that give rise to the event of space involve both conceptual structures and material forms in such a way that each is inextricably involved in the production of the other, as enacted in the lived experience of everyday life. Any account of cyberspace as lived space will have to take into account this interplay between materiality, which we tend to "place" in an infinite box of abstract space, and the conceptual and experiential qualities mapped in relational space—not as two distinct spaces, but rather as processes that take part in the articulation of virtual topographies in everyday life. Space must be understood as multiple, relational, and produced. A definition of space as dynamic and relational allows us to begin to address the interaction that occurs among language, bodies, material, and experience that maps the spatiality of cyberspace—or rather, *cyberspaces*. Further, such an account of the problem of space forces us to acknowledge that these topographies are always structured as an event, and as such, a dialectical emergence of several processes, not reducible to any one thing.

When discussing cyberspace, then, we will want to sidestep the claim that the spatiality of CMC is not real because it does not map a *real* space of physical situatedness, limited as it is to a "space in the mind." Likewise, we will want to avoid an understanding of cyberspace as simply a space of material arrangement, limited to the media devices that give substance to CMC. In place of each of these errors, we will want to find a way to discuss how materiality and semiotic structure take part in the production of cyberspace in everyday life. If we are to understand virtual topographies as performative contexts that enact, order, and actualize a set of possible relations between assemblages of bodies and assemblages of enunciations, we are left with an understanding of space—*real* space—that involves itself in dynamic, social processes. In this regard, Lefebvre's approach to spatial analysis provides an important means of extending this discussion of topographies as performative events to an understanding of the eventlike quality of all social space. Lefebvre defines social space within a field of three lines of force: material "spatial practice," conceptual "representations of space," and experiential "representational spaces" (*The Production of Space* 33–46). Social space incorporates all three of these dialectical forces, and the production of one is always implicated in producing the others.[46] Spaces are emergent, dynamic events brought about by a confluence of conceptual structure, material form, and lived practice. Thus, one cannot speak of virtual topographies as merely conceptual representations of space without also addressing the material and experiential processes implicated in the production of networked social space.

Lefebvre's focus on the *production* of space—its status as an emergence rather than as a preexisting given—provides an important theoretical grounding for an analysis of networked social space as an event: a dynamic relation of processes rather than an inert container for things. It places a discussion of space within a framework that allows us to understand the "event of space" in its richest sense, and also to address the problem of cyberspace more completely. Any spatial analysis of CMC within (or as a) social space would have to take into account all three of these spatial productions. A spatial analysis of cyberspace would need to take into account the conceived, the perceived, and the lived spaces of networked social interactions: the cramped fingers and carpal-tunnel wrists; the laptops in coffee shops and terminals in public libraries; the bubbles and bursts of IPOs and URLs; the cyberphilic hype and the technophobic dread. Lefebvre argues that social space consists of numerous heterogeneous spaces that do not coordinate in any total system, but rather present multiple emergences, types, and arrangements. For Lefebvre, "The form of social space is encounter, assembly, simultaneity. . . . Social space implies actual or potential assembly at a single point, or around that point" (*The Production of Space* 101). These scenes of "interpenetration" are not simply conceptual contradictions; they are conflicts in social space itself. Amidst these juxtaposing spaces rests the dialectical potential for emergent spaces that escape from a culture's dominant social space. The conflicts we encounter in mapping virtual topographies—smooth and striated cyberspaces, spaces of control and spaces of flow—reveal the heterogeneous and heteromorphic processes involved in the production of networked spaces of everyday life, mapped by the fault lines of conflicts in conceptual structure, material form, and lived practice. Cyberspace not only provides the potential for novel social formations; it simultaneously provides a space of colonization and capitalist expansion. I would also suggest that while "cyberspace" reveals a site of (dialectical) spatial conflict that produces differences, it likewise provides an example of how these differences can be captured within the territorializing power of modernity's abstract, co-ordinated space. While Lefebvre found a moment of crisis in the urbanism of the late 1960s, one can likewise turn to the social production of online space to understand a similar tension in contemporary network society.

This description of space as a process or an event (rather than as a thing or a container for things) may still seem to some degree counterintuitive. In its Newtonian version, after all, space is what comes *before* objects, allowing them to stand in proximal relation to one another. Thus objects *in* space define an *area* of space, but space qua space is always *there,* inert and inactive. A relational view of space would ask us to consider how space itself is *produced* by dynamic processes. The resistance to this approach, I would argue, is itself related to the dualist tension that gives rise to the problem of space: namely, the belief that physical space and social space define distinct realities, one tied to materiality and the other a domain of representational processes—semiotic, linguistic, sociological, etc. Understood as a conceptual process, it might be easier to accept that representations of space are produced by the structures of signification that we use to talk about and think about space. Likewise, it seems less of a stretch to maintain that as a lived structure, social space is produced by the everyday experiences of individuals who involve themselves in these social structures. At the level of materiality, however, the assumptions of Newtonian space assert themselves in full force: objects are located in real space—abstract, infinite, and inert—but the objects themselves have no impact upon space itself. If we are to accept space as dynamic and relational—and recognize the impossibility of reducing "space" to either side of a dualist divide—we will have to acknowledge that even in its material form space is *produced* as an event involving multiple processes.

As a specific example, we might think about how the material form of "the network" is inseparable from the processes that give rise to its conceptual structure and lived use. What's more, we will have to acknowledge this material form is itself an articulation of material processes, not a pre-given thing. The nodal function of the Internet suggests a network structure something akin to a web of points connected by wires. The machines and cables that make up this "web" present a highly redundant network of material links between routers, servers, and (ultimately) personal computers. But the materiality of this network must include not only the machines and cables, but also the *act of transmission itself* that instantiates network communication. In effect, the dynamics of the network map a material structure that is at once virtual and actual. This material process is itself implicated in and by a *conceptual* framing of the network as a web of nodes, reinforcing an ideology of traffic and circulation in which point-to-point communication occurs. The network per se, however, never *takes place* in a material form qua static system, though it is actualized as such within conceptual structures and lived practice. It would be more accurate to speak of *materially enacted* networks—structures of connection that are dependent upon the material nodes that are activated by a series of routings. In this regard, *the material form of the network is inseparable from the processes that give rise to "the network" as both conceptual structure and lived practice.*

Likewise, treating cyberspace as social space—as an event involving the relation of material, conceptual, and experiential processes—forces us to focus on the *situation of communication* and the *spaces enacted by communication.* Such an approach differs radically from many of the accounts of CMC in the 1990s, in which, as David Holmes notes, the materiality of the network was treated as a conduit for communication rather than as an enactive, situated event (28). Simplistic issues, such as where computers are located or the kinds of practices that are available to individuals who access digital networks, suggest that the social context of CMC is highly relevant to the production of cyberspace. This is expressed in assumptions of what it means to be online, not only in access to material structures but also in the sorts of bodily knowledge that become literally incorporated in the user. As such, the ability to "multitask" on the computer suggests something far more complex than the term implies. Right now, as I complete revisions on this manuscript, I am sitting in my office at my college. It is registration week. I have five applications open—a Web browser, an email application, a word processor, and two separate interfaces for the student information system. Occasionally a student arrives in my office with a registration problem. I toggle from my manuscript to a report screen for class enrollments and then to the registration application. After the student leaves, I check my email, respond to a personal message from a friend, and then return to editing this very page. Each interaction—with networks of information, with my manuscript, with the student at my desk—articulates a set of spatial relations that order and delimit me within social forms and structures, both personal and institutional. The computer, then, provides not a single point of interface but, rather, multiple zones of interaction that situate me within multiple articulations of social relations. As a *space*, networks define a conceptual structuring of relations mediated by transmission, a material form that is at once situated at points of interface at the same time that it distributes material access, and a lived practice that makes these distributed relations seem "natural." In this regard, cyberspace is not *where* these relations take place, it is *the "where" enacted by these relations.*

The situation of cyberspace as a real space, mapped in relational terms, is perhaps clearest in instances where the networks of communication explicitly relate to the networks of everyday life. With a "buddy list" or AOL Instant Message, for example, the network of computers reinforces the idea that at the same moment that I am typing at my computer, somewhere else another person is doing the same thing. This logic of contemporaneous use certainly emphasizes that time and space are not separable features here, but are part of what gives space its eventlike structure.[47] This relational network produces a space that, while enacted by individual use, is likewise caught up in emergent global structures, both on- and offline. The network space enacted between individual users via CMC is in a very real sense inseparable from the globalized networks of traffic, tourism, and industry that bring individuals together in physical proximity for both work and play (David Holmes, 27). Protocols such as buddy lists and instant messaging reinforce the enactive nature of these networks, that *one's own* set of connections is always virtually in place and actualized at any given moment within a globally distributed network. In this figuration of lived practice, however, the "global" network matters less than the representation of cyberspace as a familiar terrain in which the material form of CMC serves to strengthen the "ties that bind." Cyberspace becomes *my* cyberspace. These topographies reinforce the sorts of social spaces in which preexisting connections are strengthened: a virtual world fashioned as a walled-in city, in which all the digital landmarks are familiar.

The situation of such networks in spaces of everyday life also emphasizes that cyberspace is still caught up in the physical location of individuals at computers, as well as in the daily habits of use that reinforce chatting online and instant messaging.[48] These mappings are virtual topographies to the extent that the potential for a networked social structure is enacted and actualized within the daily practices of individuals connecting with network technology. Furthermore, this network of familiarity penetrates the formal institutional structures of social space as well, from the office cubicle to the networked computer classroom, such that the personal can irrupt from within the public—and vice versa—at any moment.[49] In this regard, one can map virtual topographies in the workplace that differ noticeably from traditional models of the flow of information, in that distinctions between formal and informal channels, for example, become increasingly fluid. The anecdotal accounts of personal emails distributed to organizations as a whole likewise suggest that the space of networks within daily corporate life enacts a proximity that is at once public and private, discrete and pervasive. Email structures organizational communication around highly efficient informational exchanges, yet just as likely are the circulation of office jokes, bogus virus alerts, and discount offers, as well as virus attachments themselves that deterritorialize these networks of control, rupturing "my" cyberspace through topographies of dissipation and dissemination.

In a similar fashion, "the Web" not only describes a concept of space, it also maps relations of materialities and lived practice that produce a social space. When an advertisement on television or in print asks potential customers to "visit our website," the call to space begins with a metaphor embedded in a verb of motion, but it also implicates a material investment on the part of both the company and the consumer, along with a lived practice in which magazine browsing and Web browsing occupy overlapping spaces of everyday life. Virtual topographies of the Web enact spaces of everyday life by articulating the material forms, conceptual structures, and lived practice of networked social space. Perhaps this is most clear in Web sites that have a particular call to spaces away from the computer screen. For example, in many cities in the United States, and indeed worldwide, traffic reports are available online, as is, in some instances, access to closed-circuit television cameras recording the flow of traffic through cities. Such an ability to monitor highway space via the Internet implies that the individual at the computer is, virtually, the individual at the wheel of the vehicles circulating (or failing to circulate) through city streets. The social space of a Web site such as this clearly involves itself in the material structures and lived practices that assume circulation as a matter of daily life. In a similar manner, the Mapquest.com Web site provides more than an electronic archive of local maps and driving directions, available to its users "anywhere"; the site maps out the spatiality of networks that has become the spaces of everyday life in the developed world. It would be rather ironic to maintain that networked technology makes geography irrelevant when discussing a Web site like Mapquest.com, in which distances between physical sites make the online site necessary.[50] More accurately, the site enacts a space of "mobile privatization" that is at once a matter of computer networks and highway networks. In fact, to the degree that an individual finds himself *in transit,* Mapquest.com becomes an increasingly important site in the spaces of everyday life. By no means do all Web sites enact this sort of space, but clearly a cluster of sites similar to Mapquest.com articulate a lived practice of both geographic and informatic flux in which the spaces of everyday life occur very much "on the fly."

Certainly, much of what we might describe as the dominant social space of CMC suggests a privileging of "free exchange" that is hardly inconsistent with the everyday life of the wired middle class and the economics of networked markets. As such, the "information superhighway" and the "World Wide Web" present a version of what Lefebvre would call a technological utopia: a libratory and mercantile virtuality rooted firmly "within the framework of the real—the framework of the existing mode of production" (*The Production of Space* 8–9). What's more, the material form, conceptual structure, and lived practice of "the network," enacted as cyberspace, is entirely in keeping with the networks of daily life that are mapped by a middle-class urban and suburban everyday life, and a social space articulated by a flow of bodies, goods, and information (38). Suburban enclaves, highways, centers of industry, strip malls, etc., produce a network of circulation that deeply penetrates the experience of the everyday, on and off the 'Net. In this regard, cyberspace is nothing new, to the extent that it allows for the articulation of this dominant social space. In perhaps its most prevalent form, this dominant spatiality of the network suggests a lived space in which the user occupies a position of *control,* an input/output relation to flows of data. Search engines and Web portals, in particular, set up this relation between user and material resources, calling upon a representation of cyberspace as a comprehensive, comprehendible system. The operational space of such Web sites intimates that the millions of servers online are, in effect, *there for my use.* The Web site produces information that is shaped by my actions. This is an information space in which the computer enacts networks of connections that correspond to my operations: the command-control-communicate world of cybernetics. As a representation of space, it enunciates an ideology of networked libertarianism that imagines the user in control. This is the "control revolution" of information technology envisioned by Andrew Shapiro:[51]

> No one is in control—except you. And if you're fairly new to the Net, then it may well feel frenzied and unmanageable. You're not powerless because someone else is pulling the strings, though. You're just beginning to realize that the strings are there for you to pull yourself. (30)

Here, then, is the technological utopia of a network society: in material form, the global network serves as an extension of the personal computer; as conceptual structure, the user-as-operator steers his cybernetic vehicle through a wealth of information; and as lived practice, the network itself serves as the workroom and the playground of a virtual middle class.

This cybernetic topography of the operator-in-control also presents itself in its inverse: cyberspace as a social space that is *out of control*. The most common manifestation of this representation of space involves the online impostor. Here, mastery of the material resources of the medium implies the potential for some *other* to deceive or to prey upon hapless users. Thus the news in the mid-1990s gave sporadic reports of sexual predators cruising teen chat rooms, and in cyber-criticism, the oft-told tale of Judy, a male psychologist who adopted an online persona of a female quadriplegic shut-in, served as both cautionary tale and critical reflection on the position of the subject in online discourse. Even in advertisements, such as the digital camera company that (humorously) depicts how photo editing can improve online romance, the suggestion is that one's mastery and control of digital technology implies potential control over *another* in a networked social space. Identity theft, as both neurotic concern and actual reality, serves as the exemplary instance of loss of control, in which some *other* occupies your networked "seat of command."

One can also identify competing virtual topographies that do not reduce to a binary of control/out of control. In contrast to the lived practice that gives rise to both the cybernetic subject and the identity-stealing hacker, network structures provide for what Mark Poster has called a "culture of underdetermination" and a distribution of identity.[52] In a number of articles, Poster has argued that the Internet provides for an opportunity to rethink the structure

of the subject-position as it has been articulated in modern political and social thought. Arguing that "the Internet is more like a social space than a thing
so that its effects are more like those of Germany than those of hammers,"
Poster notes that the assumption of a modern subject-position treats the Internet as "an effective tool of communication" (*What's the Matter with the
Internet?* 216). Poster, however, sees the Internet's potential to articulate alternate subject-positions and novel power relations. The "distributed subject"
no longer controls flows of information but takes part in the flows themselves,
produced by and producing events of exchange. In an odd way, "identity" becomes a kind of virus or "meme" (to use Richard Dawkins's term) in the social
space of networks, disseminating and dissipating within this network of flows.
These viral circulations suggest a different sense of space, flow, and interaction.
The Schmich-Vonnegut dissemination provides an exemplary instance where
a name marks a *circulation* rather than a subject, or rather circulation itself
produces a virtual subject-position that is actualized at the point of reception.
Since a dominant social space of CMC structures practice around efficiency
and control, it should come as no surprise that deterritorializations often appear as system failures of some sort: the Schmich-Vonnegut confusion (in its
most literal sense) marks cyberspace as a "lawless swamp." And it is the very
banality of this slippage that bears noting: that *one's own name* can function
online as a node of dissemination that overwhelms the forms, structures, and
practices of autonomy and control, be that through spam, viruses, or simply
the unreciprocated hypertext links pointed to one's Web site that map a user
into a network of flows. While foregrounding an ideology of agency and control, the enacted networks of cyberspace also produce spaces of dispersal and
dissipation that cannot reduce to spaces of control.[53]

In attempting to understand the processes that articulate cyberspace, we
should pay attention to the conflicts that emerge not only in representations
of space, but in material form and lived use. When discussing cyberspace as a
space of control or as a space of dissemination, for example, matters of access
to resources are significant considerations. The issues raised by discussions of
the "digital divide" (in both its global and its local forms) ultimately suggest
disparities in the spaces of everyday life mapped by lived daily interaction with
network technology. The success and failure of cybercafés in various locations
worldwide, and the variety of forms and usages that these wired public sites
enact, suggests the complexity of these emergent spaces of CMC. A "public access" terminal certainly marks a material form distinct from a home or a work-

place computer; but this singular material point of access also enacts a range of interpenetrating virtual topographies, articulated through its heterogeneous relations with conflicting conceptual structures and lived practices. The case of the Central Library in Atlanta provides a telling example. In response to a heavy demand on resources by homeless patrons, the Atlanta-Fulton Public Library System spent over $18,000 of federal grant money to provide a downtown shelter with laptop computers and a wireless Internet connection (Sansbury H1). In an interview in the *Atlanta Constitution,* Anita Beaty, executive director for the Task Force for the Homeless (which operates the shelter) explicitly describes Internet access as an issue of social access: "Computers and cell phones are the possession of people who have the money to purchase them. ... We need computer terminals in all the facilities where homeless people are because they can access resources after hours" (Sansbury H1). The brief article goes on to make several points worth noting. First, while Beaty insists that the computers are not seen as a trade-off for keeping the homeless out of the library, the article acknowledges a history of "complaints about hygiene" and fighting, indicating the resistance of the space of the library to accommodate "public access" in its broadest sense. Second, having access to email and Web-based resources is described by librarians and homeless advocates alike as an issue of *empowerment* and *enfranchisement* in society. The actions of groups dedicated to the eradication of the "digital divide" in effect map cyberspace as a space of control—where access is an inalienable right of an enlightened citizenry; at the same time, this social space actively resists modes of access that appear as "disruptions" to the structures of everyday use enacted by a dominant virtual class, treating any irregularities as "noise" and as a threat to system performance. Access must remain proper, and hence *proprietary.* Cyberspace presents spaces in conflict to the degree that these two structurings of social space—spaces of control and spaces of dispersal—play themselves out in competing directions. The question becomes a matter of understanding varying processes at work in the production of cyberspace, and hence the multiple, interpenetrating spaces that emerge as a result.

Conceptual Processes of Cyberspace

Clearly much of what was written on cyberspace in the 1990s focused heavily on conceptual processes, at the expense of the material and the experiential. The tendency to treat cyberspace as mere metaphor makes the error of abstracting semiotic systems from their material and pragmatic context, thereby enunciating a "space in the mind" without reference to the processes that bring bodies and material into the everyday practice of individuals in a networked society. A more complete spatial analysis of CMC would consider how conceptual structures interact with material forms and lived practice, without extracting these systems of signification from material and experiential contexts. The most useful analyses of representations of space will call explicit attention to the ways in which conceptual processes interact with material form and lived practice. For example, in discussions of MOOs and MUDs as virtual worlds, one would do well to be suspicious of declarations that these "worlds of the mind" liberate users from the strictures of space and time.[54] In contrast, one would want to understand the play that occurs between signifying systems, material forms, and lived, cultural practice in the production of these social spaces as virtual worlds. We would also need to maintain an understanding of space that is relational and dynamic, such that it is "the *relationship* between internal mental constructs and technologically generated representations of these constructs" that produces cyberspace as spaces of everyday life (Reid 166, italics added). Instead of suggesting a hallucinatory/illusory quality to cyberspace, such an analysis would foreground that space itself (cyber or otherwise) is a production that occurs as a result of the interaction of mental constructs and material forms, enacted in lived practice.

Differences in virtual topographies present themselves, in part, as conflicts in representations of space: "smooth spaces" emerging that disrupt the organized "striated spaces" of the point-to-point network. The representation of space implicated in the network-as-grid suggests a conceptual structure of space that is dominated by principles of point-to-point circulation. As both a material articulation of CMC and a lived practice of network use, a striated topography maps a cybernetic space in its most literal and etymological sense, providing a vehicle for steering the user through what William J. Mitchell has called the "city of bits." And certainly "the city" serves as a representation of space to the extent that it calls upon a specific set of material and experiential relations in the production of networked social space. The virtual city, as with the traditional city, presents "the striated space par excellence" by organizing flows into a system of nodes and circulations (Deleuze and Guattari 481). As a representation of space, "the city" serves to signify a locus of exchange in which the computer functions as a vehicle or tool of efficiency. In many regards, this representation of the city is the culmination of the technocratic urbanism of the 1960s and 1970s that Lefebvre reacted so strongly against in books such as *Right to the City* and *The Urban Revolution*. This vision of urbanism was epitomized for Lefebvre in Le Courbousier's rationalist city of traffic and circulation. The city can only function in this capacity to the extent that it enunciates a representation of space associated with rational control. In instances such as AOL's Digital City (recently renamed CityGuide) sites, cyberspace overlaps lived urban space to the extent that links on a page provide users with information about shopping and dining establishments in their local communities. The city online, then, presents itself as a searchable, clickable version of the city offline. In a more transcendent vision of controlling technology, GlobeXplorer.com allows its users to navigate a cybernetic urban space from above, providing street maps and aerial photographs down to the detail of one's own neighborhood. As the slogan for GlobeXplorer.com suggests ("Now, seeing the world is at your fingertips"), such representations of space bring the visual, the tactile, and the kinesthetic together in a symbol of the city tamed by the controlling urban "operator."

But "the city" also serves to signify spaces of wanderings and hidden places. In *The Urban Revolution*, Lefebvre suggests that "planning" and rational urbanism "colonize" the city, in part, by turning the "spontaneous theatre" of the streets into places of traffic and circulation (29).[55] Lefebvre maintains that the city, while dominated by a social space of urban planning and capitalist exchange, belongs to the order of human *use*: "places of simultaneity and encounters, places where exchange would not go through exchange value, commerce, and profit" (*Writings on Cities* 148). While the rationalist city speaks of circulations and flows, Lefebvre argues that: "The eminent use of the city, that is, of its streets and squares, edifices and monuments, is *la Fete* (a celebration which consumes unproductively, without other advantage but pleasure and prestige and enormous riches in money and objects)" (*Writings on Cities* 66). As one would expect, the conceptual processes involved in enacting "urban" virtual topographies are heteromorphic, leading to conflicting articulations of the city as a representation of space. The urban shows itself in a radically different representation of space when cast as a "transphysical city" of changing "liquid architecture" that forms and dissolves based on user interactions (Novak, "Transmitting Architecture"). The competing conceptual structures amount to conflicts in what Mike Crang calls an "urban imaginary" that has significant effects on how the virtual city *takes place* via CMC. Crang points out that "agora" and "forum" provide a conceptual structuring for CMC that understands the public spaces and public spheres of the city as "visualizable, organizable spaces," and in doing so articulates cyberspace along similar lines (87). The aerial maps of hometowns signify both the user's location in that space and his control over it. In contrast, Crang points to the possibility of an urban imaginary that would structure CMC as "labyrinthine space," a representation of space based on rupture, not autonomous, controlling presence. The strangeness of these interactions, and the possibility of unplanned, spontaneous gatherings, suggests an electronic urbanism that will not reduce to the rationalist cybernetic city. The urban, then, takes differing forms online—enacting cyberspace through differences in conceptual processes, material forms, and lived practice.

To speak of the conceptual processes of the virtual urban, we are indeed invoking metaphor, but in doing so, we are calling attention to how language involves itself in material form and lived practice. These conceptual structures are significant to the extent that they delimit lived practice and invoke material forms in ways that are often contradictory to other modes of "being online." The urban presents itself as heteromorphic articulations mapped in the spaces of everyday life in a networked society. As representations of space, the conceptual processes suggest not only an arrangement of ideas, but an arrangement of material forms and experiential practices. The competing conceptual processes have significance—a significance beyond signification—precisely because the conceptual structures are processes involved in enacting a social space within a networked society.

Material Processes of Cyberspace

Certainly it is tempting to unmoor our considerations of cyberspace from materiality, to get caught up in the flow of digital information. But social space is a tangle, a multiplicity, involving bodies, infrastructure, and activity—as well as representation. In addition to the conceptual processes that enunciate representations of space, we will also want to understand how material processes provide a focal point for the event of cyberspace enacted in heteromorphic virtual topographies. "The network" that maps what Lefebvre calls the "globalization of the city" materializes in the everyday life experience of globally networked home computers (*Writings on Cities* 208). Cyberspace is not only a conceptual structure but an actuality of material form that has a very real existence as a network of phone lines, T1 connections and T3 backbones, broadband cable and DSL lines, and wireless routers. The material form of virtual topographies does not enact a space that annihilates or supplants geography, although material articulations of "the world itself" are altered in the production of networked social space. Spatialities of "proximity" still exist, but the material processes of cyberspace give rise to an altered metric for "near" and "far." The emergence of Tuvalu onto the WWW provides an intriguing example of this restructuring of remoteness. Tuvalu is a small, relatively unknown chain of islands occupying ten square miles in the South Pacific, that possessed some very valuable electronic real estate: the .tv domain name. In this regard, Tuvalu is very much *on the map*. In a 1998 National Public Radio (NPR) interview, Jason Chapnik, president of the Toronto-based dotTV marketing firm that has since purchased the .tv domain name, describes the brainstorming session that got the company going. Looking for the "ultimate top-level domain name" to market the sale of Internet addresses, the team came up with the letters "TV"; only then did they discover the existence of the tiny islands, to which InterNIC had assigned the .tv domain site (Chadwick). The digital mapping of .tv onto the flows of capital and information that circulate on the WWW in this regard did precede the territory—not as a Baudrillardian simulation, but as an altered relation between material form, conceptual structure, and lived practice. In this instance, geographic proximity lacked significance compared to one's proximal situation within a network of data flows, Internet Service Providers (ISPs), and high-demand Internet protocol (IP) addresses.

Certainly the integration of what had once symbolized absolute remoteness—the antipodes—into a global communications network provides a compelling example of what Fredric Jameson and David Harvey see as a compression of space and time in a postmodern world. As Ken Friedman notes, consciously avoiding the image of a cyberspace unmoored from a social space of material form and embodied experience, the global urbanism of virtual cities places even the most remote (in his instance, Nordic) locations as material nodes into a "space of flows" and informatic exchange that "become the governing flow that controls the shape of the world." Businesses were fast to recognize the potential for a commercialism that could penetrate every household in a way far more dizzying than television, through a material super-saturation that Jameson describes as a "postmodern hyperspace" that is everywhere and nowhere at the same time (44).[56] By way of the Internet, "the market" is no longer any *place* but an ever-present virtual/potential opening, materially enacted in network flows. While McLuhan had imagined a global village, Chapnik and other Internet entrepreneurs of the 1990s materialized a global city, held together by a network of information flows. This does not mean that locality no longer matters, but rather that the material relations of space have become dominated by a logic of connectivity. Thus, in a "network society," the network itself provides a fundamental structuring for social and economic forms.

Much of what we could say about material processes that take part in the production of cyberspace parallels what Manuel Castells notes as a growing dominance of a networked "space of flows" in place of a geographic "space of places," resulting from the rise of informational structures of transnational capitalism. Castells argues, particularly in *The Rise of the Network Society,* that the restructuring of an economy based on new technologies and on a networking logic gives rise to material processes that in effect restructure social space.[57] This restructuring is profoundly global,[58] but "global" in the sense that it is now defined as a dynamic of flows. Following in a Lefebvrean tradition, Castells maintains that space is produced, and therefore is defined, as an event of relations and as an "expression of society" (*The Rise of the Network Society* 410). In a network society, the dominant processes involve the production of and control over a global "space of flows," a space that simultaneously networks and disperses geographical locations (393–98).[59] As a system, it is autopoietic rather than mechanistic, in that the network structure itself serves as a fundamental unit (165). As such, "position" or "location," defined at the scale of the individual, national, or corporate entity, is structured within the network as a materiality of flow (147). Conflicting virtual topographies suggest not only conflicting representations of space but conflicting articulations of a materiality of flow. One finds, then, that global networks in their material articulation "reinforce the social cohesion of the cosmopolitan elite, providing material support to the meaning of a global culture" at the same time that disenfranchised groups, from right-wing extremists to Zapatista rebels, find a new sense of position and situatedness within a global space of flows (364).[60] In each instance, conflicting virtual topographies involve real differences in the articulation of material relations on a global scale, actualizing very different spaces of everyday life.

Any complete spatial analysis of cyberspace would therefore need to take into account the material processes of CMC as they take part in articulating what Mark Poster calls "a new regime of relations between humans and matter and between matter and non-matter" (*What's the Matter with the Internet?* 176). An analysis of the spaces of hypertext, for example, must take into consideration not only how networks of linkage suggest an altered representation of space (rhizome, highway, etc.), but how a complex nexus of materialities is enacted by a "point-and-click" practice. Thus, Kathleen Burnett argues that the material networks and conceptual framework of an electronic "scholar's rhizome" might lead to a shift not only in "writing space" but in the networks of social power exhibited in the academy by faculty hierarchies, journal reputations, and university press rankings. In the classroom, students who have been given material access to networked computers and electronic databases find that the "library without walls" materializes in an open field of undifferentiated texts, where serious scholarship and the most frivolous of postings occupy the same information space. Any spatial analysis of cyberspace would have to take into account these competing material processes, and the material form that they enact in the production of a networked social space.

Experiential Processes of Cyberspace

Taking the preceding two sections together, it should be increasingly clear that the spaces of cyberspace provide a kind of mapping of interacting material and conceptual processes. One cannot consider the concept of space without also thinking in terms of the material forms that interact with these conceptual structures. The relation between the material and the conceptual gives rise to a constellation of sorts, what Donna Haraway has described as a situatedness: a material and semiotic universe (*Modest Witness@Second Millennium* 116). Without attempting to privilege one term over the other, we might further acknowledge a third term in this dialectic—a term marked by the lived mappings of both material forms and semiotic structures. This third term focuses our analysis of space on the experiential practices that enact and embody these material and conceptual processes.

The measure of the lived will have to be more subtle, in that any analysis is always poised on the brink of a dizzying descent of scale whose limit is the singularity of the situated individual. That said, one can still look for cultural patterns of lived use that help to foreground these heteromorphic virtual topographies of everyday life. At one end of the scale, we will want to be sensitive to the "embodied knowledge" that CMC calls forward: simple actions—such as knowing the speed of a "double click" or understanding the navigational framework of multilayered, multitasking windows—require an incorporation (in its most literal sense) of knowledge that situates the user in relation to both material forms and conceptual structures. This habitus, to use Pierre Bourdieu's term, suggests not only an embodiment of knowledge but also that the material and conceptual structures that make up these forms are enacted by situated actors within a social field. In other words, not only are the lived spaces of cyberspace produced by material and conceptual processes, the material forms and conceptual structures are themselves produced by experiential processes that stand in a situated relation to these structures and forms.

Bourdieu's discussion of habitus provides an important rubric for understanding how practice actualizes social structures while at the same time being delimited by these social structures. He defines habitus as "systems of durable, transposable *dispositions* . . . predisposed to function as . . . principles of the generation and structuring of practices and representations which can be objectively 'regulated' and 'regular' without in any way being the product of obedience to rules" (*Outline of a Theory of Practice* 72). Habitus accounts for strategies of engaging social space—never fully improvised or scripted— that are determined as a range of possibilities and actualized in the particular. Bourdieu stresses the importance of the word "disposition" in this definition, because it implies both a corporeal and a cognitive orientation. Practice occurs, he writes, as a "dialectic . . . of incorporation and objectification" (*Outline of a Theory of Practice* 72). Practice incorporates objective social structures as a set of bodily and conceptual dispositions, which in turn provide strategies for actualizing these structures in social space (*Pascalian Meditations* 130). Habitus as a collection of dispositions describes "a particular but constant way of entering into a relationship with the world which contains a knowledge enabling it to anticipate the course of the world" (*Pascalian Meditations* 142). One learns to incorporate and actualize strategies in the play of practice, which in turn give access to a field or a position in social space. Habitus, in other words, provides entry into particular fields and particular positions within social space, thereby granting access to particular forms of cultural capital.

At the most basic level of analysis, a study of online dispositions would have to give an account of the structural relation of user to computer that places the user in the role of information operator. As both corporeal and cognitive orientations, virtual topographies first and foremost assume a certain fluency with human-computer interaction. The degree to which technological knowledge is overlooked as a precursor to "entry" into cyberspace suggests what Bourdieu calls "misrecognition"—the process by which those within a field of power only recognize a system of value in a euphemized form. We might think of this "comfort" with CMC as a kind of *interface disposition:* those corporeal and cognitive strategies that predispose the user to relate to the screen as both a visual and a tactile object. Likewise, we would want to take into account the *operational disposition* that defines an input-output relation with the interface, and that expresses itself in such minute bodily acts as knowing the proper speed to "double click" a mouse, as well as globally embodied strategies such as the posture one maintains before the keyboard and the screen, defining a corporeal zone of interaction between the user and the network. As lived practice of cyberspace, these dispositions function as strategies that are misrecognized incorporations of values that allow a "virtual class" to negotiate a position within a networked digital world. We would want to ask how this sort of capital exchanges within a larger social field: the degree to which a network habitus points more toward entry into an elite class of "digerati" or an "information working class" of network capitalism.

In addition to an analysis at the scale of the situated individual, we will also want to consider cyberspace as mapped by the cultural forms that structure our understanding of lived space. In other words, to turn again to the instance of the "virtual city" as an example, we will want to engage not only the embodied dispositions that provide individuals with the cultural capital to take part within a networked urbanism, we will also want to examine the fields of power that structure the modes of exchange that are available to individuals within cyberspace as a space of everyday life. As Jonathan Sterne notes, a cultural studies approach to the Internet emphasizes the *situation* of the medium in everyday life ("Thinking the Internet" 275). The competing topographies of cyberspace in everyday life—the naturalized and normative assumptions that come into play, in both material form and conceptual structure, in defining what it means to "be online"—become the very points of analysis for understanding cyberspace. Such an analysis would highlight the significance of social forms in situating a variety of lived practices of cyberspace.[61] The everyday life experience of cyberspace would, from a cultural studies perspective, force an analysis of how practices of access reveal structures of social space. Sterne concludes: "The politics of access are not simply a matter of getting more people online. It is also a matter of how, when, and on what terms people are coming online, and what they discover upon arrival" ("The Computer Race Goes to Class" 209).

In this regard, virtual topographies reveal cultural topographies, enacted by the variety of practices of everyday life. Even when, as Stephen Doheny-Farina advocates, network technology is used "to serve, not to transcend localities" in building civic structures, these networked civic structures in effect reveal the cultural structures that map social realities of difference on a local, national, and global scale (127). As David Silver notes in his analysis of the Blacksburg [Virginia] Electronic Village (BEV), one can find structures that celebrate a diversity of ages (dedicated lists for K–12, as well as senior citizens) and a diversity of businesses (from local shops to national chains), but structures of difference by way of race, gender, and sexuality have been "routed around" (144–45); what might otherwise appear as minor interface issues (points of entry into a community portal), in effect discipline the Deleuzian minor, thereby limiting the possibilities for actualizing heteromorphic social spaces lived out by a range of users. This cultural studies approach to virtual topographies would focus on what de Certeau calls "modes of operation or schemata of action," which, while enacted by individuals, cannot be reduced to singular autonomous acts (xi). "Everyday practice," then, would help to reveal the operational structures of networked culture in its actual form, as well as the virtualities that exist as possible modes of deviance, challenge, or appropriation.

In 1960s Paris, Guy Debord and the French Situationists resisted the "planning" ideology of the organized city by bringing to the fore the experience of the urban as a confused, heterogeneous, labyrinthine space (Sadler 22–33). Unlike the circulation and flow of traffic, people, information, power, etc., of the planned city, situationist psychogeography provided mappings of *dérives:* driftings through multiple, confusing urban topographies that connected the material form of the city with experiential practice.[62] This theory of the dérive, along with Lefebvre's insistence on the ludic use of the city,[63] has important consequences for a spatial analysis of networked social space: namely that the "space of flows" instantiated by the dominant social space of CMC might likewise present spaces of everyday life that resist this logic of circulation, exchange, and maximum performance. In its simplest form, aimless "netsurfing" on the WWW suggests a kind of "drift logic"; with complete disregard for a "logic of maximum performance," Web users can find themselves involved in interactions with vast material resources that prove *aimless* and *unproductive.* Steven Johnson has developed this line of argument, drawing explicit parallels to the contrast between the "crooked Parisian streets" of the Latin Quarter and the "broad, straight lines" of Haussmann's boulevards (63–64). As an example of this image of the ludic city online, Johnson turns to the Palace, an environment for synchronous communication, with the added feature of visual representation of presence—users can select and/or customize their own personal avatar. Unlike the "surfer" metaphor associated with the Web, Johnson argues, the Palace puts the user in the role of Baudelaire's *flaneur,* "drawn to the 'kaleidoscope of consciousness' found among the teeming masses prowling those metropolitan streets" (67). Within just a few years, however, it would have been hard to take too much encouragement in this version of the ludic city, presented at www.thepalace.com. Bought out by Communities.com, the Palace was by 2000 billing itself as "the first real-time, interactive, rich media network" and promising to "packag[e] content, audience, advertising and e-commerce . . . to create an enhanced sense of place and permanence that uniquely enriches the community experience" (Communities.com). In effect, the ludic had become lucrative. The Palace presented its users with a choice of "channels" organized around topics (TV, music, romance, etc.), as well as special-event real-time "chats" with celebrities ranging from teen pop stars to dotcom CEOs. As such, we find "the city" reduced to highly organized channels of space, having more to do with scheduling and programming than "spontaneity and encounter." We can, however, still identify—in this interplay between individual practice and the social structures that delimit practice—a mapping of how experiential processes take part in the production of networked social space.[64]

As with the analysis of material forms and conceptual structures, the lived practices enacted by experiential processes reveal the production of heteromorphic cyberspaces. What's more, the interaction between the material, the conceptual, and the lived emphasizes that each cluster of processes is inextricably caught up in the produced/producing relation of the others.

(Cyber)Spaces in Conflict

The sort of spatial analysis that I am suggesting highlights that the event of cyberspace is material, conceptual, and experiential—that it is mapped by conceptual structures, material forms, and lived practice. This approach to an analysis of cyberspace resists the temptation to separate the material from the symbolic, and, as such, it comes a long way in addressing the problem of space raised by cyberspace. In addition, such an approach foregrounds the necessity of treating cyberspace as a heteromorphic event rather than a homogenous object or a place marker. Rather, the analytical approach inspired here by Lefebvre—and augmented by a Deleuzian reworking of speech act theory,

Castells's analysis of the material forms of network society, and Bourdieu's discussion of habitus—suggests that space itself, on- and offline, is heteromorphic in its productions.

Certainly we can identify a dominant social space associated with cyberspace, one that privileges the network as a coordinated system of market relays, placing the user in a lived space of "total control." Yet the range of events and situations involved in the mapping of virtual topographies makes cyberspace resistant to homogenous descriptions. If we can identify (to modify Lefebvre somewhat) "a [cyber]space that is *other*," such spaces exist not "beyond" this system but as articulated events, enacted within the very same nexus of material, conceptual, and experiential processes that give rise to a dominant social space of control, efficiency, and network capitalism (*The Production of Space* 391). These points map sites of contradiction in space: not a standing tension so much as a mutual interpenetration of space and "counter-space" (367). In contrast to the "isotopia" of cyberspace as open market/agora of ideas, the enacted virtual topographies of competing material forms, conceptual structures, and lived practices suggest a "heterotopic" cyberspace of multiple, interpenetrating articulations (Lefebvre, *Writings on Cities* 113).[65] The heterotopic maps an interpenetration of spaces in conflict that, in Deleuzian terms, both deterritorializes and reterritorializes the spaces of everyday life.[66] But these conflicting topographies do not spatially *oppose* each other; rather, they are implicated in the co-emergence of competing and interpenetrating social spaces. Cyberspace, as material form, conceptual structure, and dispositional practice, marks one such scene of conflict in the social space of a network society.

The value of .tv as virtual real estate provides an example of the sorts of contestations of cyberspace occurring online. While this piece of virtual real estate has value only once it has been "coordinated" by a logic of performance and circulation, it also marks the potential for a heterogeneity of sites that allows "difference" to maintain significance in the production of cyberspace. On one hand we are given an example of how difference is "*produced* in space through the simple logic of uneven capital investment" (Harvey, *Justice, Nature, and the Geography of Difference* 295). While the increasing power of media conglomerates such as Time Warner over the commercial terrain of the Internet, along with the radically diminished list of sites attracting a majority of browsers to the Web, suggests that cyberspace bears all the trapping of the corporate culture of American consumer markets, the billions of sites that Google or Alta-Vista count exert a heterogeneity that counteracts the homogenizing crush of a dominant corporate culture. One must also take account of the distribution of cyberspace as material form, conceptual structure, and lived practice on a global scale, allowing for heteromorphic articulations based on the situated singularity of those local-yet-global sites. This is perhaps the greatest lesson of the Ejército Zapatista de Liberación Nacional's (EZLN) appropriation of the Internet as a means of political resistance—that the global space of flows radicalizes the global and the local alike. It also accounts for why *terror* now takes the form of the distributed network. One can imagine the cluster of media corporations that will be attracted to the .tv domain name. But the Internet also allows for a proliferation of zones of difference conducive to a range of lived experiences (hence the persistent fear of perversion and corruption online), all the while allowing such spaces to abut with, connect to, and contradict other emergent spaces of everyday life.

The relation of the heterotopic to the everyday, then, is always by way of a spatial interpenetration that both deterritorializes and reterritorializes lived space. In some instances, these heterotopic sites mark true "counter-spaces": sites of contestation involving lived space of its users (Lefebvre, *The Production of Space* 367).[67] Yet these "minor" sites can never escape from the disciplining of the "major," the dominant social space that organizes material form, conceptual structure, and lived practice in an attempt to transform these sites of resistance into "induced differences" that remain instrumental within its logic circulation and control.[68] If an analysis of cyberspace reveals heterotopic sites, it does so because these spaces are implicated in the articulation of two competing and interpenetrating social spaces. Lefebvre's dialectical method identifies a critical moment in the dominant social space of the twentieth century, marked by the contradiction between a global space of localized function and a local "need" for systemic homogeneity (*The Production of Space* 355–56). By exploiting this contradiction, he argues, a new "situational" space could emerge that would preserve the singularities of localization, while at the same time opening them up to global structures of difference (363). Certain aspects of online space do seem to coincide with this description of a "situational" or "differential" social space. Virtual topographies do, after all, enact a kind of local access that at the same time disperses and disseminates at the widest level. In doing so, however, they map articulations of space played out at the level of everyday life. As such, a spatial analysis of cyberspace will reveal the dynamic tensions between the disciplines and indisciplines of virtual topographies, not the final "state of affairs" of the social space of modernity.

Cyberspace and the Spaces of Everyday Life

To understand the lived significance of cyberspace, it is important to recognize that these competing, contradictory social spaces are not merely productions of a media event or figments of a popular imagination. Called by any name, these virtual topographies involve real bodies, real material investment, and real social interaction. The current chapter has attempted to identify a tendency in CMC scholarship to perpetuate a form of dualism that separates cyberspace from real space, treating it as a conceptual structure. By drawing on a view of space as relational and dynamic, rather than abstract and passive, I have attempted to rethink space as an event produced by material, conceptual, and experiential processes. An examination of conceptual structures, material forms, and lived practices reveals that cyberspace is indeed enacted in heterogeneous spaces of everyday life. Furthermore, a critical analysis of these processes reveals the productive relation of each in the other. These heteromorphic virtual topographies do not coordinate into any overall system, but rather interpenetrate each other, producing spaces in conflict.

Without question, the rise and spread of CMC in the last decade of the twentieth century was—and continues to be—a significant cultural event. As such, one could have expected the degree of hype and dread that surrounded "cyberspace" as it moved from a science-fiction reference to the spaces of everyday life. In providing a theoretical framework for an analysis of cyberspace, it is my hope that this current project will take part in a larger reassessment of the cultural impact of network technology in contemporary society.

VIRTUAL WORLDS AND SITUATED SPACES

TOPOGRAPHIES OF THE WORLD WIDE WEB

I N THE PREVIOUS CHAPTER, I have attempted to justify considering CMC, and in particular the Internet, as a produced social space, understood as a dynamic event brought about by heteromorphic material, conceptual, and experiential processes. In this chapter and the following chapter, I attempt to situate this theoretical framework in relation to specific forms of CMC currently dominant on the Internet, namely the WWW and email. Given the divergent and often contradictory virtual topographies that result from these forces of spatial production, it would be difficult if not impossible to suggest a comprehensive map of cyberspace in all its conflicting articulations. In contrast, by focusing on two dominant modes of CMC, and by sampling the material forms, conceptual structures, and lived practices that enact these topographies, I can provide an account of prominent patterns in the production of spaces of everyday life in a networked society, along with the spaces of conflict that reveal contested sites of spatial production.

Although the Internet involves a range of modes of communication, the WWW and email remain by far the most common modes of CMC. And while email has been around a longer time and has been adopted by a larger segment of the population as an everyday practice, it was the WWW that came to represent the global implications of cyberspace in the 1990s. In less than ten years, from Tim Berners-Lee's public release of HTML standards to the dot-com crash of 2000, well over a billion pages entered into the domain of networked texts we call the World Wide Web. Today "the Web" enacts a material form that is simultaneously global and individualized, allowing a personal computer running a browser application to access networked servers "anywhere"[1] in the world. Thus the Web is presented in the mass media as the great leveler by providing individuals access to a global medium of production, distribution, and consumption. In addition to providing a material form for a "worldwide" space of flows, hypertext also enacts conceptual structures that foreground the user as an autonomous controller/operator of global resources. Browsing, as a lived practice, articulates a space in which the network situates the user in an operational relation with "the world." This vision of cyberspace as a space of control represents a dominant ideology of the Web, but the heterogeneity of globally distributed Web sites also allows for articulations of cyberspace that challenge this representation of space. As a research methodology, a "systematic" overview of Web sites would not only be impossible, it would take part in a conceptual structure that represents cyberspace as a diverse terrain in its instances, but as *essentially* homogenous in abstraction. In contrast, a method of sampling that is in a very fundamental sense idiosyncratic and random would suggest the singular, situated nature of heteromorphic virtual topographies. Such an approach would also foreground the eventlike role of lived practices as both operational strategy and embodied knowledge in the production of virtual topographies.

At its simplest, every Web site attempts to establish a sense of place—that you have arrived *somewhere*. What marks this space as such has less to do with the geographical context of the site than the relation that it maintains with other sites and documents. As fewer sites take up a greater percentage of user hits, a common terrain begins to develop online as a normative topography of a virtual class. According to a report by Jupiter Media Metrix, as of summer 2001, 60 percent of U.S. user-time online was spent at sites owned by fourteen companies. While these figures include time spent chatting, emailing, and messaging, not simply browsing, the pattern suggests that while Google and AltaVista search literally billions of Web pages, users spend a majority of time at well-known, well-traveled sites—sites affiliated with large corporations.

Thus Time Warner and its related company sites (including AOL) account for nearly one-third of use time. At the same time, however, this point-and-click interface that produces a "space of control" for the user also maps the potential for a social space in which multiple, often contradictory practices find expression within the material form of global network technology. Each Web page in effect presents a virtuality, the potential to enact a network of connections to other sites. By no means do all these sites stand in equal relation to one another. But at the same time, each enfolds the others in the potential for contact. In the commercial world, sites strive for "stickiness"—a measure of how long you stay at a site and how entangled you become in a site's various pages. As a result, commercial sites often enact a topography that is best described as a kind of "virtual world": a closed, comprehensive, self-contained globe. There's plenty of territory to discover, but ultimately all meridians lead full circle. At the same time, the concept of a virtual world is only possible within the material and experiential processes that situate this topography within a "global imagination" of the WWW as a space of flows: namely, a network of interconnecting servers and the potential for a user to reach this site from anywhere at any time. In form, structure, and practice, then, the Web is both globally expansive and locally situated. It places users in a global space of flows, yet it articulates a lived space of idiosyncratic practice, one defined more by the *potential* for linkage than the actual connection.

Underlying the WWW (in its current form) is a structure of hypertext that allows for the linking of documents at various servers worldwide. This hypertextuality serves as the basis for the event of cyberspace via the WWW by literally calling forth a material relation of computers, servers, and network infrastructure from a lived practice of pointing and clicking. As such, it would be worthwhile to examine the spatial practices of hypertext per se as a prelude to a wider discussion of the production of a networked social space via the WWW.

Hypertext and the Spaces of Information

From its prehistory in Vannevar Bush's description of the Memex machine through its best-known incarnation in the WWW, hypertext has been theorized as a spatial medium. Hypertext presents an altered understanding of what Jay Bolter has called "writing space," by allowing writing itself to become topographical. While writing assumes a spatial orientation (left-to-right, top-down), hypertextual writing occurs in or at different fields or sites, with the connections between sites marked by "links of association."[2] The documents laid out in hypertext suggest a space comprised of a network of linkages, which the writer adds to and the reader traces. But this understanding of the "network," as discussed in chapter 1, is as much a representation of space as it is a material form and a lived practice. This representation of a network of linkages treats the connections between pages of a hypertextual field as a reified structure: a network of nodes. However, there is no *material* link between two pages, only the potential for one (every "dead" link attests to this fact). As such, the materiality of the *link* does not enunciate itself on the screen in glowing blue letters, but rather in the embodied experience of the user whose eye is trained on the screen and whose hand deftly types, scrolls, and clicks. In fact, there is no reason to treat the link that occurs by way of clicking on the screen as more or less direct than the link that occurs when a user "points" the browser to another page by typing in a URL. The spatial practices of hypertext *do* enact a network, but that network need not present itself strictly as a reified "web" or a "net." Thus browsing the WWW does indeed provide users with access to a range of sources, distributed both geographically and topically, but the "connections" that link them are always potential, not *actual,* until they are articulated though an enacted relation at the point of embodied interface. In this regard, hypertextual cyberspace is a relational space, actualized in lived practice. On any given page, the potential exists for multiple mappings, but any given linkage enacted by a user amounts to an ordering and a territorialization of both material form and semiotic structure. As an event, then, hypertext suggests both virtual structures of potential and actual enacted writing spaces. In fact, hypertext as a material form, conceptual structure, and lived practice provides a valuable model for the eventlike quality of space in general, and the dynamic, relational qualities of cyberspace in particular.

The event-network of hypertext that I am describing is fundamentally virtual in the sense that these pages stand in a relation such that at any given time a connection between any two sites could occur by way of lived practice. This virtuality reframes discussions of dangerous content on the Internet by forcing us to reconsider how hypertext enacts an actual information space as an event-network. Toward the end of his book on virtual state structures, for example, Jerry Everard speaks of the Internet as a *tool,* explaining how his daughter can conduct primary research on NASA transcripts in a networked environment that will also give her access to "home pages for Barbie dolls and the

Simpsons" (128). But Everard here seems to have lost sight of his own discussion of the relation between states and identities, forgetting, as Mark Poster has suggested, that the Internet is more like Germany than a hammer. In the social space produced by the user pointing and clicking her way through various sites in a globally distributed network, the very possibility for errant or "perverse" connections is inseparable and indistinguishable from its global, "universal" potential. From the perspective of an information space, then, there can be no real distinction between appropriate or inappropriate linkages or sites. It should be no surprise that while hypertext allows for the spread of a "scholar's rhizome," it also gives rise to a crisis of sorts in college classrooms as teachers increasingly encounter problems addressing the validity of sources on the WWW. In a discussion of how online pornography often frames Internet censorship debates, Everard notes: "The chances of children accidentally blundering into such sites seems in fact smaller than a child accidentally wandering into an adults-only night-club or sex shop" (131). Where the analogy breaks down is that "zoning" cannot really exist in the virtual topographies of hypertext, nor will setting up warning posts declaring "18 or over" keep any user from enacting a space, through lived practice, that would link, for example, NASA Mars photos to a pornographic site. Such a vision of the spatiality of hypertext runs contrary to the ideology of the information superhighway, where connectivity equates with efficiency and productivity. As an event-space, these topographies of control attempt to discipline the material, conceptual, and experiential processes of hypertext by articulating the actual at the expense of the virtual—producing an efficient, "high performance" network of nodes. Yet gaps and fissures will always exist as indisciplines, minor practices, and deterritorializations. The very "tools" that suggest a relation predicated upon meaningful or authorized connections provide their own ironic revenge. With XML tags, it is certainly possible to create a site that will "pop up" in a search engine regardless of one's search criteria. And in its inverse, spaces of control enacted by "Netnanny" and other gatekeeper programs (which Everard mentions) may very well present blockages that impede the "appropriate" connections intended by the user.[3]

As a virtual structure, hypertext suggests a universalizing and thereby globalizing medium. By making links from text to text or site to site, the user literally maps, by way of lived practice, a cluster of material and conceptual connections within this universal archive. Tim Berners-Lee makes clear throughout his book *Weaving the Web* that, from his perspective, the WWW functions as a transformative technology specifically by its ability to function on a global, universal level enacted by the individual user. The Web is, for Berners-Lee, a *space* that is both informatic and social, weaving ideas and individuals together in mutual relations. Describing his early thoughts on the Web (and its origin as an in-house program at CERN called Enquire), Berners-Lee writes:

> *Suppose all the information stored on computers everywhere were linked,* I thought. *Suppose I could program my computer to create a space in which anything could be linked to anything.* All the bits of information in every computer at CERN, and on the planet, would be available to me and to anyone else. There would be a single, global information space. (4)

As a space of potential, Berners-Lee describes hypertext as an all-encompassing medium, on both the planetary and informatic scale. In effect, hypertext conflates these two scales in the vision of a "single, global information space." This space functions, for Berners-Lee, as the equivalent to Newtonian abstract space: a container for "bits" of information.[4] As such, the user occupies a position of control, manipulating these "bits" in an abstract space of potential in which "anything could be linked to anything." In addition to these traces of a Newtonian abstract space, one can also find intimations of the "Liebnizian conceit" in the dominant spatiality of hypertext, which locates the user in abstraction from and as master over a universe of relations. The user remains *outside* of this space (transcendent rather than immanent) and in control of these connections, invoking once again the cybernetician's fantasy of the controller/operator who commands planetary resources.

For Berners-Lee, the global reach of hypertext and the individual autonomy of the user are integral, inseparable elements of the Web as an information space, allowing it to function as "an intimate collaborative medium" (57). This apparent contradiction is a defining feature of the spatiality of hypertext: it is a medium that is global and "intimate" at the same time. Furthermore, in its collaborative, productive mode, Berners-Lee describes the Web as fundamentally a social space. He writes: "I designed [the Web] for a social effect—to help people work together. . . . The ultimate goal of the Web is to support and improve our weblike existence in the world" (123). In effect, Berners-Lee acknowledges the network structure of society that computer technology augments but did not create. The Web exploits the networking logic of a space of flows, and in doing so, it reinforces these same "weblike" forms, structures, and practices that give rise to a network society. As a spatial medium, then, hypertext is ideally suited for the dispositional practices and operational strategies of individuals in a social space that is increasingly globalized. While the spatiality of hypertext implies a global scale, it is likewise mapped and enacted in the lived practice of individual users controlling these planetary flows. For example, in describing the future of the WWW as an emergent "Semantic Web,"[5] Berners-Lee writes:

> Imagine what computers can understand when there is a vast tangle of interconnected terms and data that can automatically be followed. The power we will have at our fingertips will be awesome. (185)

There is a definite ideology at work in this conception of cyberspace that on one hand foregrounds the catholic structures of a global information space while at the same time it privileges the agency of the individual, be that as Enlightenment subject or as cybernetic operator with "awesome" powers in hand. "Control" serves as an order-word that disciplines the relation between the global/universal and the individual/intimate in a social information space, with no room for errant lines of flight and outlying data.

While Berners-Lee is responsible for the appearance of hypertext as the WWW, the vision of hypertext as a global, universal medium predates the Web in Ted Nelson's originary vision of hypertext as information space and transformative technology. In Nelson's vision, the universal machine becomes a universal space, with the computer functioning, in effect, as "one great repository [in which] everything will be equally accessible" (*Literary Machines* 1.15). Hypertext, in other words, would serve as "a universal instantaneous publishing system and archive for the world." (2.4). Nelson is interested in information storage and retrieval, but clearly his understanding of hypertext makes a strong connection between the "structure of ideas,"[6] the material production of technological systems, and the lived practice of reading and writing. As such, his vision of hypertext is very much a vision of a spatial medium involved in the lived spaces of everyday life. The mission statement for Nelson's Project Xanadu (www.xanadu.com) calls for "a world of deep electronic documents" and describes a version of hypertext (the true version, Nelson would argue) in which individual pages enact structures of connection on a global scale, conceptualized as a depth (one document emerging from and interpenetrating another) rather than just a breadth (one document linking to another). While Nelson tends less toward an organic vision of global hypertext, as a spatial medium he still describes it as a *world* of information in which users are *deeply involved.*

The structure of Nelson's thoughts on hypertext, built around the slogan "everything is deeply intertwingled," suggests that the medium draws the user into a universe of ideas.[7] This vision of a "world of deep electronic documents" becomes a literalized space for reading and writing, a space in which literacy takes the form of an interpenetration of globally distributed texts.

While the conflicts between Nelson's and Berners-Lee's conceptions of hypertext are not insignificant, it should be worth noting that the point of contact between the two visions of hypertext is its universality and its global reach. The structure of hypertext, then, is very much a matter of space—not only a medium for presenting spatially arranged texts (the topographic writing that Jay Bolter describes), but literally a machinic and semiotic assemblage that places communication and geography in lived relation. The dominant virtual topography of hypertext is produced by a representation of space that is both global in its scope and individual and intimate at the point of interface. Its material form locates the user at a screen, yet through a visual-tactile interface—the point and click—it situates the user within a globally distributed network of texts. As lived practice, hypertext also depends upon a practice of interaction: creating texts that respond to the user's demands and commands. This is an ergodic text, to use Espen Aarseth's term, to the extent that it suggests a malleable medium in which the user participates. Hypertext structures a relation between the virtual and the actual, translated into the global and the situated, by way of experiential processes that enact a relation between texts. At its most virtual, the WWW presents an indeterminate domain of connectivity—connections leading anywhere. As an event enacted by a specific user, however, the Web provides a space that situates the individual and the act of browsing in very singular ways. In this regard, even something as banal as a "dead link" is not to be overlooked, but understood as taking part in mapping spaces of everyday life.

Virtual Worlds and the Global Imagination

The dream of control, epitomized by search engines and net filters, suggests a specific structuring of hypertext as a global, intimate medium. At the scale of the individual, it suggests the autonomous subject with the world at his fingertips. At the same time, however, the conflation of information space and geographic space suggests a coding and mapping of the planet as a whole through flows of data. As such, the networked computer functions as a technology that is indeed transformative to the extent that it provides an altered material, conceptual, and lived relation between the individual and "the globe." The spatiality of hypertext, particularly as presented on the WWW, provides a means for rethinking the way we understand the social space of global networks. The user of these networks finds an opportunity to position everyday life within a global framework. But that user is hardly "everyone": at present no more than 15 percent of the global population (ClickZ Stats, "Population Explosion!"). The spatiality of the WWW, then, involves a set of non-coordinating processes that warrant further analysis: its position within an understanding of "the global," as a material, conceptual, and lived framework for the developed world; its resistance to the flows, levelings, and heteromorphic forms that the network instantiates in its potential for enacting encounters; and the means by which, at the scale of lived experience, these topographies interpenetrate the everyday lives of citizens in a networked world.

As several authors have noted, perhaps most notably David Harvey, the global network structures in place today via high-speed data lines and computer servers take part in a history that has its origins in the fifteenth century with the rise of market capitalism and European imperialism. As such, the spatiality of hypertext as both global and intimate space is caught up in this history of "the globe" itself as a social space—its emergence as a dominant representation of space, intertwined with the material processes of nautical commerce and the lived experience of imported goods, narratives of exploration, and a bidirectional colonial influence. The medium of the map provides a historical instance of how "the globe" occurs in modernity, not merely as a *concept* but also as a material form and a lived practice. While it would be overly simplistic to suggest that the medium of the map and the medium of the Web are identical, I would argue that a comparative analysis of both media would help clarify how cyberspace takes part in the material, conceptual, and experiential processes that gave rise to "the globe" as a space of everyday life in the West.

In many ways, one could argue that the history of modernity is the history of the globe. The system of modern mapping began to emerge in the early fifteenth century with the arrival of Ptolemaic maps in Florence (Harvey, *The Condition of Postmodernity* 245). Earlier, navigational *portulans* recorded coastal outlines and subjective accounts as recorded by ships' pilots. As Harvey notes, the move from portulan to cartographic grid (from chorography to geography) introduced a mathematical and perspectival abstraction that could depict the world as an "objective" whole (246–49). This geometric abstraction allowed "global position" to emerge as a coordinate property of the world itself, separate from any individual's experience of place. Calling particular attention to the rise of perspectival optics at this moment in the West, Samuel Edgerton comments:

> The portulans did not furnish a geometrical framework for comprehending the whole world. The Ptolemaic grid, on the other hand, posed an immediate mathematical unity. The most far-flung places could all be precisely fixed in relation to one another by unchanging coordinates so that their proportionate distance, as well as their directional relationships, would be apparent. (quoted in Harvey, *The Condition of Postmodernity* 245)

Ptolemy's grid provided a conceptual framework for *ordering and determining* the globe, even if pilots could not yet actualize this system. European navigators had a representation of space, but they had yet to find the spatial practice that would enact that structure as a lived space. Increasingly dependable compasses led to the introduction of "rhumb lines" on portulans and sea charts: renderings of magnetic headings radiating from various ports of call and depicting linear routes of navigation (Albuquerque 36–37). These lines, however, had little to do with determining a fixed point at sea; instead, they marked lines of movement *between* fixed points. By 1485, Portuguese navigators had determined the technical means for calculating latitude based on both solar position and polestar position (Albuquerque 38). Over the next century, the quadrant, the astrolabe, and the cross-staff would allow pilots to establish latitudinal location along a set of determinate geographic lines encircling the globe.

As early as 1567, when King Phillip II of Spain offered the first of several rewards[8] to anyone who could determine *el punto fijo*—fixed point—during nautical navigation, European states began to conceive of and actualize the globe as a space of action. If Foucault is correct in claiming that the emergent epistemology of the seventeenth century involved a "spatialization of knowledge," then certainly the quest for the *punto fijo* provides a clear example of how space, power, and knowledge intersect in "the map" ("Space, Knowledge, and Power" 254). By the early seventeenth century, European politics and global politics were becoming increasingly intertwined. The ability to determine a fixed point would allow the emerging colonial powers of Spain, England, and France to dominate the seas. At the same time as this quest for the *punto fijo* was occurring, the Thirty Years' War placed Europe in a period of border disputes, boundary mappings, and national reifications. Just as the Thirty Years'

War would reify Europe, so too would a system for determining longitude reify a global system of fixed points.[9] In fact, Louis XIV reportedly complained that with the redrawing of France based on principles of longitude derived from the Jovian moons, he lost more territory to cartographers than he gained with his troops (Howse 16). By the mid-seventeenth century, longitude had become an elusive obsession. In effect, Europe had already created a representation of space that was based upon a coordinate system of fixed points. It had yet to realize this representation within the lived space of navigation. It is not until the mid-eighteenth century, with Harrison's chronometers, that longitude became an equally determinate point, leaving two centuries during which pilots and cartographers searched for a means of determining "fixed point" on the globe.

The development of modern cartography in the seventeenth century in many regards amounted to a mapping of Cartesian space onto the globe: a coordinate system in which "position" occurs at the intersection of two axes as a fixed (determined and determinate) point. Similar to the grid system, a Cartesian conception of the world implies a transformation of the globe into a space in which every point on the map is a determinate entity; everything is mappable and no place can exist that cannot be mapped. The world becomes a comprehensive globe in which nothing is hidden and everything can be put in its place. As map coordinates become increasingly more determinate, the relation between the individual, the map, and the world becomes increasingly a matter of abstraction. This epistemology of the modern map is quite literally Cartesian in its dualist separation of the knowing "I" from *res extensa.* Unlike the medieval map, the modern map depicted an abstracted view of the globe. Frank Lestringant notes in his study of Renaissance mapping that the shift from chorography to geography amounted to an "upward displacement of one's point of view" (5). For Renaissance cosmographers, this "upward displacement" re-created the eye of God. Mercator, for example, in the late sixteenth century speaks of engaging in "cosmographical meditation": observing in cartographic representations of the world the patterns of a providential order (quoted in Lestringant 45). A century later, the transcendent point of view implied by the coordinate map is no longer the all-encompassing eye of God; it is the all-encompassing eye of abstraction, calculated determination, and mathematical extrapolation. Nor is this "eye" subjective. What Lestringant calls the change in scope between pre-Renaissance chorography and early modern geography amounts to the disappearance of individual perspective in global mapping. Space, in other words, becomes abstract and objective. It also gains what Lefebvre calls the "illusion of transparency": that space is "free of traps or secret places. Anything hidden or dissimulated—and hence danger-ous—is antagonistic to transparency, under whose reign everything can be taken in by a single glance from that mental eye which illuminates whatever it contemplates" (*The Production of Space* 28).

The abstraction of space to the global perspective introduced its own theo-retical framework that set up conditions of possibility that were then actu-alized by empirical experience. As in the Borges fable (co-opted by Baudril-lard and countless others), the modern map provides an abstraction that rests upon the possibility of a one-to-one representational correspondence with the world. The map allows the experience of place only in the abstract; in parallel, place in the world increasingly becomes determined by location on the map. For Lestringant, the nautical space of the ocean provides an ideal image of the intersection between the experiential and the abstract. On the blank surface of a featureless ocean, geographical place ironically appears more definite as a mathematical and cosmological abstraction represented by a point on the map. The pilot, fixing his longitude and latitude on the open sea, experiences this act of "global location" firsthand; in effect, he positions himself *in* the map, not in front of it (Lestringant 15). This experience of location as a projection within abstract space (Lefebvre's "anaphorization") is indicative of a reversal of the relation between map and world. In the modern cartographic project, the map becomes predictive of position rather than simply descriptive. This sort of re-lation can exist only within a comprehensive globe. It is also conditioned upon two Cartesian principles: the dualist separation of cogito from material exten-sion, and the transformation of space into a mathematical coordinate abstrac-tion. In a system in which everything is mappable, what is *actually* unmapped has already found its place on a *virtual* map (as terra incognita). This logic of the map follows a Baudrillardian trajectory to where the map *becomes* the world; today, the Borges fantasy comes true as the Global Positioning System enshrouds the globe in a fine mesh of radio satellite transmissions, marking every spot on Earth as a potentially mappable point. While a pilot once looked to the heavens through a quadrant for absolute cues, now satellites provide us with an absolute eye with which to look down on the world.[10]

The "globe," then, doesn't merely represent the world; it describes a social space that connects material form and conceptual structures with lived prac-tice. Cartography as a practice provides a literal mapping of these processes in the modern West. And the processes of globalization at work in the contemporary moment are very much rooted in this history of the globe itself as a social space and in the global technologies that take part in actualizing it as a lived space of practice. When we enact a relation to the WWW framed as a spatial medium with universal scope, we are in effect articulating processes that map the planet as a network of flows. The connection between the history of cartography and the spaces of hypertext is probably most clear on a Web site such as GlobeXplorer.com, which, in addition to taking a name that situates itself within a Western colonial imagination, provides users with aerial photographs of local neighborhoods with the click of a mouse. Much as the pilot navigating the seas would locate himself first on the map and then in the material expanse of the sea, the Web provides an interface between conceptual representations of space and lived practice, under the control of the user. Through the use of a site like GlobeXplorer, the user can be both "eye in the sky" and object on the map, as a satellite photo of one's own neighborhood appears on the screen. The user is both inside and under the scrutiny of panoptic technology. Here, it is not just a matter of cybernetic space replacing geographic space; rather, the technology invoked by the global imagination of the WWW facilitates the global flows that are already in place, placing the user in a position of control on a global scale. The cybernetic vehicle drives—and is driven by—material forms and lived practices that already conceive of the world as a network of flows.

Much as the map provides a technology that helps enact "the globe" as a lived space, the Web provides a vehicle for placing these global technologies within individual control—as materiality, concept, and lived practice. While mapping sites make this connection explicit, this same logic is very much in place at search engine and directory sites (and many other Web sites) that enact spaces of control, placing the autonomous subject at the wheel of a cybernetic vehicle. If we think about the representation of cyberspace as a space of control, in light of this history of the globe, it becomes apparent that the possibility of an economic, political, and social structure unmoored from geography is paradoxically dependent upon an understanding of the global as a conceptual, material, and lived structure. In its most literal sense, the overlapping of the geography of the planet and the material form of the Internet provides a first step toward understanding what we mean by "global" in a network society. To this extent, "maps of cyberspace" highlight material processes that take part in the production of spaces of everyday life. Martin Dodge and Rob Kitchin's work, along with Matthew Zook's "Zooknic Internet Geography

Project" (www.zooknic.com), to cite two particularly useful examples, provide a variety of cartographic techniques that begin to trace these material processes.[11] In these instances, the map serves literally as a representation of space that reveals processes of material form and lived practice. Even rather simple maps of worldwide host density provide a sense of how "the globe" presents itself online as material form, conceptual structure, and lived practice. The map of the globe, then, when presented electronically, becomes a map of flows of power. While by the year 2000 the United States had dropped to the 50 percent mark in number of host sites on the Internet, it still dominated the World Wide Web (Zook, "Percentage of the World's Domains in the Top Twenty-five Countries, January 2000"). More tellingly, perhaps, of the top ten domain names tallied by the Internet Systems Consortium in its "Distribution of Top-Level Domain Names by Host Count, January 2001" report, six of the original G7 countries made the rank (.fr came in at number 14). The top three, in order, were .com (36.35 million), .net (30.89 million), and .edu (7.12 million). While these domains conflate other countries, they are primarily U.S.-based.[12] In all, at the start of this decade, G8 countries accounted for a little more than three-fourths of all the domains online, and while the number of domains in developing countries increases each year, G8 countries continue to dominate the 'Net.[13] As Everard notes, the networked colonialism of the Internet now allows nations to penetrate other geographical territories without actually departing from the defining borders of the state (50). In the same way that the quest for fixed-point navigation established a means for European powers to actualize a comprehensive global space, the development of a global "space of flows" dominated by developed nations provides a technology that maps the world as a space coordinated by a geography of domains that establish *dominion*.

These maps of material forms, especially in the context of a discussion of a history of the globe, suggest that (as Manuel Castells notes) the global space of flows is anything but worldwide. What falls on or off the map determines a structure of economic and cultural power for the users whose everyday life is most deeply involved and "intertwingled" in these spaces. According to NUA Internet Survey's calculations, as of May 2002, approximately 580.78 million (slightly more than 9.6 percent of the world's population) were online—41 percent in the United States and Canada, 27 percent in Europe, and 26 percent in Asia and the Pacific (primarily in Japan and South Korea).[14] Even to speak of a *World Wide* Web invokes a number of very problematic assumptions about what "world wide" means. When we speak of penetration into everyday life, we need to be very careful about what everyday life means, and for whom. The lived practice enacted by users of this global space creates a habitus that grants access to what it means to "be online" within a space of flows. And these lived practices do not reduce to any single set of dispositions. Thus a computer in a public library provides the material form for the divergent operational strategies enacted by a homeless individual seeking public assistance, a reader browsing online newspapers, or an adolescent trying to access restricted sites.[15] As such, the intimation of a digital global village by various Internet pundits and theorists is hardly warranted. One finds instead dispositions and operational strategies that produce situated identities and structures of community based on one's access to material form, conceptual structure, and lived practice, thereby producing very different mappings of a global space of flows.

Membership in a virtual class, then, entails not only material access, but also conceptual access to a representation of global space in its dominant form as a networked space of control. To some degree, this parallels the sort of "imagined community" that Benedict Anderson describes in conjunction with the rise of the modern nation. An important concept for Anderson is that these imagined communities are mediated phenomena, exchanged between public institutions and private experience by way of the daily practice of newspaper reading. It is the uniformity of the newspaper as topos for news that defines the identity of "citizen." He writes:

> The newspaper reader, observing exact replicas of his own paper being consumed by his subway, barbershop, or residential neighbors, is continually reassured that the imagined world is visibly rooted in everyday life. (35–36)

For Anderson, the community of citizens created by the ubiquitous practice of newspaper reading implies a public sphere that is as much "in mind" as it is in space (we shall return to Anderson, Habermas, and the problematic notion of public sphere in chapter 3), situated in an exchange of information by way of the medium of newsprint. The Web is likewise a medium that, as Berners-Lee argues, functions as an information space on a global level, which at the same time calls upon its users to interact with it. I would argue that there is a similar mapping of community implicated by mediated, global flows of information; but this representation of space or "imagined world" is marked in material form and daily practice not by the ubiquity of newspapers but by the incessant presence of computers as representations of community and communication in those same countries that currently dominate the material form of the Internet. The globe is a network, and the network is a globe—or so declare the television ads for America Online (AOL), Comcast, and Earthlink. Likewise, the presence of cybercafés and all-night Kinko's shops with hourly rentals of networked computers further suggests the penetration of this material artifact into both the lived experience and the conceptual structure of individuals in developed countries.

On one hand, clearly this is a lived space inhabited by an elite (from a global perspective) virtual class: citizens who increasingly find themselves in control of a means of communication, as both consumers and producers. This is the group Manuel Castells calls "globapolitans (half beings, half flows)" (*The Power of Identity* 69). This is also a virtual world of what Marc Augé calls nonspaces: a culture of homogenous airports and hotel rooms where the social placement of individuals has more to do with access to international flows of material, information, and capital than the specificity of situatedness. In addition to the topographies of networked social space mapped by this elite virtual class, we will also want to consider how heterogeneous lived practices might articulate dispositions that grant access to the dominant processes of social space without necessarily disciplining and reifying the social fields of power in which they communicate. While all of these practices fall *on* rather than *off* the map of cyberspace, "the global" here must refer to structures of everyday life that determine normative as well as "deviant" membership in a network society.

The Global and the Local: All the World That's Fit to Link

While Anderson foregrounds "news" as a significant structure of community in the rise of the nation-state, news itself has undergone significant changes in the last half century by way of changes in social and technological networks of communication, from the prominence of daily circulations to televised nightly newscasts to twenty-four-hour cable news stations. As Web browsing became an increasingly common practice in America in the mid-1990s, a number of mass-media outlets began to consider how to exploit this new medium. As a result, television shows, weekly print publications, and daily newspapers began to find their place on the Web. At the same time, online publications were establishing their presence on the Web, from *Postmodern Culture* and the *Electronic Journal of Virtual Culture* to *Salon* and the *Drudge Report*, attempting to define how publication would look and feel in a hypertextual environment.

In thinking about the WWW as an information space enacted by the daily lived practice of its users, the structure of "news" on the Internet takes on particular significance. On one hand, the mass-media model has been replicated online by way of CNN, *Time*, and the *New York Times* in their Web versions. But the convergence of the global and the intimate by way of the spaces of hypertext also suggests an altered relation to both the consumption and the production of news. As such, one would expect to find in the virtual topographies of Web-based news sites altered conceptual, material, and experiential processes involved in the production of spaces of everyday life within a global space of flows.

On a Web site such as CNN.com, the news parallels the twenty-four-hour news of a cable television channel, only now it is updated "continuously" with the click of a mouse. The porousness of this and many other sites by way of chat sessions, open bulletin boards, and blogs suggests a blurring of the line between producer and consumer, but this effect is incidental to the Web site. For the most part, CNN's online presence conveys a "worldview" that maintains its centralized authority for gathering, verifying, and presenting/defining the news. CNN.com presents its international news in four groupings: United States, Europe, Asia, and a catch-all World. The structure of the site amounts to something closer to Castells's space of flows, in which transnational networks structure events, here clustered in three economic zones corresponding to the North American Free Trade Agreement (NAFTA), the European Union (EU), and the Asian Pacific region.[16] One's location, then, has some significance, but the larger framework of the CNN.com site implies the dominant thrust of the Web site: situating the user within global flows of information.

As a means of *incorporating* participants of an "imagined community," access to CNN.com by way of material form, conceptual structure, and lived practice situates the user within these same global flows. Certainly the same argument could be made about CNN in its televised version. The material form of the computer, however, differs from television in its *place* within everyday life. While televisions reside in homes (and in casual restaurants and bars), the computer's ubiquity places it at home, at work, and at a variety of public venues by way of wirelessly networked laptops, pay-for-use PCs, and public kiosks. Of course, it is the network itself as a flow of information that penetrates daily life, not the computer per se. Thus with Personal Digital Assistants (PDAs) and "Web-ready" cell phones, CNN's Web site can indeed exist anywhere and anytime.[17] The eventlike quality of cyberspace also involves a temporal element, marked most clearly in the structure of CNN.com as a real-time publication. CNN presents a banner just under its Web masthead declaring the time of the last site update—in Greenwich mean time. The implication of the site is that the news is indeed to-the-minute, although the actual updates may amount to changes in layout rather than substantive news updates. While Stuart Sherman talks about the structuring of middle-class everyday life by the diurnal rhythm of eighteenth-century newspaper publication, online the *date* does not matter so much as the *time stamp*. The structure, then, is not diurnal but real-time on a global (Greenwich mean) clock, situated by users who are potentially present at a keyboard and screen, ready to read or to post at any moment. The real-time aspect marks the space of the Web page as an event that is constantly unfolding. Every click on the "refresh" button on a browser holds the potential to alter headlines or to bring updates, retractions, or breaking news.

As material form, conceptual structure, and lived practice, the dominant topography of a site such as CNN.com enacts a space that situates its users within global, real-time flows of information. Browsing the site articulates the dispositions and operational strategies of a normative virtual class, at home both at the keyboard and in a space that controls and navigates global flows. The Web makes CNN available "worldwide" (again with "the world" mapped in very distinct material and conceptual terms), and, as such, it is fair to say that the imagined communities of CNN and the WWW as a space of flows overlap significantly. But the Web also places *any* media outlet within the same space. In effect, every local TV channel or newspaper with a Web site gains access to global distribution. Why, though, would this global reach be necessary, or, for that matter, desirable? While the ubiquity of networks grants a user access to CNN from anywhere on the globe, these same global processes provide access back to highly localized virtual topographies. The *Concord Journal,* for example, is just as accessible to readers worldwide as CNN.com, yet clearly the positioning of each within a global network is quite different. While CNN brings a "world of news" to electronic readers, the *Concord Journal* promises to serve as "your Massachusetts news hometown connection." The structure of the Web, as both a global technology and a situated medium, suggests that the everyday practice of browsing "news" maps the shifting relations between the global and the local in a network society.

The *Concord Journal* is a print paper with a modest circulation in Middlesex County, Massachusetts, but its online version (www.concordjournal. com), hosted by Town Online and produced by the Community Newspaper

Company, sees its place in local space and global networks as equally important. In explaining their publishing philosophy, Town Online states:

> This is the Internet, an interactive medium that encourages participation from its users.... The goal of our Web sites is to be the online connection for the community. It will do this by providing a forum for the exchange of information and ideas in much the same way that the town common was once the focal point of daily life.[18]

With explicit reference to the community forum and the town common, this Web site actively styles itself in the image of the virtual agora, a place for gathering news but also for exchanging commentary. Note that it is the Web that now serves as "the focal point of daily life," not the town common. I find this choice of words interesting to the extent that it implies a point toward which other activities orient; while locality still signifies, it finds its *place* in a networked space of flows. Such statements reveal conceptual structures that take part in the production of cyberspace and suggest an implicit assumption about the embodiment of browsing and posting to discussion lists as a form of cultural capital with increasing value in daily life. Locality is foregrounded, but in such a way that it is an integral part of a globally distributed medium. Town Online newspaper sites explicitly attempt to function as community hubs, much as Doheny-Farina discusses, with the potential for online communities "to be employed to serve, not to transcend localities" (127). More accurately, perhaps, it seems that these sites function as community hubs to the extent that locality is *immanent* in the material, conceptual, and experiential processes that draw Web sites into global social space.

Clicking from local site to local site within the Town Online Web pages reveals a publication pattern that is apparent in print newspapers as well: many of the "local" stories are repeated from the *Concord Journal* to the *Cape Codder* to the *North Shore Sunday*. In the same way that many small-town print newspapers blend Associated Press (AP) wire stories with articles written by staff reporters, the structure of these online newspapers suggests that the "local" news for these various communities coincides to varying degrees with regional, national, and international news. The very definition of "local" is already under flux in local town newspapers, but locality still signifies, in the literal and figurative appearance of the newspaper, "at your doorstep." But when this locality is placed within the global structurings of the WWW, readers become connected to that sense of location and locality from anywhere in the world. With the ubiquity of the computer and the network within a structure of society based upon the flows of information, there is the potential for readers around the world to be in touch with their local news. And the "local interest" is undeniable—newspapers at Town Online provide, among other features, youth baseball reports, classified advertisements, and calendar events listings. With print circulations in perennial decline, online we find a burgeoning of electronic newspapers. Yahoo's directory of online newspapers, for example, lists over 9,400 newspapers arranged by country, state, and region, with well more than one-third of the papers originating outside the United States. And each of these papers enjoys the same potential for global publication as CNN.com. The proliferation of such Web sites suggests a social space in which the networked computer might be more available to the potential reader of the local newspaper than the print paper itself.

As mentioned earlier in the context of Tuvalu's sale of its .tv domain name, remoteness becomes restructured by a global network of flows and the potential for worldwide distribution. As with the material, conceptual, and experiential processes that gave rise to the globe as a social space in the sixteenth and seventeenth centuries, the remotest parts of the world enter into relation with colonial and imperial powers by way of cultural and economic networks of exchange. In contrast to this history of the globe as an economic and cultural form, however, the immanent power of the network means that localities caught up in its flows *enact* these structures but are not entirely *dominated* by them. With the virtual topographies of the WWW, in this instance enacted through globally distributed local news, the globally remote enacts a highly situated space, but one that is immanent to, not dominated by or isolated from, the network structure of social space. In Annie Proulx's novel *The Shipping News*, for example, much is made of the remoteness of Newfoundland in general, and, more specifically, of the Great Northern Peninsula to which the main character moves. The fictional newspaper that he works for, which specializes in local gossip and front-page photos of highway wrecks, is modeled after the real-life *Northern Pen*, located in St. Anthony, Newfoundland, and now available online through password subscription. The news in the *Northern Pen* is without question local: headline news includes a story on local unemployment rates, a piece on an upcoming festival in St. Paul's, a story on waste management plans for the region, an article on cod-fishing licenses, and a report on a seafood company's appeal of a court decision. With a print circulation of 6,000, the home page for the online edition (northernpen.hypermart.net) recorded over 30,000 hits to the site as of summer 2001. As of summer 2003, the editorial page still boasted a circulation of 6,000, whereas the Web site recorded over 50,000 hits.[19] Granted, these figures are to some degree incomparable (since there is no guarantee that "unique" hits are actually equivalent to separate individuals receiving the paper), but it does suggest that this rather remote newspaper receives a significant number of visitors and takes part in a networked space of flows. What's more, its (now-defunct) guest book recorded a large number of readers who were former inhabitants of the Great Northern Peninsula and who now live elsewhere, suggesting not only the global distribution of local news but the distribution of "locals" themselves to other parts of the world. These complex relations between the global and the local, the integral and the remote, complicate how we understand the relation between network technology and the social space of "community hubs." Nor does it allow for the clear distinction Doheny-Farina makes between online communities that "serve" rather than "transcend" locality.

The local has by no means disappeared in the networked spaces of everyday life; rather, it too has become a site of global flows of information. At the same time, what counts as the global is also localized by the specifics of situatedness that give rise to the space of flows. In other words, it makes sense to speak of "the global" as a lived space only in its enacted, actualized form; the global is always immanent in the material, conceptual, and experiential processes that give rise to it. As the presence of local newspapers in global circulation implies, the user of the Web is both situated by locality and "at home" in the space of flows. In his discussion of the local in relation to working-class culture, Darren O'Byrne defines localities as "constructions of a tentative social order in a world of flows" (74). Combining the work of David Harvey with that of Roland Robertson, O'Byrne defines globalization both as a material process of "time-space compression" and as a cultural process (conceptual and experiential) of "globality," which is "built on an image of the globe itself as an arena for social action" (75). Access to globality, and hence to the processes of globalization, are for O'Byrne measures of cultural capital, which is unevenly distributed in any given social space (76). This framework has significance for a discussion of how the WWW functions in the production of virtual topographies that are both global as a space of flows, and situated within local, enactive environments of embodied, everyday use. Global and local, far from maintaining a binary opposition, become interpenetrating modes of articulating cultural capital for individuals living in a networked social space.

Roland Robertson's ideas on globality and the cultural processes of globalization are worth further consideration in a discussion of the lived practices of the WWW. Robertson approaches "world image" in an expanded, Weberian sense, in contrast to strictly economic or materialist discussions of global systems (*Globalization* 23–24). This world image is both virtual and actual, noting "how the world is variously and often conflictfully regarded as *possible*" (75). The globe, then, enacts very different spaces, depending upon one's situated locality and disposition. As his use of the term "glocalization"[20] implies, Robertson sees the global and the local as inextricably connected in the globality that defines the world as a livable space. As such, the global is defined by both the networked spaces of flows and the particularities of situated enactions of that same network. He writes: "The globalization process itself—the rendering of the world as a single place—constrains civilizations and societies . . . to be increasingly explicit about what might be called their *global callings* (their unique geocultural or memorable contributions to world history)" (*Globalization* 130). Robertson is explicitly interested in understanding the "world as a whole," yet he also foregrounds the complex relationship between local features and global forms. In doing so, Robertson makes the point that even the antiglobalization movement is very much involved in a world image, in that it presents a vision of how the world should be as global community or as society.[21] Thus the current cultural moment reveals "a massive, twofold process involving *the interpenetration of the universalization of particularism and the particularization of universalism*" (*Globalization* 100).

Certainly there are some contestable points in Robertson's argument (his dependence on the concept of "human condition,"[22] for example), but the important element worth extracting here is his understanding of the interpenetration of the universal and the particular, the global and the local. This indeed seems to be the case with virtual topographies of the WWW, where global and local processes are immanent in the network itself, and, as such, take part in producing heteromorphic cyberspaces. At sites such as the *Concord Journal* or the *Northern Pen,* "the local" situates global networks to enact locality on a global scale. In contrast, on Web pages that enact global spaces of control, such as at CNN.com, the user engages in a lived practice that ablates the local by making the global immanent in use. CNN provides to-the-minute news from around the globe at the user's command, but the situation of the user is treated as irrelevant. Furthermore, these sites, while calling upon a space of flows, function in all their "stickiness" as virtual worlds, an all-encompassing globe of its own mapping.

But the relation between the global and the local, the universal and the intimate, is marked on the Web by a hypertextual space that is directed not only toward consumption but toward allowing the individual user to mark her position within these same flows of information. While CNN.com or even Web versions of local papers re-create a mass-media model, the potential to "talk back" to the medium is always present.[23] In some instances, the "letters to the editor" section expands to the point of becoming the corpus of the medium itself. In contrast to CNN, Slashdot (www.slashdot.org) and the Independent Media Center (IMC; www.indymedia.org) provide radically different structures for what it means to disseminate news within a community. Indymedia. org's home page describes itself as "a collective of independent media organizations and hundreds of journalists offering grassroots non-corporate coverage. ... a democratic media outlet for the creation of radical, accurate, and passionate tellings of truth." The supporting media groups have a distinctly antiglobalization thrust;[24] yet (as Robertson notes), this antiglobalization focus, and its position contrary to transnational media conglomerates, makes sense only by providing individual users with the material access to global flows of information, coupled with a concept of a shared global space and a lived practice of browsing on and posting to global networks via the Web. Indymedia.org places a premium on *reportage*—such that the situation of the journalist-eyewitness makes the story credible and worthy of circulation—not on some abstracted standard of zero-degree objectivity. As an arrangement of material form, conceptual structure, and lived practice, then, Indymedia.org enacts a network for its users that places the individual voice within a global space of flows, allowing (or rather interpellating) the firsthand account that, in the eyes of its contributors, the major media outlets aren't reporting.[25]

Central to the publication ideology of the Independent Media Center is the concept of "open publishing," allowing individuals to place their own reports into a global flow conceived of as a "decentralized and autonomous network" of sites around the globe. In the words of the Washington, D.C., Independent Media Center, readers are always potential writers, and, hence, potential "media producers," situated quite differently from the corporate media: "Come join us and become the media." Distributed publishing processes are at the heart of Indymedia.org's editorial policy. At many of the distributed IMC sites around the world, pages addressed to potential news providers declare: "Indymedia is a democratic newswire. We want to see and hear the real stories, news, and opinions from around the world. While we struggle to maintain the news wire as a completely open forum we do monitor it and remove posts."[26] By design, these sites are highly porous in the sense that the line between article and comment is fairly invisible. That blurring is, of course, by no means unproblematic. During the first half of 2002, for example, Indymedia.org increasingly came under criticism for the number of anti-Semitic postings that began to appear in response to the escalation of violence in Israel and the occupied territories. As Naomi Klein noted in a *Globe and Mail* column: "Every time I log onto activist sites such as Indymedia.org, which practice 'open publishing,' I'm confronted with a string of Jewish conspiracy theories about 9/11 and excerpts from the *Protocols of the Elders of Zion.*"[27] As a topography, this blurring suggests a space in which situated voices—even those motivated by ideology, prejudice, or hatred—determine the production of a global space of flows. There is a legitimate sense that these sites are in contradistinction to both mass-media outlets and the sorts of contained virtual worlds of CNN. com or its parent company, Time Warner. As a map of global flows, then, Indymedia.org takes part in the WWW as a medium with planetary reach, but in doing so, it situates itself contrary to the functioning of corporations in that same space. The global here is always enacted in relation to a situated user, lived through a practice of point-and-click consumption or interactive publication. At the same time, all the posters to a site such as Indymedia.org take part in a wired world of developed countries within which cyberspace is very much a space of everyday life. In the case of Indymedia.org, the network is an essential counterpoint to the globalizing structures of the G8, the World Trade Organization (WTO), and the International Monetary Fund (IMF). This community of resistance is at the same time a community that is enmeshed within the same global network.

Clearly we cannot reduce topographies of the Web to a single set of relations in social space, given the significant differences in the produced spaces of everyday life between Web sites enacted as "global portals," such as CNN.com, and sites that create a nexus of global flows, such as Indymedia.org. Even the concept of "interactive" differs between these two topographies—either as a medium of point-and-click control or as a medium of collaborative exchange. The global itself functions in two very different relations to individual use marked by embodied knowledge and operational strategies. At the same time, the "intimacy" of these virtual topographies is quite different. At sites of collaborative production, the specificity of one's own situation is foregrounded as the site of information exchange. In spaces of control, however, with the user operating as Leibnizian god, intimacy involves the creation of networked spaces that function as a personal world: a monad topography. To a degree, the possessive individual[28] becomes the possessive user, engaged in an interface with global networks mapped as "My Netscape," "My AOL," and personalized Web portals.

To focus our discussion on the everyday life experiences of these processes of spatial production, it is worthwhile to look at one of the more popular on-line sites that takes part in producing a monad topography of cyberspace. Claiming to be the "The world's biggest everything," Amazon.com attempts to encompass a space of global reach, putting books (and other goods) within a terrain of individual control. This confluence of global flow and personal space is typical of the virtual topographies enacted by the global imaginary of the WWW.

My World (Wide Web)

Of all the companies that did phenomenally well during the "dot-com bubble," Amazon.com has fared far better than most, including AOL in its merger with Time Warner. While it suffered catastrophic losses in stock price when the bubble burst, by the first quarter of 2002, its stock had returned to prices equal to those posted just prior to the start of the buying frenzies of late 1998. A year later Amazon.com stock had nearly tripled, recouping almost half its all-time-high closing price. What's more, it remains a well-visited site among a range of users, with a presence online that surpasses that of the major brick-and-mortar chains. In addition to providing a popular site for buying books, Amazon.com provides an exemplary instance of a virtual topography of control, and, in particular, a version of a networked lived space articulated as a personalized virtual world.

When pointing my browser to Amazon.com, whether I am aware of it or not, I find myself redirected to another page, one that has been designed just for me. The Web site *addresses* me: "Hello, Mark Nunes. Check out the new recommendations area. (If you're not Mark Nunes, click here.)" The site hails the reader (in an Althusserian sense), and then addresses the user with an imperative. This combination of hailing and imperative repeats itself on multiple screens, establishing the user as the computer's, or the Web site's, interlocutor. In a similar fashion, the site addresses the user in several locations in the second person (for example, the link titled "Your Recommendations"). In this regard, the site as a whole addresses itself to its user, creating a space that bears famil-iar trappings. In addition, the site provides links that address the computer—first-person statements that place the user in the position of rhetor. These are labels for other personalized pages (such as a link titled "My Account"), as well as questions the user is likely to ask to maximize the performance of the site (such as the annoyingly gen-x "Where's My Stuff?" link).

This mapping of Amazon.com as "my space"—a trend carried through to the Windows operating system's "My Computer" and "My Documents" icons—has some important consequences for understanding the spatiality of CMC as virtual world.[29] The computer becomes a device in which communi-cation serves to instantiate certain preconceived forms of actions and, hence, hypertextual paths. Margaret Morse refers to this form of mediated address—from the radio announcer's imperative to the TV news anchor's gaze directed at "you"—as an interactivity in the place of intersubjectivity (6–7). Extending the work of Raymond Williams, Morse sees highways, malls, and television as instances of virtualities of "distraction": forms of mobile privatization that produce "a partial loss of touch with the here-and-now" (99). To some extent, one could argue that the personalization of a site like Amazon.com likewise produces a mobile privatization, or, more accurately, a privatization of a global space of flows. Williams defines mobile privatization as "an at once mobile and home-centered way of living" (26). The Web as social space fulfills this func-tion, yet the dichotomy between mobile space and home space is increasingly less clear in the privatization of spaces that are themselves spaces of flow. While the automobile takes personal space and mobilizes it, the privatization of a global space of flows in effect makes the world itself a personal space for the user, enacted via networks of control.

Part of this privatization takes the form of constructing Amazon.com pages that are dynamically generated for the user. At the center of *my* Amazon.com home page, for example, the link titled "Your Recommendations" leads to a page suggesting titles that may be of interest to me, including, on this par-ticular day, Pierre Lévy's *Collective Intelligence*. These titles are generated by purchase patterns of other users who have bought the same or similar books. From the standpoint of cybernetics, this sort of "information mining"—cull-ing out between five and fifteen books from Amazon.com's catalog of over 4 million titles—can succeed in two ways: on one hand, it can suggest a list of titles that the user is interested in purchasing; on the other hand, the list could suggest books that the user already owns. In either case, the user experiences the "Your Recommendations" page as a space designed personally for the user. Once again, the user is hailed and addressed by this site: here as a *profile*. As the user points and clicks through the site, the Web pages of Amazon.com increasingly bear the user's marks, as if traveling through very familiar territory. To fine-tune recommendations, the site also provides users with the ability to rate books they have purchased, to rate the titles recommended, and to acknowledge the books that he or she already owns. In effect, the dialogic relationship between the computer and the user increasingly maps a cybernetic circuit of output and feedback, striving to actualize a site that eliminates anything that falls beyond the circumference of the user's monadic virtual globe.

In a similar way, Amazon.com's dynamically generated pages provide a sense that the Web site that the user visits is, in effect, unlike any other Web site for any other user. Amazon.com tracks recently viewed pages and compares these titles to the purchase patterns of other consumers, producing "The Page You Made," designed to: "help you find what you want and discover related items." Elsewhere, the site promises a page "By you, for you, in real time." Likewise, the "Friends and Favorites" section allows users to "Build your personal network of Favorite People and watch this page come to life with opinions and recommendations." In addition, users can create a profile page, formerly called an "About You Area": "the *place* at Amazon.com where others can learn more about you" ("Friends and Favorites," italics added). The construction of pages that are personalized and privatized increasingly creates the experience that Amazon.com is *your* space, that the vast resources of networked computers, search engines, and extensive databases are there "by you, for you, in real time"; and in real space, one might add. The virtual world of Amazon.com is paradoxically open and closed at the same time: closed increasingly as a domain, *my* space; yet open to vast flows of information, linked materially, conceptually, and experientially. The "My Amazon" page in this regard is very much a monad—reflecting an entire networked world through a privatized cybernetic filter. Yet this site also suggests other worlds out there as well. The network of "friends and favorites," "purchase circles," and "listmania" lists calls attention to the proximity of other likeminded individuals: hailings of other users that serve as nodes within a hypertextual flow. In this regard, the site presents yet another version of cyberspace as an "agora of ideas" (after all, as an earlier version of the listmania FAQ told us, everyone is entitled to a list—they are "free, democratic, and fun"). This FAQ goes on to explain: "Your lists will appear on your About You page. People can check out your other recommendations by clicking on your name at the bottom of your list—this will take them to your About You area" ("Listmania Lists").

But these lines of community are, in effect, already mapped long before I begin clicking, much as my choices for book recommendations are generated from correlations with my previous purchases and interests. And with each click, the site further determines and actualizes the terrain of my virtual world. Perhaps it's just an academic's monomaniacal reading habits that give rise to such a familiar territory of suggested titles and recommended authors, but through a logic of cybernetic feedback, in conjunction with a Web site that attempts to make Amazon.com *my* Amazon.com, I find myself within an increasingly determined virtual world, a topography in which ultimately I will only be exploring links that lead down well-worn paths. As an encouragement to get users to create their own Listmania lists, the site cajoles: "After all, who knows better what you like than you?" Since this list ultimately becomes part of a cybernetic feedback loop that will fine-tune my privatized world of Amazon.com, the answer seems to be: *the site itself.* And, of course, Amazon.com has generated thousands of other virtual monads, privatized and personalized to other users, networked together, certainly, but each a distinct topography of linkages.

With networked privatization, the world increasingly becomes a mapping of my own perspective. At the same time, this comprehensive, personal world makes sense only within a lived space enacted by a user in front of a computer, at home or at work, ordering goods from a site such as Amazon.com, providing a credit card number, and then receiving a doorstep delivery within a matter of days via networks of highways and air routes. While the virtual world of My Amazon maps a monadological topography, my position within this virtual world is still highly situated by global material and semiotic processes that make such a topography possible. The global and the local here translate into the universal and the personal by way of a networked privatization of the Web. The interactivity and cybernetic feedback have the effect of creating a virtual topography for the user that is at the same time intensely organized around personal space and instantiated by way of global flows of information. In this regard, the global is indeed a monad, and whatever connections exist on Amazon.com by way of "friends and favorites" or "purchase circles" are produced from the situated perspective of the user who controls this world of information.

Yet even within this highly "sticky" site, one can find gaps in which lived practice emerges that runs contrary to the practices set out by a space of control. As a somewhat minor example, the Amazon.com marketplace offers a different kind of structure of community in the sense that it creates a forum in which users can both buy and sell goods. Amazon.com prompts the user with an assessed value for previously purchased goods, and then provides users with the technology to recirculate their goods to other users. In this regard, Amazon.com takes part in a space of flows that opens up to larger network structures, yet at the same time assures the centrality of its own site, by way of its site security. To some extent, then, we can find traces of an agora on the Amazon.com site, but in a form that foregrounds the comings and goings of individuals and information, not the "coming together" of individuals at a focal point of community. The structure evoked here suggests a form of peer-to-peer exchange that was epitomized in the brief period before Napster was shut down for copyright infringement. What made Napster work—and what makes the Amazon.com marketplace work—is the presence of a significant number of individual users placed within a space of flows, with access to computers and a comfort with online interactions. Napster functioned more as a node than as a virtual world, in that it existed solely as a point of contact for peer-to-peer routings between users. The same could be said of the Amazon.com marketplace. Unlike the spaces suggested by "My Amazon," the marketplace provides a fluid structure that is situated more specifically by the connections enacted between buyer and seller, not between a potential buyer and his own purchase patterns. Certainly all the trappings of Amazon.com's sticky site are still in place—information fed into databases, the call of other product arenas, etc.— but the space enacted here by linking individuals in a network of lived practice does not limit itself to a closed, virtual world.

Situated Spaces and Networks of Everyday Life

In April 2002, Napster had yet to launch its new service after its gutting by the court ruling. On its Web site (www.napster.com), it had the following posting:

> We're getting closer to a settlement with the major record companies that would clear away our legal troubles and secure a good range of music for the Napster community, but we're taking some more time to make sure we get the very best deals we can.

The Web site refers to the peer-to-peer network as a "community," though even at its heaviest traffic, Napster provided little in the way of what is normally discussed as a "virtual community." It had chat rooms and bulletin boards, but these functioned at a superficial level. Instead, it seems that the "community" referred to here was *an articulation of the network structure itself:* the potential for a peer-to-peer space of flows, actualized in the moment of exchange. The "global" here is not important; nor, really, is the local, in the sense of shared investments in similar interests. Neither virtual "world" nor "tool" for locality, the peer-to-peer community is immanent in the network of flows itself. There is an anonymity to this practice, but at the same time, these exchanges derive from the coming together in lived practice of individuals who are themselves situated within these networks of everyday life. The linkages and exchanges that are facilitated through the virtual topographies of the electronic marketplaces of peer-to-peer networks and Amazon.com suggest instead that, in networked social space, "anonymity" does not efface the situatedness of individuals, nor does "community" preclude ephemeral contacts and rapid exchanges.[30]

In its most widely accepted form, the virtual agora takes part in a representation of space in which the WWW maps a hypercomplex network of interconnected sites—a matrix of stable, navigable points. In acknowledging the heterogeneous and heteromorphic nature of these sites, one might also acknowledge an alternate arrangement of material, conceptual, and live processes—namely, a network that is emergent and enactive, and therefore never simply a "network of circulation and communication" (Lefebvre, *Writings on Cities* 98). As such, each Web page functions less as a node on a web than as its own "enacted environment," producing linkages according to principles quite distinct from Lyotard's "logic of maximum performance." While peer-to-peer networks provide a clear example of this altered understanding of networked social space, many sites on the Web provide similar instances of enactive networks of material form, conceptual structure, and lived practice. For example, the various clusters of sites known as "WebRings" (www.webring.com) appear to present an orderly arrangement of likeminded sites, organized hierarchically by topic. Yet each Web ring shows itself to be an assemblage of interconnected sites in which the linkages between various Web pages produce disjunctions and differences as much as lines of filiation. As a social space, this arrangement of sites into a network based on loose, changing, and at times idiosyncratic connections suggests a resistance to the dominant social space of

control. Rather than producing a space of regulated traffic, these linkages produce a space that enacts the potential for fortuitous, singular *encounters*.

When browsing the Web, by no means are we limited to exploring the
closed boundaries of virtual worlds. Nor does every topography function
in complicity with the nonspaces and nonplaces of a virtual class (thus, as
Castells notes, Zapatistas and right-wing militias find a place for insurgency
within the global space of flows). While open publishing sites like Indymedia.
org certainly present an example of a topography in which the Web serves as
a nexus of flows rather than as a closed world, even some corporate sites offer
instances in which the WWW provides for cyberspaces that resist closure while
articulating a lived space of singularity and encounter. At BabyCenter.com, for
example, one finds a site that is very heavily invested in an economy of banner ads (Pampers, Gerber, Toys "R" Us) and product sales (with its site slogan,
"cradle and all"). The BabyCenter.com site—one of a number that provides
new parents and parents-to-be with information on childrearing—in several
instances resembles what you would find at Amazon.com. The site hails you
and asks you to log out if you are not "you." While Amazon.com profiles its
users based on purchase patterns and patterns of consumption, BabyCenter.
com situates its user within the identity of "parent," where the defining relation is to the child's anticipated or actual birth date. One can navigate the site
according to a timeline from preconception through pregnancy, delivery, and
childhood development, or one can explore areas devoted to expert opinion,
recent parenting-related news, or topic-based discussion lists. In effect, the site
attempts to organize its users along a continuum of presumed shared experiences—a taxonomy of everyday life of childbearing and child rearing.

Upon logging onto the site, the personalized page of "My BabyCenter" provides links to specific information on "How Your Baby's Growing" and "How
Your Life Is Changing." Clearly there's a kind of normalization of parent and
child in these blurbs (with reassuring reminders that every child and parent is
different, of course). The site also makes clear its assumptions about the underlying shared experience of its users. A pop-up window, for example, asks
parents to shop the BabyCenter store for "top rated products." The emphasis on top rating (while not indicating who has rated these products, or by
what criteria) implicates an underlying logic of the site: that the parent visiting
BabyCenter.com is searching for "the best" for his or her child. Likewise, the
store's slogan, "Products parents love. Answers parents need," connects information and expert advice with consumerism. Typical links literally combine

these two aspects of parenting (for example, a cycling banner link that reads: "Don't Miss: Great ways to soothe your toddler's fever. . . . Win a $1,000 Gap-Maternity shopping spree!"), suggesting that caring for one's child is inseparable from buying for one's child.

But in the midst of all this consumerism, I find traces of a topography that resist the monadological enclosure of a virtual world. The major difference may be that the comings and goings on Amazon.com ultimately involve themselves in consumption and purchase, whereas at BabyCenter.com, the networks that are enacted, while situated within a consumer marketplace, do so within the context of everyday life experience, which includes but is not limited to commercial exchange. While the BabyCenter.com site clearly articulates certain expectations of middle-class childrearing, consumption, and lifestyle (and assumes membership in a virtual class "at home" in networked social space), the spatiality of the site is very much the product of the interaction of situated individuals who take part in these exchanges.[31] BabyCenter.com provides a page that lists a range of topics, and each topic links to a page that offers articles, "Ask the Experts" pages, "Life Stories," and links to bulletin boards. Any one of the articles provides information that has been "approved by the BabyCenter Medical Advisory Board," often followed by a much longer section of parenting tips—a bulletin board of firsthand experiences with childrearing.[32] Likewise, Web-based chats function as "peer support," with discussions structured for (among other things) both working and stay-at-home moms, teen and single parents, couples trying to conceive, "Moms on Bedrest," and "Pregnancy and Infant Loss." Some chats deal with advice, such as "Picking a Practitioner" or "Sleep Deprivation," while others serve as "Birth Clubs" for mothers sharing due dates or actual delivery dates.

In scrolling down the list of bulletin-board entries by parent after parent (mostly mothers), an aspect of the actual writing space becomes apparent: as a layout of text, the ads that border the top of the page have disappeared, and all that appears in my window is the personal stories of mothers and babies. At times these postings read as personal confessionals: anecdotes of one's own experience. In other instances, they appear to be in dialogue with one another. The most distinct feature, however, is that the space is one that is literally structured by individual encounters. These pages also suggest the idiosyncratic[33] nature of their position within a network—not a structure of organized flows, but rather a situated enaction of specific networks, with openings outward. These network openings are quite literally beyond the closure of BabyCenter.

com. While Amazon.com allows its reviewers to post email addresses in its "About You" pages, the structure of BabyCenter.com allows users to post active email links *within* their discussion postings, along with links to external Web sites, in effect encouraging a connection of parents outside of the closed circumference of a virtual world. The mappings of connections *start off* as the output of profiling and a taxonomy of parenthood; but what develops between parents is a topography enacted by shared everyday life, mediated by the material networks that are a part of that everyday life, and conceived in the form of a "virtual community" of exchanges and singular encounters.

And it is worth noting that those shared spaces of everyday life are very much embodied spaces, marked by the corporeality of pregnant or nursing bodies—as well as typing and clicking fingertips. While the site gestures to include fathers, the various hailings of the site ("You're ___ weeks pregnant"; "What do your baby's movements feel like? Share your take") provide an ordering of sorts that defines and delimits the user as "woman" and "mother." The site likewise hails diverse embodiments of "mother": a taxonomy of discussion lists for women of color, single mothers, working mothers, gay and lesbian parents, adoptive mothers, and mothers of various (or no) religious affiliation, including Christian, Jewish, Islamic, Buddhist, and pagan.[34] Of equal importance are the misrecognized hailings—the ones that address the reader without even being spoken. While the Web site groups shared experience by religion, sexuality, and age, it remains silent on its assumption that BabyCenter.com mothers are comfortably positioned within a virtual middle class (one cannot find a discussion list for "computer-free parenting"). Likewise, the "Great Debates" discussion boards, which BabyCenter.com hosted in 2001 and 2002, reveal an understanding that the primary struggle in contemporary parenting involves the role of outside influences in parenting (medical or pharmaceutical interventions), yet with very little concern over the impact of media. By number of postings in April 2002, the "Breastfeeding OR Formula Feeding" debate accounted for nearly half of the postings (2,207). The next three most-popular debates concerned natural childbirth (614 postings), circumcision (548 postings), and immunization (513 postings). Very little debate occurs at the level of one's membership within a set of values that situates the parent within a virtual middle class; in fact, the least-debated topic involved concern over media consumption, in the form of television viewing (61 postings).

The unspoken habitus that situates all of these discussions is the ability to use the computer in this fashion, which delimits these users perhaps far better than the user profiles derived by cybernetic circuits of inputs and outputs. Likewise, the site assumes mobile privatization as a common experience revealed in its most literal sense by the site's frequent emphasis on travel, including bulletin boards devoted to travel topics and articles such as "Eight smart on-the-road (and in-the-air) strategies for expectant moms." The frame of shared experience for users, then, is specifically one that connects access to Web pages and access to travel networks, a pattern that I have noted above. In other words, the more one has access to cyberspace, the more one can assume spaces of everyday life that involve geographic mobility as well. Still, while structuring an everyday experience of a normative virtual class, BabyCenter. com also provides a Web site that opens to participation in a community that is immanent in the event-space of the network itself, and is not limited to interpellation as controller/operator in a closed virtual world. The structuring of commerce takes precedence, but the site also has indisciplines that allow for errant lines of flight beyond the "sticky" confines of expert advice and point-and-click shopping. Rather than creating a virtual world as monad, one can find a network structure in which nodes of flow function as the primary structure. The "intimate" here is not just a matter of personalized control mapped by "My BabyCenter," but rather the specificity of individuals engaged in the production of a collaborative social space.

Outside of corporate Web sites, one can find similar Web pages in which the situatedness of individual voices within global network structures takes precedence over the material, conceptual, and experiential processes that give rise to monadic spaces of control. In this regard, the work of Amy Koerber on alternative mothering sites and rhetorical spaces provides an appropriate counterpoint to an analysis of BabyCenter.com. Koerber argues that a collection of Web sites (linked by Feminist Mothers and AlternaMoms Unite Web rings) provides spaces in which mothers can enact a politics that challenges both the dominant American feminist vision of empowerment through work and the patriarchal image of the submissive, passive mother. Further, Koerber argues that the resistance produced by such Web sites occurs not through claims to agency, but rather through giving voice to the disjunctions and discontinuities in these two subject-making systems that make claims on female identity. She writes:

> Rather than thinking of resistance as a question of uttering meaningful sounds that a stable, Enlightenment-style subject utters clearly enough to break through the

noise of everyday life, to understand resistance in cyberspace, we must consider
noise—the disruption of meaning itself—as a form of resistance. (219)

Drawing on the work of Lorraine Code, Koerber conceives of an online community such as Hipmama.com as a "rhetorical space," defined by Code as "fictive but not fanciful or fixed location, whose (tacit, rarely spoken) territorial
imperatives structure and limit the kinds of utterance that can be voiced within
them with a reasonable expectation of uptake and 'choral support'" (quoted
in Koerber 221). These Web sites, then, provide a space that is difficult to find
in contemporary society: a space to speak of the feminist practice of motherhood (Koerber 223).

Note, however, that in calling upon the concept of rhetorical space, Koerber
perpetuates a division between the space of communication and "real" space
(hence defined as "fictive but not fanciful"). I would extend her argument to
suggest that these rhetorical spaces are indeed real spaces of everyday life. In
other words, by providing a space in which women can develop a discourse
that explores and exploits the current contradictions between dominant discourses on feminism and motherhood, these Web sites enact a space that is
materially formed by way of computers and networks, conceptually structured
as a shared, collective endeavor, and lived in the daily practice of hypertextual
links, bulletin-board posts, and email correspondence. As such, these rhetorical spaces are very much lived spaces. Koerber writes:

> The online mothers seek space for themselves in the gaps that exist between the
> dominant discourses that compete with each other to dictate what a good mother is
> in our society. In doing so, they make noise that thwarts these discourses' attempts
> to maintain dominion over mothering through prescriptive definitions of what a
> good mother should be. (225)

As "gaps," these spaces are maps of "error" on one hand, to the extent that the
"noise" produced by such indisciplines conflicts with a cybernetic vision of
communication as efficient exchange. What's more, the lived spaces of resistance mapped by women who post to and visit these sites are by definition
highly situated: not only by the embodied spatiality of pregnancy and "motherhood,"[35] but also by the specificity of that position within the global flows of
information on the Web, as defined against normative formations of gender,
race, sexuality, and class.

Not only are these Web rings "open systems," as Koerber notes, they are
fundamentally produced by the situated understandings of individuals who

join these rings, enacting asystemic, at times aberrant, undisciplined connections (220). The sites tend to share values that define the rhetorical space as such—anticonsumerist, doctor-skeptical, for example—but the undercurrent has more to do with their situation as singular sites that enact social connections: "that the information they contain is based in real experiences of motherhood, rather than textbook-style prescription about what mothering should be" (Koerber 230). While hints of this same resistance occur within BabyCenter.com (the voice of mothers in contradistinction to the expert opinions that the site itself foregrounds), the Web rings that Koerber describes are themselves enacted spaces that map out a space for women who *embody a lived practice* of networked, feminist mothering. These are not merely "connections" by way of a medium; they are enactions of lived space in a networked society. What's more, the production of this rhetorical space is inseparable from the production of a lived space of network interaction. In its own community forum, Hipmama.com describes its mission as:

> A place that mamas of color, bi/lesbian/poly mamas, very young mamas, mamas on public assistance, sex worker mamas, single mamas, artist mamas, socialist mamas, green mamas, anarchist mamas, and pro-choice mamas identify as their community and home. By entering our discussion community, you agree to recognize and respect our standards and values. ("Mission Statement of Hipmama.com")[36]

Clearly there is an expectation of a consensus of value, but the range of "identities" claiming membership to this space implies an openness where conflict may well arise. Unlike BabyCenter.com's topic/identity approach, which attempts to organize, and potentially to limit, these discourses to a closed community, Hipmama.com provides a space for noise as well as information.

The emphasis on lived context and overt exploring of the points of conflict within the community also provides the basis for the production of space. From its main page in spring 2002, Hipmama.com linked to a Maegan "la Mala" Ortiz poem titled "Slip," in which the author responds to the "harmless" use of a derogatory word by a contributor to an online list. Drawing a comparison between the "slip" of a (presumably "disembodied") word onto a list and her own experiences with the physical assaults she and her community have experienced, Ortiz concludes:

> And with my brown baby on my hip
> and all these memories running through my head
> you have the nerve to ask me not to be pissed,

to read it as an exercise in academic semantics?
Well fuck you,
Shit.

Matters of rhetoric, experience, assumption, etc., are not glossed over; nor
is this "public sphere" something in which bodies no longer matter. Instead,
the community articulated by these crossings of situated individuals suggests
something closer to the "coalitional politics" Judith Butler describes, which
"do not assume in advance what the content of 'women' will be. They propose
instead a set of dialogic encounters by which variously positioned women articulate separate identities within the framework of an emergent coalition"
(*Gender Trouble* 14).

Globes, Gaps, and the Space of Flows

We see, then, that not all Web pages situate users within the same spaces of
everyday life. The Web functions within material, conceptual, and lived processes that are best described as a space of flows. The global reach of these networks in material form has significant consequences for social space, as does
the required representation of social space as potentially global. The practice
of browsing provides an embodied disposition that signals access to a field
of cultural capital. The "virtual class" is signified by familiarity with technology embodied in the pointing-and-clicking apparatuses of cyberspace. The
injunctions in advertisements to "just click" or "just point your browser to ..."
imply that these actions are simple. The virtual class may not be the digirati of
media producers so much as those who have access to a means of information
production in the most basic sense—their daily lives take part in the space of
flows that dominate a networked social space. At the same time that the Web
enunciates this space of flows, it is likewise providing the material, conceptual,
and lived processes for situated spaces in which the intimate and the personal
emerge as discursive structures. Such Web sites do not define the user as a
global, virtual citizen, but rather establish the space of the Web as highly personal, disjunctive, and often in opposition to global structures.

In this tension between a dominant topography of a space of control
and the indisciplines that arise through the singularities of heterogeneous
sites and situated practices, one can find spaces of "noise" that map networked social spaces in conflict. Amazon.com assumes I want what I have. An

operationalized, monadic relation to virtual worlds of information demands that "output" limit itself to the protocols of input. As Norbert Wiener notes in a cybernetic reading of legal systems based on precedence, "the technique of the interpretation of past judgments must be such that a lawyer should know, not only what a court has said, but even with high probability what the court is going to say" (110). Topographies of control function along a similar operationalized line, in which ultimately, in a Baudrillardian moment of the hyperreal, output precedes input in the form of Amazon.com's "Your Recommendations" link. But something seems to be profoundly lacking in this moment of extreme performativity, precisely in its attempt to banish the outlier and eliminate errant lines of flight from my virtual world. There is a certain pleasure, after all, when I get back not what I expected but a discourse that is no longer my own. These are indisciplines of communication that cannot be reduced to a cybernetic logic of performance.[37]

In short, we need to account for the random, unintended messages that constantly make claims on us, other than those we set forth in a program of command and control. As a representation of space, we would need to acknowledge the conditions of possibility that express themselves quite literally as "noise," as indisciplines that deterritorialize the spaces of control that dominate dispositional practices of Web browsing. Part of the solution certainly involves following what Katherine Hayles has called "Shannon's choice": namely, the decision by Claude Shannon to establish a direct, rather than inverse, relation between information and entropy. As Warren Weaver explains in his comments on Shannon's work:

> Information is . . . a measure of one's freedom of choice in selecting a message. The greater the freedom of choice, and hence the greater the information, the greater is the uncertainty that the message actually selected is some particular one. (Shannon and Weaver 18–19)

Weaver goes on to explain that the only difference between noise and signal in Shannon's cybernetics is selection; noise is "spurious" information (19). More than anything else, it is the between-ness of entropy that distresses Wiener: neither signal nor noise. In the same passage in *The Human Use of Human Beings* where Wiener discusses a cybernetics of the law, he maintains that "the greatest opportunity of the criminal in the modern community lies in this position as a dishonest broker in the interstices of the law," operating outside of or between two systems of information (111). The virtual, as a mark of indiscipline, "underdetermination," or deterritorialization marks a zone of the criminal for Wiener.[38] For Shannon, this gap between signal and selection marks a space of "equivocation," what Weaver calls "an undesirable . . . uncertainty about what the message was" (Shannon and Weaver 21). In either system of cybernetic control, however, there is still no place for indeterminacy per se: the virtual itself as a field of the possible.

Might we not find a way to mark this gap between determinations, this space of the outlier, as a space of potential?

The aberrant Web site or the outlier on a search engine's results page calls attention to the fact that systems of information are constructed, or more accurately, *enacted* by my own situated, networked interactions. As such, the outlier presents a very different opportunity, both in information mining and in our everyday experiences of networked interactions, to identify what conditions of possibility exist even within the most controlled, monadic articulations of cyberspace. *Any* query would enact the potential for new structures, not simply calculable, predictable results. The "noisy" outlier once again reveals the virtuality of the network, an essential feature of emergent, enactive hypertextuality. Freed from the image of a reified, nodal network, the WWW as an enacted, emergent network allows for a relation between human and computer that does not reduce to a matter of input/output, nor does it play out the cybernetic fantasy of absolute control. These are networks that do not *represent* a relation between points of affinity but actively *construct* them in competing, multiple forms.

While Amazon.com strives to re-create my digital footprints everywhere I go, the outlier suggests lines of flight that enact novel networks of information. Under the cluster of books by Pierre Levy that Amazon.com recommends for me, I find the following curious title:

United Nations Conference on Straddling Fish Stocks and Highly Migratory Fish Stocks: Selected Documents

This is an "error," of course, the *wrong* Pierre Levy, a misdirection never intended for *me*. But it also suggests a mapping of connections that disrupts the input/output relation of cybernetic feedback: "if you are not Mark Nunes, click here." Cracks appear in my virtual world, threatening to rupture its circumference.

Sitting in my office at home, well past 1:00 a.m., with my family asleep upstairs, I click on the blue letters and wait for the page to load.

EMAIL, THE LETTER, AND THE POST

T SHOULD COME AS NO SURPRISE that email ranks as the most common means by which individuals engage in computer-mediated communication. In fact, according to a Yankee Group survey of U.S. households online, 68 percent of American users ranked email as "their top online activity." In volume, email is equally impressive: the number of emails originating in North America per day outpaces U.S. Postal Service (USPS) volume by over 1,000 percent.[1] According to IDC, an information technology research firm, daily worldwide emails were at 31 billion in 2002 and will reach 60 billion by the year 2006. Perhaps the rapid, widespread uptake of this mode of communication is best explained by its familiarity as a practice. Letters, mailboxes, addresses, and delivery routes define a well-established social space within the developed world. Like carrier routes connecting distant ports, the Internet, in its figuration as a digital postal system, connects sites in a point-to-point network of dispatch and destination. Email occupies a paradoxical relation to space, however, marking distance as both necessary and irrelevant; dispatch and destination must be noncoterminous, but the distance between termini must be more virtual than actual. In this regard, electronic mail, with its (ap)proximate immediacy, appears as the telos of "tele-graphe": now the letter can be "here" and "there" at the same time. But email also reveals a relation to the letter and "the post" that suggests alternate topographies of correspondence. While simulating a network of determinate, point-to-point contact, email also sets up a social space that is more distributive than connective. Firsthand experience and apocryphal stories abound that suggest communication from post to post hardly amounts to a "secure dispatch." Viruses, spam, and misdirected "reply to's" appear as errors or aberrations within the systematic coordination of point-to-point communication, but these processes at the same time articulate spaces that suggest competing virtual topographies of everyday life in a network society.

As an event of space, the arrangement of material and conceptual processes that give rise to the lived practices of email exchange produces a social space that is an integral part of a network society. At a basic level, email foregrounds exchange itself as a spatial process, and, more specifically, the relation of processes of exchange to the production of the networked social spaces of modernity. An analysis of these processes would reveal that "networked social space" hardly depends upon the material, technological form of computer-mediated communication; in fact, I would argue that email in its dominant social form simulates the material processes of "the post" that predate email by more than three centuries. In other words, the routes and mailboxes that email approximates are themselves, in effect, a technological stratum that is very much embedded in the history of the production of social space of modernity. My interest in email as an articulation of social space is twofold. On one hand, email suggests an altered arrangement of material, conceptual, and experiential processes that maps both the disciplines and indisciplines of social networks in a "postmodern" society. On the other hand, it provides a coda of sorts to a history of postal networks, one that places the virtual topographies of cyberspace in a larger historical context of modernity.

To begin, let us start our spatial analysis of email with a discussion of another postal invention, one that played a prominent role in the production of the altered urban social spaces of early modernity.

The Post

In 1682, William Dockwra found himself facing twenty-two charges placed against him by the Duke of York, including £10,000 in damages (Robinson 74). At issue was what Dockwra, a merchant of growing reputation in London, described in his defense as an "invention" to assist in the daily lives of the city's merchants and residents; as such, he argued, he was protected by a 1623 statute granting him "the benefit for fourteen years of any new contrivance for the public good" (Robinson 74). Dockwra's invention was the London Penny Post. The Duke of York charged that, two years earlier, when Dockwra established a private system of delivery, he violated the 1660 Postal Act that established a monopoly on the carriage of letters in England. His advertisements for "A Penny Well Bestowed" promised a

> New Design contrived for the great Increase of Trade, and Ease of Correspondence, to the great Advantage of the Inhabitants of all sorts, by Conveying of Letters or Pacquets under a Pound Weight, to and from all parts within the Cities of London and Westminster; and the Out Parishes. (quoted in Robinson 70–71)

In place of a central post office as a point of dispatch, Dockwra served London with "receiving houses" numbering in the hundreds, with hourly foot delivery to houses and businesses throughout the area (Robinson 71). Not surprisingly, given the profits involved, the Duke of York won his case against Dockwra, and the London Penny Post became a part of the greater post office.[2]

To some degree, Dockwra was justified in claiming that his Penny Post was an "invention." Obviously the carriage of letters as a matter of governmental correspondence predates the Penny Post back to antiquity. On the Continent, modern "royal posts" had been in place for over two centuries, most notably Louis XI's horse-based courier system in 1464, and the famous Thurn and Taxis postal monopoly established by Emperor Maximillian in the 1490s.[3] At this time, regular, private delivery was for the most part a matter of business limited to universities, merchants, and banks, each of which had its own carrier system for the delivery of letters. In England, the Post Office officially began in 1516 with Henry VIII's appointment of Brian Tuke as "Master of the Posts," who, following upon continental models, established set stations or "posts" for the exchange of mail horses. The goal was, in Tuke's words, "to provide able men well horsed to carry all such letters . . . from post to post with all diligence by night and day" (quoted in Robinson 9). The result was the establishment of a system of postal roads originating in London and leading in five directions: to the north, toward Dover, to the west, toward Bristol, and toward Chester (Robinson 16–20).

According to Robinson, documents exist showing that private letters were carried on these post roads as early as the 1580s, but it is not until the first half of the 1600s that a marked increase occurred in private correspondences (16, 23). In 1633 and again in 1635, the first proposals appear petitioning for the development of a postal delivery system that would extend beyond the post roads. In 1635, a "Proposition for settling . . . packet posts betwixt London and all parts of His Majesties dominions for the carrying and recarrying of His subjects letters" resulted in a proclamation that established a national mail system: letters would be put in bags and left at the closest post along the post road, addressed to specified "by-post" towns; horseback couriers would then carry these bags from post road to by-post town; finally, letters beyond the by-post towns were carried on foot to market towns within a ten mile radius (29–32). This proclamation also established a postal monopoly, with express restrictions on the unauthorized carriage of letters in England.[4]

By Dockwra's time, England had six post roads that "were like the spokes of a great wheel, the hub being London with the six spokes of uneven length radiating from this center" (Robinson 64). As a system of delivery, the post functioned as a network of dispatch sites, with London serving as the central point of exchange. Quite contrary to this arrangement, Dockwra's Penny Post established a network with literally hundreds of points of dispatch and thousands of points of delivery. His "invention," in other words, altered the spatial arrangements of a postal network. This network structure of point-to-point contact was beginning to emerge throughout England in the materiality of roads, in the lived practice of exchange markets, and in a growing conception of a national, urban identity. While the "information superhighway" may seem to epitomize the technophilia of America in the 1990s, the roads of seventeenth-century England created the equivalent of a bandwidth restriction on the growing demand for correspondence beyond the six post roads. Increasingly, from the mid-1600s onward, *circulation* became a structuring concept in both the material form and the lived practice of modern social, cultural, and economic life. As the practice of postal exchange developed, so too did the material processes that helped articulate this and other forms of circulation as spaces of everyday life. Thus a major project for the royal cosmographer in the 1670s was the improvement of by-roads for the express purpose of facilitating movement of people, goods, and letters throughout England (Robinson 62-67). At the same time that the pursuit of fixed-point navigation increasingly determined the forms, structures, and practices of a modern global social space, as discussed in chapter 2, the relation between public and private entities in England and on the Continent began to emerge as a network allowing for circulation and flow. We find, then, that far from being a product of twentieth-century computer technology, "the network" is very much a product (and process) of modernity, which begins to emerge as early as the seventeenth century.

By 1680, the year Dockwra's "Penny Well Bestowed" advertisement appeared, a fairly well-established system was in place for the conveyance of letters along the main posts out of London. But as Robinson points out, "a Londoner could send a letter to Edinburgh or Exeter or even suburban Barnet with little trouble, but the Post Office offered no provision for sending a letter from Westminster to Blackwall" (70). Dockwra's invention provided a system whereby individuals engaged in the habits of everyday urban life could communicate directly with one another in an expedient, efficient manner. As such, his Penny Post provides for us a map of the emerging urban network of modernity, a lived space of merchants, banks, and private citizens in need of frequent, daily contact. This network structure became a network of the nation in the eighteenth century—in England and throughout what would increasingly be conceived of as the "modern world." By 1756, England still maintained six post roads, but now thirty major and ten minor crossroads existed, allowing efficient delivery between towns independent of the London central office.[5] As of 1773, however, London was the only town with home and business delivery (Robinson 192). It was not until well into the nineteenth century that a national postal network of home-to-home delivery was in place throughout England, and, by this point, a recognizably modern dominant social space was firmly established in a recognizably modern world.

The Network

From the seventeenth century to the present, postal networks have promised the potential (if not the actuality) for rapid, efficient exchange from dispatch to destination. What was significant in Dockwra's "invention" was not just the speed at which he promised to convey correspondence; rather, it was the restructuring of social space enunciated by rapid and efficient point-to-point exchange, a restructuring that understands the network itself as an integral part of everyday life. This network structure, I would argue, is deeply involved in the material, conceptual, and lived processes of modernity that by the nineteenth century would produce a dominant social space for the dominant social class. Dockwra's network describes the processes of exchange that allow for the flow of goods, capital, and information essential to modern capitalism and to an urban bourgeois lifestyle. To the extent that email presents a familiar mode of communication, it does so by taking part in the production of modernity's dominant social space of the network. The "digitization" of the letter, delivery route, and mailbox, then, is somewhat unimportant to the production of the dominant social space of modernity, as long as it continues to articulate a lived space of rapid point-to-point exchange. Such practices suggest that the social space of email is nothing new, but, rather, a culminating expression of a desire for the immediate delivery of missives from dispatch to destination.

In *practice and representation,* then, Dockwra's Penny Post is not too far removed from the network of point-to-point communication simulated on the Internet via email. In fact, one could argue that email surpassed telegraph and telephone networks in efficiency and speed precisely because it emulated the postal networks that Dockwra had introduced in the seventeenth century, which distributed deliveries to multiple points of dispatch rather than relying upon centralized points of exchange. As the story goes (becoming, as it has, a part of the "history of the Internet" folklore), it was Paul Baran, a RAND Corporation researcher, who in the early 1960s became interested in redundant networks and the survivability of a communications system after a nuclear war. Inspired by the neural net research of psychiatrist and Macy Conference regular Warren McCulloch, Baran came up with a design for a network that would, in theory, be robust enough to survive partial catastrophic damage. Baran called this structure a "distributed network," in contrast to the centralized and decentralized network structures common at the time (Hafner and Lyon 57–59). In a centralized network, all communication passes from a single hub out to its periphery. In a decentralized network (such as those in use by the phone company at the time), multiple hubs communicate with each other, each of which is responsible for communicating with its own peripheral points. In contrast to either of these structures, Baran suggested "a network of interconnected nodes resembling a distorted lattice, or a fish net," in which every point potentially served as a node of dispatch and delivery (Hafner and Lyon 58). Each node would provide a limited number of links to other nodes, the result being a network in which any point of delivery could serve equally as a point of relay and dispatch.

To apply this twentieth-century vocabulary to the seventeenth-century postal system: with the establishment of the post roads in England, up through the 1660 postal charter, the post office served primarily as a centralized network, with London as its central hub. As an increasingly effective system of by- and cross-post roads developed in the late seventeenth and early eighteenth centuries, the postal system shifted from a centralized network to a decentralized network. In contrast, Dockwra's "invention" blanketed London with receiving houses, initiating in concept, form, and practice what approximated a distributed network. While the city was divided into a number of district sorting-offices, which would then deliver the letters to private addresses (thus functioning somewhat as a decentralized network), the Penny Post provided hundreds of points of dispatch, which would in turn deliver to thousands of points of delivery (and then return-post these letters as well), thereby articulating a rudimentary point-to-point distributed network that would serve as a space of practice for urban everyday life (Robinson 71).[6]

   The history of "the network," from Penny Post to point-to-point protocol (PPP) offers an important account of the social space of modernity, as material form, conceptual structure, and lived practice. To return to the language of Deleuze and Guattari discussed in chapter 1, the network operates by capturing flows into a striated space of point-to-point contact. As a representation of space, the network of modernity is allocative and coordinated: each node serves as a point of delivery and distribution in a comprehensive system. As lived practice, it provides a structuring of experience in which exchanges and flows of information, goods, and capital occur over a geographic expanse that at the same time maps the flows of everyday life. And in its material form, it provides an expression of relations in which circulation and flow are actualized as spatial events. But by no means is the social space of "the network" limited to a postal mapping of carrier routes and dispatch hubs. The growth and spread of the newspaper in seventeenth- and eighteenth-century England was very much entangled in the material, conceptual, and experiential processes that also gave rise to the growing number (and growing population) of towns along the by-roads and crossroads of England (B. Harris 105). The spread of markets likewise helped to create a network in which towns served, as Bob Harris notes, as "nodal points in commodity and product markets that were becoming national in focus" (23). Clearly, the production of the social space of modernity involves a dialogic relationship among a number of urban processes, including the improvement of roads, the development of coffeehouses, the spread of market towns, the connection of urban locales to foreign markets, and the spread of credit networks (B. Harris 23–25).[7] These networks of point-to-point contact and rapid exchange take part in the production of the networked social space of modernity. In this history of the modern network, then, email provides an intensification of modernity's social space, not a rupture. With email, the network itself becomes foregrounded as a space of everyday life, articulated through a cluster of practices involving dispatch, delivery, and (im)mediate exchange.

Email simulates and actualizes this system of point-to-point connection as a lived space. But as an enacted network of exchange, email dispatches packets across the global/geographical space of networks and phone lines in a manner far removed from this site-to-site postal mapping of dispatch and delivery. While these material arrangements are not without impact, the dominant social space mapped by email persists in a simulated virtual topography of direct site-to-site transmission both as a representation of space and as an everyday practice. What was perhaps most unique about Baran's distributed network, and what clearly differentiates it materially from Dockwra's network, would in fact be transparent to its users at points of delivery and dispatch: namely, its redundancy. A message traveling from point A to point B would *not* follow a rigid, coordinated path, but would instead search for the route with the lightest traffic. Here the "immateriality" of the letter (or rather, its material articulation as an electronic exchange via global networks) does have some relevance to the social space it produces. Baran's network was "revolutionary," to borrow the rhetoric of Hafner and Lyon, not only in its distributed structure but also in its transmission of the signal in fragmentary "message blocks," each of which would search out its own expedient path to its destination (59–60).[8] Email does not render geography irrelevant—in fact, as noted in earlier chapters, email gains importance as a lived practice the more one has access to other global processes of transportation and exchange. But the enacted space of exchange articulated in material form by a distributed, redundant network suggests that in a space of flows, it is *traffic rather than distance* that holds spatial significance—and that social space itself occurs as an event rather than a thing. The distributed, fragmented material form of the enacted event-space of electronic transmissions allows for the production of a space that does not reduce to a networked "space of places," to use Manuel Castells's term. While continuing to simulate what Fredric Jameson describes as the "logic of the grid" of classical capitalism, the Internet, linked as it is to a capitalism of "the multinational network," results in a space that "involves the suppression of distance ... and the relentless saturation of any remaining voids and empty places, to the point where the postmodern body ... is now exposed to a perceptual

barrage of immediacy from which all sheltering layers and intervening mediations have been removed" (410–13). In this "hyperspace," each node, in effect,
is everywhere on the network "simultaneously." As such, the electronic means
of delivery and dispatch, while allowing for an "immediate" post, also suggests
an arrangement of space that does not reduce to a point-to-point, coordinated
network. As a virtual topography, then, electronic mail ends up disrupting the
postal space it seeks to simulate.

The distributive, dissipative properties of the electronic letter give rise to
material, conceptual, and experiential processes that articulate altered spatial
relations between "dispatch" and "delivery." While presenting the simulation
of a unique *correspondence,* the reproducibility of any electronic transmission
implies the potential for multiple addresses. The letter never arrives "uniquely"
but as a potential multiplicity under the guise of a unique address.[9] While a
chain letter via the postal service figures as an anomaly in the system, the principle of multiple, often anonymous correspondences forwarded "directly"
to specified addresses provides a daily structuring of one's experience with
email. Hoax letters, either as intended to deceive ("Help me wire $1,000,000 to
your checking account") or as well intentioned ("Delete the following .exe file
IMMEDIATELY!"), circulate in a network of dissemination in which a *personal
address* can replicate itself indefinitely to an indeterminate number of recipients. Certainly, to some extent, "spam" mimics the bulk-rate junk mail that
gluts traditional postal systems, but unlike postal mass-mailings, each point
of electronic delivery potentially serves as a point of dispatch within a wider
field of dissemination. In actuality, I receive an email *addressed to me,* but, at
the same time, any email is always *virtually* a chain letter. Much as the map of
hypertext discussed in the preceding chapter depends upon the potential for
linkage (not only actual linkages), the topography of email maps a virtuality in
which a personal address always holds the potential for relay within a space of
dissemination. The interpellation of the electronic address not only arrives in
the hailing of a subject heading, but it passes on and through my personal addresses to an undefined network of others.

Virus-warning spam, "Nigerian 419" scams, and incidents such as the
Schmich-Vonnegut commencement speech demonstrate the peculiar, dissipative nature of electronic transmission, in which *correspondence in its most
literal sense* often fails. Email enacts a paradoxical space of communication.
On one hand, electronic mail takes the form of personal correspondence—
a literal co-responding of persons.[10] At the same time, this place of personal

correspondence is very much a medium of publication and dissemination—a potential present in every electronic dispatch. Katie Argyle, for example, describes how the CyberMind Listserv functioned as a personal space of mourning when one of its members died suddenly. At the same time, she and others realized that these personal correspondences were "placed in an extremely public forum. Anyone could have copied them. . . . There were no guarantees that these private lamentations would stay amongst the grievers" (135). These emergent network structures speak not only of altered writing spaces, they suggest shifts in lived social space, mapped by shifts in how the public and private are articulated in everyday life. One space does not negate the other; rather, in the spaces of everyday life produced by email, the public and the private, the personal and the indiscriminate enact altered spatial (and hence social) relations.

Mail groups and Listservs provide a particularly compelling example of this altered relation between public and private correspondence, and the general problem of *correspondence* raised by CMC: namely, that when I receive an email, I have no guarantee to whom it was addressed. On a Listserv, any member of a group can dispatch a letter to the entire subscription list. At times, this dispatch functions more like a message in a bottle than a "true" postal envoy: something cast out at a distance in the hope of some (random) response. But list correspondences also frequently produce "addressed" dialogues between two or more individuals, creating the appearance of determined point-to-point contact. Even in these instances of apparent dispatch and arrival, however, the potential exists at every moment that an undetermined recipient (any of a number of silently participating "lurkers") could irrupt from within this point-to-point correspondence and carry the letter off, so to speak, to new potential destinations. In this figuration, email no longer serves as a system of dispatch; it now functions within a space of dissemination. Each envoy proliferates: received at multiple addresses and open to the response of multiple recipients. To this extent, the electronic letter maps a network space that is no longer determined by point-to-point contact. The immateriality of the electronic letter "materializes" a certain poststructuralist insight on writing: that the letter *always* disseminates.

As a space of writing, this literalized dissemination made possible by way of electronic discourse suggests a network structure at odds with even the most distributed of networks, which still depends upon the notion that what gets sent will arrive at its "proper" destination. Mark Poster notes:

> The electronic mark, as opposed to the graphic mark, permits a deep reforming of the space/time coordinates of writing and reading throughout everyday life. The electronic mark radicalizes the anti-logocentric tendencies that deconstruction argues are inherent in all writing. The change from graphic to electronic mark permits the wide diffusion of electronic writing throughout the social space and undermines the temporal limits of pre-electronic writing. (*The Mode of Information* 123)[11]

The postal network operates under the conduit fallacy to the extent that it treats the materiality of the post as essential (by way of its faith in the integrity of the letter as object), but ultimately insignificant, since it merely functions as a vehicle for communicating correspondence between dispatch and destination. We can no longer operate under these assumptions to the extent that diffusion and dissipation serve as general principles of circulation for email. "The letter" itself undergoes a material, conceptual, and experiential restructuring that maps this shift in the production of the spaces of everyday life in a network society. To understand the social spaces produced by and producing this arrangement of electronic dispatch, then, it is worthwhile to explore what becomes of "the letter" when it is articulated as an electronic exchange across a distributed network.

The Letter

The traditional post treats the letter as a material singularity, one that (hopefully) remains passive in its transport from point of dispatch to point of destination. It assumes, and asks its users to assume, that the letter maintains its integrity, neither mutilated nor unsealed during its journey from A to B. Email challenges these assumptions in its shift from material transport to digital transmission. Signatures, seals, and other marks of authenticity take on a radically different form once the letter becomes "pixilated." Encryption keys and electronic signatures attempt to preserve the integrity of transmission with reference to the digital form of the letter, not to its material singularity—a coding that precedes its material appearance as pixels on my screen or characters on a printed page. Such assurances no longer depend upon a metaphysics of presence but rather on a Baudrillardian metaphysics of the code. In fact, as a third-order simulacrum, the electronic graphical mark provides no guarantee of even a static image, much less an "authentic" one: the text that appears on my screen in a given font with given margins may arrive elsewhere appearing quite differently, based on the configuration of the recipient's computer. The letter, then, is not a *thing* that arrives but an event that occurs: an articulation of code into material form as marks on a page or pixels on a screen. As Jay Bolter notes, typography no longer marks the permanence of the printed page or of the published word: "electronic writers sense that their writing and therefore their typography is always subject to recall and change" (67). The form of electronic writing, then, emphasizes dynamics rather than permanence, transmission instead of stasis. In both private communiqué and public discourse, the electronic writing space is not *occupied* by the text; rather, the letter *harbors* in this space.

The electronic letter functions less as a material artifact than as a medium. The handwritten letter carries an elaborate signature of presence, concluding with the author's signature. Even a typed letter with AutoScript signature does more than convey a message; it conveys an official material presence, political or otherwise, in the form of the letter that actually arrives. The same cannot be said about telewriting, however, in which what arrives is *materially different* from what was sent. Consider, as a point of comparison, other forms of telewriting, in which transmission takes precedence over material transport. The telegraph, for example, translates an original letter into a code of "dots and dashes," only then to reconstitute the message at the point of arrival. But the *letter itself* no longer arrives, only its message. The fax machine operates by the same principle: the original remains but the message transmits. With email, however, the "original" seems to have disappeared, leaving only the transmission. In fact, the "material presence" of the letter at the point of dispatch—electronic marks on the computer screen—has already been codified. The letter *communicates* but it no longer stands as an original and as a point of origin. Yet the *image* of the letter as original and as originary mark exists on the screen as a simulation of material presence. The electronic letter provides an exemplary instance of a Baudrillardian simulation: a model without original that provides the blueprint for infinite iterations of "the same."[12] As a production, it is always already a reproduction; its dispatch is always a circulation and a publication. One might argue that the persistence of email's appearance as unique material presence is nothing more than a cultural archaism: our nostalgic hesitancy to accept the rupture in writing space that has already occurred by way of this medium. On the other hand, this archaism could reveal a foundation for the postal economy of dispatch and arrival: that the postal space of point-to-point contact *demands* a displacement of presence, either actual or simulative, from dispatch to destination. The metaphysics of the post (to turn a phrase) provides a conceptual structuring and underpinning for the production of a social space in which the object, be it letter or commodity, must circulate freely, yet with assurances of integrity. In a networked social space, then, in order for email to function as "the post" in the absence of a materially present letter that arrives at its destination, it must simulate an original, transmit its message, and then simulate the intact arrival of *the same letter* at the point of receipt.

We find, then, that the letter occupies competing positions within inter-penetrating social spaces. On one hand, as simulated presence, electronic correspondence allows for an apotheosis of the postal relay, a convergence of absence and presence. Instead of challenging logocentrism, as Poster and others have argued, electronic writing would function as the telos to writing's history as absent presence: immediate, transparent, and therefore transcendent. At the same time, the dispersive, dissipative qualities of electronic correspondence rupture the metaphysics of the post that depends upon determinate communication from dispatch to destination—the *arrival* of the letter. The challenge in mapping the material, conceptual, and experiential processes of email, then, is understanding that these apparent contradictions in constatives are in fact scenes of contestation in the performative production of space. Perhaps this is one reason why the letter, electronic and otherwise, has a significant position in Derrida's work, especially in *The Post Card*, where he shows explicit concern in its role as a communication medium. Through a series of love-letter postcards and essays on Freud, Derrida argues (contrary to Lacan) that "a letter can always—and therefore must—never arrive at its destination" (*The Post Card* 121). The possibility of a private correspondence slipping away, far from being an aberration in the postal economy, is for Derrida the "condition . . . that something does arrive" (121). In other words, mediation is always risky business, though as *technē*, it seeks to erase the marks of risk through claims of immediacy and transparency. By further complicating the social position of "private address," email calls attention to both the desire for secure, point-to-point delivery and the rupturing of a metaphysics of the post initiated by dispersive mediation.

In *Archive Fever*, Derrida touches upon the effect of the electronic letter as a "postal technology":

> Electronic mail today, even more than the fax, is on the way to transforming the entire public and private space of humanity, and first of all the limit between the private, the secret (private or public), and the public or phenomenal. It is not only

a technique, in the ordinary and limited sense of the term: at an unprecedented rhythm, in quasi-instantaneous fashion, this instrumental possibility of production, of printing, of conversation, and of destruction of the archive must inevitably be accompanied by juridical and thus political transformations. These affect nothing less than property rights, publishing and reproduction rights. (17)

Derrida suggests that the letter, once it becomes an electronic exchange, forces a radicalization of "the history of the post." The postcard/*carte postale*, for Derrida, is emblematic of this relation between writing and space, in its position as "half-private, half-public, neither the one nor the other" (*The Post Card* 62), but this radicalization of social space is only suggested in Derrida's writing. Poster elaborates on this claim and sees in Derrida's focus on the electronic letter a challenge to political and social frameworks:

> To the extent that the mode of information restructures language and symbols generally into a configuration that is aptly termed "virtual reality," the particular form of the messianic, of our hope for justice, must go through this technological circuit and must account for the difference between writing and e-mail, dissemination and the Internet, the parergon and the World Wide Web. ("Theorizing Virtual Reality" 55–56)

For Poster, the most significant result of electronic writing is the way that it "disperses the subject so that it no longer functions as a center in the way it did in pre-electronic writing" (*The Mode of Information* 100). The "immateriality" of the electronic letter, coupled with the computer network's potential to disperse the subject, provides a mapping of a virtual topography that resists the dominant network structures of modernity. At the same time, it also seems clear that, rather than destabilizing "the word," electronic writing attempts to simulate it perfectly. In traces of the electronic letter, then, we find competing representations of space and conflicting lived practices—a mapping of multiple topographies.

But rather than limiting our analysis of email to its immaterial, enactive qualities, it is worthwhile to consider how this distributive, dissipative potential for electronic correspondence participates in conceptual and experiential processes to produce spaces of everyday life. As a mapping of lived space, I would argue that email suggests both a dominant social space that reinforces social relations of modernity's networks of exchange, as well as a restructuring of these relations through the production of altered spaces of everyday life. The shifting status of the letter, as electronic and digital correspondence, keeps CMC from simulating the postal system as material, conceptual, and lived processes. As such, the sorts of practices entailed in email correspondence should suggest networks of social space that both affirm and resist the point-to-point network of modernity. To clarify the sorts of social spaces produced by and producing the electronic post, it is helpful to return once again to Dockwra's "invention" and an analysis of the social spaces in which this network arose.

Closets and Post Roads

As Robinson notes, the letter in England prior to the 1600s served primarily as a vehicle for royal correspondence. In the first half of the seventeenth century, the number of personal correspondences began to increase rapidly (Robinson 23). Dockwra's Penny Post and the establishment of efficient by- and cross-post roads in the 1680s are, in part, responses to the growing volume of letters distributed by post. By the start of the eighteenth century, the London Penny Post was carrying a million letters a year, boasting "nothing can be more exact, and 'tis with the utmost Safety and Dispatch, that Letters are delivered at the remotest Corners of the Town, almost as soon as they can be sent by a Messenger" (quoted in Robinson 85). What's more, the lived practice of letter writing, and dispatch by way of the post, increasingly became an everyday activity in the eighteenth century, especially for those most caught up in the emerging networks of the nation.

In his discussion of the history of the novel, Ian Watt notes that the practice of personal letter writing grew in popularity in England from the 1680s into the 1700s, eventually achieving "cult" status amongst the middle class (189). Not coincidentally, this period also marked the rise of epistolary literature that both mirrored and modeled personal letter writing. With their shared focus on inner consciousness and personal experience, the seventeenth-century private epistle and the English epistolary novel serve for Watt as artifacts that reveal changing social relations in early modern England. Watt writes:

> By the time of [Richardson's] *Pamela* the majority of the literate public cared little
> for the traditions of courtly rhetoric and used letters only for the purpose of sharing their daily thoughts and acts with a friend; the cult of familiar letter writing, in
> fact, provided Richardson with a microphone already attuned to the tones of private experience. (193)

While the novel borrows from the epistle to become a medium that focuses on the individual and on his or her "interior life," both media reflect a larger cultural shift occurring in late-seventeenth-century England, one marked by forms and representations of privacy. In spatial terms, this shift marks a transition toward containment and compartmentalization in the production of social space. Watt notes that letter writing, both in the novel and in actual social practice, often occurred in the closet, an image of feminine privacy and individuation (188). At its most distinct articulation (one that carries well into the nineteenth century), the private letter maps a social space of a feminized domestic sphere, distinct from a market sphere of male business correspondences and bills of sale. The coordination of these spheres occurs by way of an increasingly complex articulation of the networks of modernity. Thus, the eighteenth-century epistolary novel "unrolls in a flow of letters from one lonely closet to another," mapping a social space involving private, domestic space; public roadways and delivery routes; and a concept of social networks of exchange (Watt 189). To this extent, the social practice of letter writing articulates the networks of modernity as a lived space—individuals in private, corresponding by way of a national, public communication system.

The social space suggested by Watt via the epistolary novel corresponds with shifts in urban social space occurring in concert with the spread of postal networks, public roads, and other modes of circulation, articulated in its inverse through the production of "the private" as a space of everyday life. Increasingly, interior design of households in England reflects a shift toward a layout of private rooms equipped with locks, and public receiving rooms (Habermas 44–46). Homes also find their place within a coordinated public network as houses gain numbered street addresses to aid in postal delivery (Watt 182). In form, representation, and practice, the post articulates a nexus of sorts between public and private space. The lived spatial experience of novel reading and letter writing is entangled in the emerging spatial practice of locked doors, street numbers, and closets, and a modern conceptual representation of a network of point-to-point communication. As a material form, then, the letter quite literally negotiates between public networks and private addresses, and, in doing so, it takes part in the production of the public and the private as social space. The map of this social space can be traced out in the (well-founded) seventeenth-century fear that no letter was safe as it passed through the central London office.[13] Robinson notes: "As the public came to use the facilities of the Post Office more freely, it was to grow much more concerned over this violation of the secrecy of correspondence" (55). The letter and post, then, provide a medium through social space that articulates the relation—and distinction—between the private and the public. In his discussion of the "archetypal eighteenth-century activity" of letter writing, Simon Varey makes a similar point: "Writing letters is simultaneously an individual and a social act: individual because it expresses the self, social because it communicates with other 'selves'" (184–85). I would make explicit, however, that this social space of private "selves" in commerce with other "selves" via a public network is itself produced by and producing the material, conceptual, and experiential processes of the seventeenth and eighteenth centuries. As the lived practice of letter writing gains prominence as a process involved in the production of social space, the post increasingly serves as a scene of interpenetrating articulations of the public and the private. The Postal Act of 1657 established a general post office with the state's, not its private citizens', interest in mind: to "discover and prevent many dangerous and wicked designs, which have been, and are daily contrived against the Peace and Welfare of the Commonwealth, the intelligence whereof cannot well be Communicated but by letter" (quoted in Robinson 46). Within a generation, the post office appeared to its citizens not as a protective agency of the Crown but as a potential threat: a public institution capable of violating private space.

The fact that "violation of the private" would occupy the concerns of eighteenth-century citizens implies that as a representation of space, the public and private are already articulated as distinct zones of social space. What's more, writing, mediated by either postal network or printed publication, served as an "interface" that both distinguished and bridged these two spaces of everyday life. As Varey points out, in the novels of Richardson the threat of a "violation of personal space" is threefold: through an unwanted entry into the private room, through the violence of rape, and through the unsealing of the letter (187). All three elements define a social space of the private, possessed by the individual. Likewise, the popular published diaries (fictional and authentic) and epistolary novels of the period played precisely on this binary relation between the public and the private, mediated by the text. Given this concept of the text as a zone of mediation, the novel reader occupies a dual site: as both intended private addressee and intervening public eye. While this novel form suggests that writing serves as a medium connecting interior spaces, at the same time, writing circulates only because of its function as a public/published medium (Watt 189). Both novel and letter, then, reveal aspects of late seventeenth-century social space in England, and, by extension, in Enlightenment Europe. As Lefebvre notes, one can only begin to recognize social space from within the midst of the processes that give rise to its articulation (*The Production of Space* 79). Both the representation of a "postal space" as a mental concept and the representational spaces of epistolary novels and letter writing suggest that by the 1700s an abstract social space of partitioned private space and circulating public space had already been produced. The spatial practice of locked doors and closets, along with the demarcation of public world and private life, function as part of the fragmentation of this abstract space that accompanied the rise of a middle class and the ascendancy of modern capitalism:[14] a localization of social function around a fundamentally binary relation of inside and outside. If one can begin to theorize the private during this period—personal space, private property, the "proper" in general—it is because the late seventeenth and early eighteenth centuries had already produced a social space that initiated these relations, placed in communication with one another through complex networks of roads, postal routes, and market exchanges.

In an analysis of this articulation of the private and public in negotiated, separate spheres, a large body of literature has developed on the rise of what Habermas calls "a public sphere whose decisive mark was the published word" (16). While Watt calls attention to the relation of the post to the rise of a "private subject" position, Habermas focuses on how these systems of traffic—newspapers, letters, and commodities—put a "public" in communication with one another. As a social space, the public sphere describes, in its Habermasian formulation:

> The sphere of private people come together as a public . . . regulated from above against the public authorities themselves, to engage them in a debate over the general rules governing relations in the basically privatized but publicly relevant sphere of commodity exchange and social labor. (27)

Most significant to our discussion (and most commented upon) is Habermas's notion of coffeehouses as nodes in their own right for the circulation of "news" and the debate of ideas. The most relevant of this material draws upon a study of coffeehouses and newspapers in the eighteenth century as a means of establishing a domain of public debate. Here again the letter as a mode of communication has a central role. On one hand, Habermas confirms Watt's discussion of the rise of the epistolary novel and private correspondence (49). But, in addition, letters served as a vehicle into the public sphere in the form of "letters to the editor" via the newspaper and the coffeehouse (Habermas 42). By the middle of the eighteenth century, the triweekly and daily newspapers had greatly expanded their coverage of political concerns of the day, with much of the debate taking the form of published letters from a community of readers (B. Harris 38). As Stuart Sherman points out, the newspapers of the late seventeenth and early eighteenth centuries stood in part "as a site for correspondences between writers and readers"—and, therefore, amongst a public of readers (120). Here the letter still circulates, but it does so within a public sphere: from public subject to public audience via public medium.

What is relevant here, in this notion of the public sphere, is the degree to which writing takes part in the production of social space, and how that social space is articulated through a material form of postal and publication technologies; a conceptual structure of "the public" and "the private"; and a cluster of lived practices involved in reading, correspondence, and public debate. Of less concern here is Habermas's contentious claim for a public sphere defined as disinterested and open to all comers (36–37). In this regard, as Michael Warner and others have noted,[15] it is not the technology of writing in and of itself that articulates a public sphere, but the relation of this technology to discursive systems involved in the reproduction of fields of social power. The press, then, serves an emblematic function in the production of eighteenth-century social space in its relation to material form, conceptual structure, and lived practice, but it does not determine the relation of processes—a point well worth taking in any study of the Internet. What's more, these processes are produced in a dialogic relation with one another that gives rise to the dominant social space of modernity.

As Habermas, Sherman, and other commentators have noted, the spread of the newspaper and the advance of the postal system are by no means separate events. Robinson reports that from the circulation of the triweeklies through much of the eighteenth century, the British Post Office, in effect, served as a "news agent on a grand scale," allowing newspapers postage-free delivery on the post roads and giving local delivery profits to the postmasters (147–48). Networks of the post and networks of the news provide overlapping processes that take part in the production of modern social space. While Bob Harris points to the coexistence of other forms of communication of the news (such as manuscript newsletters and word-of-mouth reports), newspapers "establish[ed] a continuous circuit of communication, linking reader to paper, and reader to reader" and distributed on a national scale (106). In 1695, triweekly papers were leaving London on post days—Tuesdays, Thursdays, and Saturdays. A year later, the first evening paper appeared. By around the turn of the century, the first provincial papers were in press (B. Harris 10). By 1702, London's first daily, the *Courant,* was in circulation. Changes in modes of distribution and franking of papers led to a rapid increase in circulation. In 1764, approximately 1.1 million papers traveled the post. By 1782 that number had more than tripled, and it reached 4.5 million by the early 1790s, when London had fourteen dailies, seven triweeklies, and two weeklies (B. Harris 10–15).[16] By no means separable events, the forms, structures, and practices involved in the delivery of correspondences and newspapers alike via postal routes map an increasingly complex network of communication throughout this period. In this regard, what is of interest here is not so much Habermas's claim that the public sphere allowed for "people's public use of their reason" in separation from their "private" interests, but the sort of social space of circulations set up in the eighteenth century, defined by social networks, private correspondences, and public media.

We see, then, a convergence of several processes in the production of the social space of modernity, including better roads, a greater number of cross-posts, reduced government taxation, and an audience engaged in the consumption of daily news. In a fashion similar to the practice of letter writing and the literary form of the epistolary novel, the eighteenth-century newspaper suggests an arrangement of social space in which "private" selves negotiate a public space by way of a network of communication.[17] By operating in both public and private space, newspapers as material form and lived practice create a community of readers. What's more, they take part in a representation of space that is implicated in both material and lived processes. The newspaper sets up an imagined community, coordinating public and private experience by making the public seem private (Sherman 23). The everyday experience of reading and recognizing specific newspapers within specific social spaces enacts membership in what Benedict Anderson calls a "visibly invisible" community by serving as an emblematic link between the conceptual and the material (35–36).[18] Connected with these lived practices is a representation of space that structures the public as a "republic of letters." Finally, as a material practice, we have the post roads, coffeehouses, and homes—a network of a nation connecting public arenas with private spaces, occupied by individuals who navigate this public/private divide.

Email and the Virtual Agora

Certainly, in many of its figurations, email (re)institutes the public and private spaces instantiated by the eighteenth-century newspaper and by personal correspondence. Watt's description of letters traveling "from one lonely closet to another" offers an image of letter writing as a lived space connecting private domains. Email can indeed function as just such a representational space; in fact it is this image of email that has perhaps best captured the popular imagination: communication from one lonely *terminal* to another. While electronic mail originated within the work world of shared network resources, it very quickly became a popular means of personal correspondence. Hafner and Lyon, for example, begin their account of email technology with the tale of one of the original network designers using a network protocol to request that a fellow attendee return an electric razor that he had left behind at a conference in Sweden. Likewise, in the almost-mythical tale of the Internet's spread, told by Howard Rheingold and numerous others, ARPANET very quickly became a domain in which researchers, rather than sharing data, used various network protocols to exchange jokes, trivia, and personal commentary. In media representations as well, from thrillers like *The Net* to romantic comedies such as *You've Got Mail*, the Internet, specifically when used as a mode of communication (through email, chat rooms, and bulletin boards), provides a means by which people can exchange intimate details with one another. The computer, rather than figuring as a device that alienates its user and isolates her from the world, becomes instead a means of personal contact.

While, on one hand, email articulates a lived space of intimate exchange, it at the same time takes part in the articulation of spaces of control governed by a performativity principle of efficiency and speed. Here, communication serves as a relay of information. Intimacy implies a space of interiority, a privacy shared or secreted. Immediacy, in contrast, suggests not only rapid exchange but also a shared medium or *middle ground*. It is a matter of interface rather than interiors. Whereas in the eighteenth century, as Alan McKenzie notes, "the form of the letter as a separate, handwritten sheet conveyed across some distance a tangible, legible 'gift' from the writer to a specific intended reader," with email it is not the *object* of the letter that matters, only its *exchange* (5). Such lived practice privileges immediacy above reflection. That is not to suggest that email necessitates immediate response. A study of email practices at work suggests that correspondences may not be as ephemeral as they appear to be. Quite frequently, Steve Whittaker and Candace Sidner found, email in-boxes were overflowing with correspondences, often archiving threads of on-going exchanges between two or more individuals. Each letter, then, stands less as a "legible gift" than as a potential for reply, immediacy played out in ar-chival space. While the literary convention of the epistolary novel supposes a "real-time" writing,[19] email makes this convention a reality. But this image of "real-time" writing, where the *outer* public threatens to break *in* on the private at any moment, functions quite differently electronically. Now the practice of a private writing, which can occur everywhere "immediately," emphasizes that the public and private do not stand in this sort of inside-outside relation. With the epistolary novel, we read a private space used as a means of publication, the reader always functioning as interloper, reading over the shoulder of the intended addressee. Electronic writing to some degree reverses this conven-tion. With the clear potential for dissemination implicated in every electronic transmission, all correspondences—even those intended as strictly private—become a kind of publication. Personal email inverts the gesture of epistolary literature: with electronic writing, a public medium is used as a private mode by way of a "convention" of point-to-point contact. The seemingly direct com-munication is never that; at the same time, each envoy maps a potential for (im)mediate exchange in a system of efficient, direct contact.

Whereas cross-post roads in the seventeenth century marked the elabora-tion of a decentralized postal network, electronic cross-posts—via Listservs, cc's and bcc's, chain letters, and spam—map a network of lived practice that is never determinate, always in the process of proliferating new contacts. Poster argues that all "mediated media" are "communicated not simply to the ad-dressee but to an unpredictable multiplicity of readers" (*The Mode of Informa-tion* 126). In particular, electronic writing "is a distancing that multiplies and decenters the subject to the point that the reader cannot localize and specify the subject/author to any degree" (126–27). Poster concludes: "perhaps more than textuality per se, the situation of writing is today being changed. The spacing on the page of the book becomes, with electronic writing, the spacing of the message in the world" (128). More specifically, this change in spacing shows itself as a viral reproduction and proliferation, undermining the postal economy of displaced presence and point-to-point contact.

While Derrida argues that writing serves as pharmakon to a metaphysics of presence, electronic writing functions more as virus than poison/cure. The viral form replicates and spreads by hijacking host functions. In a similar way, email, while maintaining a postal economy of dispatch-to-destination/point-to-point delivery, offers a structuring of dispatch in which the letter is always replicating itself in multiple, indeterminate directions. While the letter circulates, email literally *proliferates*. In the case of an actual email virus, this viral system of dissemination becomes explicit. In mid-2002, a rash of "Klez" viruses began spreading across servers in the United States and worldwide. Klez uses an attachment to exploit Microsoft Outlook's address book, generating a new round of viral emails "from" the infected and the host, personally addressed, with a randomized subject line. The result was a virus that exploited a trust in the integrity of the singular address. As the automated processes of the virus make clear, as a space of exchange, the flows themselves are antecedents of the agents that "initiate" these circulations. It is the space of flows itself that dominates email, not the writer or reader per se. In other words, an email virus reveals an underlying viral logic implicit in every electronic dispatch. In the case of the Klez virus, the following scenario can—and did—occur:

> If Klez happens to send an email "from" a user to an email list's automatic subscribe address, the list software assumes the email is a valid subscription request and begins sending mail to the user. A mailing list for fans of the Grammy Award–winning Steely Dan band has posted an explanation directed to those who were subscribed to the list by the virus. "We are not infected with the Klez virus. We don't know if you are infected with the Klez virus. You may be. But even if you are not, someone out there who is infected has both your address and our address on their computer . . . and therein lies the problem." (Delio)

The shift in metaphor from Derridean poison to viral infection is significant. The medium itself provides a basis for a repositioning of each "address" as an unwitting "host" for further dissemination. What an email virus makes apparent is that email itself is always already infected with this viral potential. As such, the social space of email is no longer a coordinated map of point-to-point delivery but rather a zone of potential proliferating contacts, in which the situated nodes that determine the singularities of one's personal address— the folks I get email from, the lists to which I subscribe—become a matrix for determining the potential for further dissemination. Mapping such a system would involve a topography of pandemics and outbreaks, not a coordinated grid.

Email, then, enacts both a topography in which the letter simulates the immediacy and transparency of pure presence and a topography of disseminated multiples. And with these competing topographies come competing claims on the social spaces in which letter writing can occur. Electronic writing's ability to allow the public to permeate the private (and vice versa) would suggest the arrival of an alternate social space in which a binary relation between the two no longer made sense. What occurs in email is the image of the private correspondence, which is in fact public as well. More so, the medium allows for a dissemination of multiple, replicating public correspondences, with each recipient designated as the unique address. It is an unusual feature of Listservs that when posting to a list, the addresser automatically assumes the position as addressee. Although the letter arrives, it is always marked "return to sender." And conversely, each letter addressed "to me" also addresses itself personally to multiple others. As a lived practice, then, email functions as personal correspondence, but in a manner that disrupts the public-private relation mapped by earlier "postal technologies." Clearly, the lived practice of emailing is not restricted to personal contacts. The very existence of Listservs and USENET groups—dating back to the Advanced Research Projects Agency's (ARPA) MsgGroup—suggests the importance of email in structuring a "network community" of electronic exchanges (Hafner and Lyon 200). Whereas personal correspondences find themselves virtually published with every transmission, these "forums" of public exchange open up for each individual user on the private space of mainframe terminals, servers, and *personal* computers. Electronic writing, it would seem, sets up a social space in which the public continually reveals itself as private, and the private reveals itself as public.

In a similar fashion, email manages to blur processes that are both intimate and impersonal. Again, the "contact" established by way of the medium is both direct and at a distance. It is increasingly common for family and friends to "stay in touch" through CMC. When grandparents receive digital-photo attachments of their grandchildren who live 1,000 or so miles away, the "legible gift" of a letter in hand is no longer *present* as such; however, the promise of immediate contact, of bringing dispatch and delivery together, establishes the medium as a space of "authentic contact." And this same principle works in reverse. The metaphorical distance that had once separated everyday life from individuals at the center of media and cultural events no longer exists. While it still may be very difficult to get a personal conference with the president of the United States, anyone can send email to president@whitehouse.gov. Granted, the same could be said of standard postal delivery, and one's chances of the president himself actually reading your comments or concerns are perhaps about as good. But even at the level of rhetorical construction of the "virtual agora," politicians who have embraced e-government see the potential to bring constituents into a closer proximity with their elected representatives. We might question why this would be, if the post always promised such contact. The answer seems to be, in part, visible in this restructuring of social space in which public/private and intimate/impersonal have become interpenetrating spaces of everyday life. The same example could be drawn from the world of celebrities, who have always received fan mail but who, with electronic correspondence, are brought into a dialogue that breeches the viewer's world of mobile privatization, while still maintaining a mediated distance. Or to draw on a more personal example: as a college professor, I have had only a handful of students call me at my home phone number; while I (and many of my colleagues) would interpret such a call as an intrusion on personal space, on numerous occasions I have found myself responding to student email on weekends, late at night, or while drinking my morning coffee. Such a medium is invasive—holding the potential for violation—only from the perspective of a clearly defined public-private divide. But the mediation of email distances dispatch from delivery according to a postal economy, thereby maintaining an impersonal space of social distance. The result is the production of a lived space in which the public irrupts within the private and vice versa, yet where proximity and immediacy are always still *at a remove.*

Of all the representations of space called upon to account for this public function of Internet-based communications, "the agora" has probably had the widest currency, originating in the writing of Howard Rheingold, to describe his experience in building community with likeminded individuals on the WELL (Whole Earth 'Lectronic Link). Back in the early 1990s, Rheingold envisioned the spread of "informal public places" online that would serve as new community hubs in this age of encroaching shopping malls (26). William Mitchell elaborated on this trope in his 1995 book *City of Bits,* exploring what he saw as the libratory potentials of CMC:

> The worldwide computer network—the electronic agora—subverts, displaces, and radically redefines our notions of gathering place, community, and urban life. The Net has a fundamentally different physical structure, and it operates under quite different rules from those that organize the action in the public places of traditional cities. It will play as crucial a role in the twenty-first century as the centrally located, spatially bounded, architecturally celebrated agora did (according to Aristotle's *Politics*) in the life of the Greek polis. (8)

Yet while Rheingold, Mitchell, and others describe the Internet of the mid-1990s as an agora of rational social exchange, and therefore of liberation, the market function implicit in this representation of space also suggests an experience governed by circulation and exchange well in keeping with the dominant social space of late capitalism. Further, as Michael Ostwald notes, in both the mall and the virtual community, "the urban" has become a simulation of sorts that simultaneously replicates and resists the social function of the agora as a point of "cultural seepage" (132–35). The electronic agora merely provides a more technologically sophisticated version of the "private city," sanitizing the urban of its social encounters but leaving intact its function as a point of exchange and consumption (Ostwald 137). Rather than mapping a terrain of libratory potential, the emergence of this electronic "great city" just as easily points toward an experience of the urban as *hypermarket,* everywhere and nowhere at the same time (Jameson 44). In the electronic agora, the marketplace is no longer any public *place,* but an ever-present, privatized hyperpotential opening onto a commercial space of flows, articulated by a consumer practice of *browsing.*

Clearly there is a significant investment in this dominant articulation of cyberspace as marketplace. But that does not mean that some mode of "public sphere" might not in fact find expression in the forms, structures, and practices of online forums, Listservs, and electronic correspondences. We should be hesitant to assume that the foregrounded immateriality of the electronic post insures a "disinterested" *res publica,* removed from a sphere of "private" concerns. This sort of analysis assumes all too readily—MCI ads aside—that one can leave behind race, gender, sexuality, disability, etc., on "one side" of the screen. A more nuanced approach to cyberspace as public sphere would attempt to assess how a domain of exchange can exist that recognizes difference rather than eliding it in some construction of "consensus." For example, following on the critique of Michael Warner and others, James Knapp tries to identify "a public space that is made up of heterogeneous and contestatory subject-positions," but questions whether such a space exists online (182). Authority, Knapp notes, comes from the personal online; the challenge, then, is "to identify a public space in which the personal is legibly represented as political" (183). In this regard, Knapp finds some potential in a medium that "collapses the division between public and private" (187). By navigating between public and private, the "virtual public sphere" might suggest a space for community and debate. But topical arrangements of discussion groups, quite literally *topoi,* provide a spatial arrangement of people that threatens to produce spaces of control that amplify communication and contact between "like minds" while silencing aberrant voices and cutting off outlying lines of flight. While these email forums "[have] the potential to open up a space for diverse discourses, the effect of its location in a complex of specific categories is to compartmentalize differences, thereby dramatically limiting their public status" (Knapp 193). This structure would insure that "voiceless" minorities would have a space to speak, but these spaces risk self-closure and self-reference.[20] The "public," then, would only enact networks of exchange that were already authenticated. As such, critics fear, the blurring of public and private space in the virtual agora might produce only a monadic public sphere that would transform the public into "self" writ large.

What, then, would be the potential for networked social space as an articulation of a public, communal, or group enterprise? To the extent that electronic forums and Listservs articulate spaces of control, "the network" maintains a boundary in which my comments are addressed to a "public" defined by self-same principles. Rather than providing spaces of coalition and debate, structures of sociality delimited by normative constraints of "being on topic" could radically reduce the vibrancy of a "public."[21] As such, Dan Thu Nguyen and Jon Alexander note:

> In the old nation-state people met face to face and compromised on the basis of shared everyday lives. In cyberspace each precinct is virtual, and people only "meet" in it to talk about one specific thing. The old mass media were unifying media. They assembled and sustained nations with real-time theater. In cyberspace, there is no central stage; however immense, cyberspacetime is intensely decentralizing. (108)

Whereas Knapp calls attention to the striating hierarchical organizations of the Internet, Nguyen and Alexander critique the fluidity of the medium. Neither critique, however, takes into account the degree to which *the network itself* suggests a social space that, while engaging the private and the public, the personal and the political, cannot reduce to the point-to-point network of modernity. Whereas the letter, the novel, and the newspaper *negotiate* a course between the public and the private, electronic discourse *enacts* a social space that is indeed virtual: a potential for a range of dynamic relations. One's exchanges are neither private nor public; rather, they are potentially both, virtually both. Email enacts a network in which a single post can serve as publication, private envoy, or both. And upon receipt, the addressee can become another point of relay. The viruses that attach themselves to emails (and what more personal correspondence is there than the ILOVEYOU bug) spread in much the same fashion. While hierarchies of USENET groups and chat rooms attempt to organize clusters into self-fulfilling organs of discourse, the network itself allows for emergent structures in which dissipation, not organization, dominates. Structures arise that bring voices, needs, and desires into dynamic relation. Rather than producing a space of regulated traffic, these linkages produce a space that enacts ephemeral formations and conjunctions of situated users, mapping a unique potential for fortuitous, singular *encounters*.

Consider, for example, the Web site Meetup.com, which attracted a great deal of media attention in 2003 as a result of Democratic presidential candidate Howard Dean's embrace of the technology as a "rallying point" for grassroots support. In the spirit of the ad hoc construction of Indymedia.org during the Seattle IMF protests, Meetup.com provides a means for local individuals to connect within their local environment via global networks. Email provides an important link to the site, in that one registers to use the site via email and one receives notifications of "meetups" through email as well. While locality and face-to-face encounter provides a structuring raison d'etre for the site, by definition those brought into contact are, in effect, already interpellated into a networked social space that gives access to these global networks. As the "About" page on Meetup.com explains, the inspiration for the Web site was part Ray Oldenburg's *The Great Good Place* and part Steven Johnson's *Emergence*, a public space created through emergent structures of individuals responding to their own interests and ideas.[22] Unlike a classic Habermasian notion of a disinterested public sphere, however, Meetup.com structures interest headings that individuals can join (users can create their own topics as well, though the Web site must approve them). While these clusters are based on affinities to topics, the potential for fortuitous encounters exists to the extent that they enact a mode of the "public" articulated by viral processes of replication and dispersal rather than monadic processes of controlled relays and closed feedback. While existing on the Web, a site like Meetup.com in effect functions as a Listserv "majordomo" by disseminating email notifications to an indefinite network of addresses. Be it flash mobs (the Internet fad of summer 2003) or Rheingold's smart mobs, the networks of dispersal, situated in a process that articulates the public and private as emergent, enactive spaces of everyday life, give rise to social spaces that present a challenge to the dominant spaces of control that define networks of modernity, understood here as autonomous, private subjects engaged in a disinterested public sphere of politics. While a user enacts a network of connections via his situated relation to a space of flows (signing onto a list, functioning as a node of both dispatch and delivery), that user does not command the emergent networks produced by these collective processes.[23] The material form of the postal exchange as a point-to-point delivery matters far less here than the network's potential for massively interconnected, distributed communication. The conceptual structure of email likewise involves the articulation of these networks of exchange as an event, be that in the frozen "immediate" exchanges of a chain of correspondences or in the proliferation of contacts that lead to emergent clustering of individuals, through social linkages that are more viral than coordinated.

I would be remiss in discussing the parallel between CMC and the eighteenth-century coffeehouse were I not to mention the coincidental hybrid that emerged in its first boom in the mid-1990s: the cybercafé. Cybercafés take part in a range of representations that either explicitly or implicitly invoke a complex rhetoric of the public sphere. While much of the hype has since died down, these venues often appeared in the press as points of democratic access and social exchange. They were "revolutionary" information hubs, in the words of *Village Voice* reporter Mark Boal (29), and what Brian Connery describes as a late-twentieth-century recreation of the Enlightenment public sphere. Although his primary interest is in the *metaphor* of the coffeehouse, not its social reality, Connery begins his discussion by exploring how access to the Internet in a place like the (now-defunct) Horseshoe Coffee Shop allows today's users to "emulate young men of meager means . . . who used coffeehouses" to gain access to discursive communities (161). I would argue, however, that the lived practices associated with cybercafé use take part in the production of a social space that establishes a very different set of relations between "private" user and "public" network. As a dominant cluster of practices, patrons (in the United States, at least) are more likely to maintain an operational relation to CMC in cybercafés, using the computers to access email or browse Web pages in a space that is neither a private home nor a public workplace but rather a public venue that enacts personal network structures. While one might encounter "group browsing" at a café, more typical usage would probably involve brief forays onto the Internet, and then a return to a face-to-face social group. The structure of community enacted by cybercafés has very little to do with public reading, and much more to do with articulating one's position within a networked social space through a habitus that declares membership in a wired middle class.

If we were to begin to consider what sort of "imagined communities" these electronic coffeehouses suggest, it would not be the ubiquitous newspaper that maps a lived space of social reading but rather the familiarity of the computer itself as a point of access to a network of information and potential contact. Social reading is replaced by social browsing, as the computer now signifies not the coming together of a diverse populace in a public sphere but the potential for individuals gathered in a public place to connect *elsewhere*. This would explain why for Americans, both in the United States and abroad, cybercafés most commonly serve as spots to check and send email. Several newspaper articles in the late 1990s mention cafés in the context of their importance to business travelers and vacationers. For example, Dan Koeppel's 1998 *New York Times* article, "Jungle Outpost Offers Beer, Mayan Ruins and the Net," reports on the success of Eva's Cafe—a bar in Belize with Internet access that served as an important hub for international students and researchers, as well as natives of Belize. While the individuals engaging the technology differ radically in daily practice and in situation within networked social space, for both groups the cybercafé connects a remote location to a global urbanism. Likewise, in my informal telephone conversations with cybercafé owners and employees around the United States during 1999, the phrase "we get a lot of foreigners" occurred several times before I realized the significance of the statement. These cybercafés are places *in flux*. The café does not function as a point of exchange, as one would expect in the market/agora model of the public sphere, but rather as an opening onto the virtual as a network of potential contacts and encounters. Rather than serving as a kind of gathering point, the café takes part in a space that is already a globally dispersed "space of flows."

As a space of everyday life, cybercafés interpellate a wired middle class— not the digerati of a global elite but, rather, a subject-position articulated by access to and control over a global networked urbanism. Few of the cybercafés I contacted reported a significant homeless clientele. The "disenfranchised" who make use of cybercafés are merely *away from* their own computers. We might, then, tentatively suggest that rather than serving as places of gathering, cybercafés function as "spaces of elsewhere" in which the potential for displacement becomes a mode of membership in a wired middle class. What we share is our nomadism. But note also that these cafés mark scenes of interpenetrating social spaces. At Eva's Cafe in Belize, we see two very different social spaces—one tending toward a virtual middle class at home in a space of flows, and the other toward a truly disenfranchised class, communicating with relatives who, as a body of labor, have been carried to North America in the flows of transnational capitalism.[24] In my (previously mentioned) 1999 phone conversations, I found remote, developed locations such as the Whidbey Island Cybercafé likewise map a space of comings and goings for tourists, but also a place of networking for the local community. This coastal island just north of Seattle sees a lot of tourists during the summer, a number of whom stop by to check their email. But for residents, Whidbey Island Cybercafé owner Rick Ingrasci told me, his bookstore, his computers, and his community meeting room all serve to distribute information within the lived space of Whidbey Island. From Ingrasci's point of view, the computers are "an extension of our ability to network as a community."

In this regard, cybercafés provide an important site for exploring the dynamics of spaces in conflict within a network society. Dockwra's "invention" gave Europe its first distributed network; it put in place a material, conceptual, and lived space in which points of dispatch and delivery stood at the ready—a dedicated network, so to speak. Email promises the same network, but at the same time its dispersive nature and its function as a space of flows, both intimate and public, suggest an arrangement of space that is enactive and emergent, not static. In contrast to a virtual agora, we find signs of interpenetrating spaces of flows, in which either privatized displacement (cybercafés) or ephemeral, enactive formations of "the public" (MoveOn.org, Meetup.com) serve as alternate articulations of social space.

Addresses and the Purloined e-Letter

Through email, the interpellation of address creates an electronic profiling, such that I am constructed in a particular relation not only as a subject-position (recipient of an email) but within a node of network exchange that is both public and private. To take an idiosyncratic sampling from my own email account: I recently received an invitation to the 2004 International Dance Competition in Barcelona. I occasionally get email from www.dancegrandprix.com, but why, I do not know. I have no affiliation with dance programs at my college, nor have I ever participated in any dance competition. It could be that it is simply the result of a mass emailing, but given the specificity of the intended address and the presumed cost of attending an overseas event, it would seem like quite a wide net to cast. It is unlikely that this email was the result of a mass harvesting of addresses. How, then, does this email construct a viral node?

The impact of an email such as this is not merely in its arrival but in its passing on. Circulation itself—or, more accurately, proliferation—provides a conceptual structuring for both material form and lived practice of network exchange. Another email in my box at this particular moment is a call for papers on reality television. Although I may not respond to the call, I will probably forward it along to another list, or perhaps to select individuals. As such, the *proprietary* nature of the letter is always up for grabs. One's address, then, becomes a matter of private and public concern to the extent that it is both a point of destination and a point of dispatch. More so, however, in this reciprocal dispersal, there is a potential for aberrant lines of communication and points of contact. What arrives, although addressed to me, hails me in ways that, rather than matching a profile, introduces "error" into systems of performativity and spaces of control. Each such communiqué in effect situates me within an altered, enactive network in that, as with autopoietic networks, I am opened to a new virtual arrangement of potential responses. As a part of a material process enacting conditions of possibility, each aberrant letter holds the potential for relay as an indiscipline that could articulate a new subject-position within a space of flows. As a production of space, then, one finds that practices of email exchange articulate a space in which *the network itself* enacts a social space (it is, as Castells notes, a fundamental unit of the social) rather than serving merely as a conduit between private citizens or a medium connecting private spaces to a public sphere.

The spatial practices of email map an event in which the virtuality of proliferation is actualized in each dispatch and delivery (each recipient serving as a relay). Rather than *negotiating* public and private space, the electronic letter articulates a dispersal that, in its viral nature, constantly transforms the singularity of (private) address into a multiplicity of (public) dissemination. The structure of Listservs, viruses, and spam suggests that, unlike the stable subject-position assumed within modern postal relays, "address" in a network environment functions as both an articulation of a subject-position within a particular contingent arrangement and as an enaction of a potential network of exchanges. In spatial terms, then, we find that the lived practice of email defines one's relation to the network as an actualization of potential linkages: a closing off of a network of dispersal, or an enacting of reciprocal and dispersive linkages. All email holds a viral potential, and it is precisely this destabilization of autonomous agency that makes spam and email viruses a threat to the dominant social space articulated by the economy of the post.

As a case in point, the 2003 U.S. House of Representative's Reduction in Distribution (RID) of Spam bill reproduced as a representation of space much of what I have previously described as a dominant social space in a network society. In his testimony before the Subcommittee on Crime, Terrorism, and Homeland Security, Joseph Rubin describes the Internet, in effect, as a hyper-potential market: "No longer is a customer bound by geographic location to a business, but in a nano-second can travel anywhere in the world to purchase products and services that they want with just a click of the mouse." As such, spam is positioned as a "threat" to this articulation of networked social space, in part by disrupting the integrity of address assumed by a point-to-point system of dispatch and delivery: "Increasingly, consumers are getting inundated with pornographic or false and misleading email that diminishes their faith in e-commerce, undermining many of the benefits that consumers derive from e-commerce." The RID Spam bill, Rubin argued, attempts to preserve e-commerce by targeting the "bad actors"—defined by a company's willingness to misrepresent the content of a message or to "harvest" addresses by illegitimate means: "those who attempt to use fraud and deception to get consumers to open their emails or avoid Internet Service Provider (ISP) filters and obtain customer 'leads' by, in effect, stealing addresses from other online service providers." While "legitimate means" of email acquisition is never defined (nor what separates the threat of spam from market-invigorating junk mail), Rubin's testimony continues by defining the grounds for criminal prosecution under the proposed act as "when a spammer uses false header and routing information or the harvesting of email addresses." His testimony continues:

> These activities, which no legitimate company would use, harm the whole e-commerce system and undermine the faith and trust in e-commerce, taking advantage of the most vulnerable among us. Further, because these are intentional, fraudulent acts perpetrated on unsuspecting consumers, criminal penalties certainly may be appropriate.[25]

The rhetoric of vulnerability ("vulnerability" here perhaps referring to the elderly rather than to children) suggests that in the collapsing of markets to a global, hyperpotential point—one's personal computer in a private residence—e-commerce now allows for the potential of deception by opening up unintended networks of correspondence. Once again, the public and the private interpenetrate one another, with *proper address* defining the line between legitimacy and transgression.

The network space of spam, then, is explicitly a space of dispersal. All email holds the viral potential of spam, but to enact such dispersal is seen as a violation of agency. In addition to "mass mailing" spam, email users encounter, on a daily basis, "personal" spam—the forwarded jokes, petitions, and professional opportunities from well-intentioned friends and acquaintances. These proliferating correspondences provide a category that in practice is identical to spam, but one that maintains a sense of private agency, sender to addressee. While one is flagged as a systemic threat, the other is cast as a mere annoyance of the medium. Both, I would argue, provide mappings of altered spaces of the post. The RID Spam bill defines illegitimate harvesting as "us[ing] an automated means to obtain electronic mail addresses from an Internet website or proprietary online service operated by another person, without the authorization of that person" (United States, H.R. 2214). It is the cybernetic principles of information mining that, when turned against the presumed integrity of dispatch and private address, define the practice as illegitimate. But note that with the personal forwarding of email, the same restructuring of dispatch and delivery occurs. And, typically, these forwarded emails, copied with headers included, give a long list of addressees, each intended by a recipient but not necessarily at the point of dispatch. What *is* intended at dispatch is a viral dissemination: that the lived practice of email articulates a space that reaches far beyond one's private communications and into a form of public arena, or, rather, into an arena of multiple, indeterminate singular addresses. This blurring of the public and the private serves as an ontological foundation for an emergent social space in a network society.

Like the eighteenth-century writing closet, the subject's "scene of writing" at the personal computer is experienced as a personal space, but one defined less by locks and interiority, or even claims of the proper, and more by an operational disposition hailed by protocols that grant access to one's personal address. Any machine, in other words, holds the potential to generate a private space, be it in a café in Belize, in a homeless shelter, or in a college computer classroom. With email and its permeable public/private, the parallel between computer and writing closet can only carry so far. Unlike the closet, the place of the private does *not* occur within a physically compartmentalized space. The private itself has become unmoored from its binary relation with an "exterior" public; it has become an *irruptive* relation. Likewise, the public is no longer *exterior* to this scene of writing but is contained as a potential within it. All correspondences—even those intended as strictly private—become a kind of *virtual* publication. Perhaps, to clarify this shift in social space, it would be worth drawing an analogy from a similar shift that has occurred in telephony. Like an address, a phone number provides a public link to a private space. With the advent of mobile phones, however, a number connects to a *person* rather than to a place. The cell phone gives us a mode of the private that has been unmoored from its binary relation to the public, with the potential to occur "anywhere." Now private conversations can occur in the midst of the public, irrupting within the public rather than being sanctioned off.[26] The public permeates and penetrates the private at every turn. With email, this "portable" address likewise reveals how any public place—an office, a classroom, a conference center—can unfold/enfold a private place. The "private," as produced and lived, appears as a space that emerges and disappears as an actuality, but one that also remains virtually open at all times: a *potential* for an irruptive private. This same relation exists in the opposite direction, as the potential for an irruptive public.

If we think of "address" as a noun, we are describing the forms, structures, and practices of a postal space of places, which requires a distance between addresser and addressee. We are also operating within an understanding of space as a container for things. Thus, the spatial practices of the Penny Post take part in the material and the conceptual articulation of address as site of delivery—houses with street numbers, for example. With email, however, "address" functions more as a verb than as a noun, and, as such, its spatiality suggests an event or a relation rather than an arrangement of objects. Someone's address is also a *naming:* a topographic performative. William Mitchell comments at length on how the collapse of name and address makes email "antispatial," since it negates the need for stable communication (8–10). Mitchell sees this displacement as allowing for a social remapping from geographical cities to the "recombinant architecture" of electronic cities. But something more fundamental is at stake here. Address is only antispatial if we are to limit our understanding of space to a Newtonian abstract space. I would argue instead that the restructuring of address is both a product of and a process involved in a restructuring of spatial relations of everyday life in a network society. More to the point, the unmooring of the private from a spatiality of containment marks a site of contestation in the dominant social space.

One might read this "floating address," as Poster suggests, as a kind of distribution of the subject-position. The user is interpellated into network relations in such a way that "identity" emerges through the situated enaction of a space of flows (an actualization of proliferating virtual exchanges), not through stable connections to claims of presence and place. At the same time, the articulation of address in relational space could intensify the experience of the personal as a space of the cogito, distinct and separate from the external world of things. Mitchell, for example, discusses how multiple addresses and multiple identities can challenge notions of subjectivity, but ultimately these multiples serve as "aliases": parts of a "*disembodied* electronic identity" (11, italics added). The result would be an articulation of the network as a mentalist, cybernetic space of control, the terminal-as-monad identified by Michael Heim, David Harvey, and others as an underlying metaphysical construction for much of the discourse and practice associated with cyberspace. Rather than disrupting a dominant social space, such a construction of address, identity, and subject could result in what Harvey sees as a politically dangerous monadology: "the Utopian vision of being able to live the 'Leibnizian conceit' free of material constraints. . . . We can each voyage forth to the frontiers of cyberspace as mini-deities" (*Justice, Nature, and the Geography of Difference* 279–80).

We have, then, in the same phenomenon of the "floating address," two accounts of the social space of the post. On one hand, the network of immediate transparent communication, governed by principles of efficiency and control, maps a highly organized, striated topography. At the same time, the immateriality of the letter, and the porous figurations of public and private space, suggest a network structure that no longer behaves in a coordinated manner. While the postal map may ask us to figure address and destination as stable entities, the mode of action in which public and private interpenetrate and enfold one another does not allow for this sort of representation of a binary space of inside/outside. What's more, all spaces tend toward an irruptive presence, rather than functioning as stable components or compartments. As such, email in part enunciates a representation of space of partial dimensions, emergences, and enfoldings.[27] This perspective of space presents an alternative to the "illusion of transparency" that Baudrillard sees rampant in simulatory culture, and that for our purposes is best represented by the postal network of point-to-point correspondences. Lefebvre points to this illusion of transparency as being an inherent part of a mentalist conception of space that has dominated Western culture since the Enlightenment:

The illusion of transparency goes hand in hand with a view of space as innocent, as free of traps or secret places. Anything hidden or dissimulated—and hence danger-ous—is antagonistic to transparency, under whose reign everything can be taken in by a single glance from that mental eye which illuminates whatever it contemplates. (*The Production of Space* 28)

A representation of space that involves these sorts of "enfoldings" challenges the illusion of transparency. Hakim Bey, one of the earliest theorists to call at-tention to the "fractal" nature of online interactions, notes how an apparently cohesive space can have other spaces "enfolded" within it, like "Mandelbrot peninsulas" (112–13). For Bey, this representation of space holds radical and revolutionary potentials. Calling upon the same representation of space, email perhaps presents a more banal version of the same representational space: the lived enfolding of the private within the public as an everyday occurrence.

This enfolding of the public and the private in social space implies not only a change in the representational space of letter writing—the lived space of electronic correspondence, mobile addresses, and irruptive contacts—it also suggests a shift in mental representations of space. To return to our earlier dis-cussion of the metaphysics of the post and the *carte postale* of writing, the fun-damental issue in this representation of space is the notion of "detour" within point-to-point contact. For Jacques Lacan, the moral of Poe's story "The Pur-loined Letter" is that "a letter always arrives at its destination" (52–53). Lacan focuses on how the "purloined" letter is "put far off" or deferred: a "letter in suffrance" in the postal sense (43). This aspect emphasizes the "singularity of the letter" for Lacan: "since it can be diverted, it must have a course which is proper to it" (43). At the same time, this deferral and dis-placement can func-tion as a kind of no-placement: a "nullibility" of the letter that allows absence to declare presence (Lacan 38–39). In his reading of both Lacan and Poe, Der-rida expresses quite the contrary sentiment: "a letter can always—and there-fore must—never arrive at its destination" (*The Post Card* 121). The absent presence of the letter is a *desire* of the post and not an *essence* of writing. The *carte postale*, then, is a map of this metaphysical desire. In Lacan's reading, the path of the letter, its "diversion," operates as a kind of machine, "requiring it to leave its place, even though it returns to it by a circular path" (43). Lacan's cir-culation is circuitous but determined: the letter always arrives. For Derrida, it is the indeterminations of writing that lead you on, and hence lead you astray (*Dissemination* 70–71). The letter, Derrida seems to suggest, cannot be "pur-loined," because it is always already seduced. The "postal effect," then, is not one of assurance (the letter always arrives) but one of risk: the letter never arrives at its unique address. The erasure of this risk is at the heart of logocentrism, and the attempt to reveal these traces is at the heart of Derrida's deconstructive method.

This difference in understanding "the course of the letter" is essential to understanding the representations of space concurrent with electronic writing and email. Particularly in exploring these sites of contestation in the spaces of CMC, we need to consider the degree to which electronic mail sustains the postal arrangement of absence-made presence, along with the social spaces articulated by this representation of space and how email reveals other material, conceptual, and lived relations and other productions of space. To the extent that it simulates the *carte postale,* email presents a border-crossing of sorts, by way of its claim to an "authentic," immediate, and transparent written word. But the *potentials* within this mapping suggest other spaces as well—spaces in which the letter is neither purloined nor seduced because its "path" is no longer point-to-point. The space presented by email, then, is not so much a gone/there space of *fort:da,* but rather a space in which the *actuality* of presence and absence describes merely one plane within an orthogonal dimension of virtualities. Email, in other words, performs a space of potentials rather than a space of presence. Letter writing is often depicted as an act of establishing contact with another. Electronically, though, email establishes potentials in a way that denies connective spaces entirely. The interpellation of address establishes a user within a network of virtual openings, such that the connections one enacts in the actual (by way of reading, posting, deleting, and relaying) not only produce a networked subject-position but at the same time articulate a situated space of flows in a global network. Such a spatiality of potentials holds implications not only for the restructuring of "private correspondence" as lived practice but also for a restructuring of "public discourse." Electronic mail does not guarantee reciprocal "correspondence," but, at the same time, each "envoi" is indeed an envoy, a message/messenger at the ready. As such, electronic mail establishes a different sort of representation of space, one based on possibility and potential rather than on claims of presence. In place of the Lacanian singularity of the letter, or a Derridean desire for the "unique address," email as lived practice maps a social space of situatedness, an articulation of flows within a global network that both distributes a private subject and makes a global public a personal space.

Virtual Posts/Enactive Networks

At one point in "Envois," Derrida turns to the dispatch of M. Boiurgeu, inspector for the French post office, to discuss the possibility of an "omnipresent" post that would make this one-to-one contact ubiquitous and transparent by way of electronic communication. For Derrida, this ubiquity is a "terror," but it also holds a revolutionary potential:

> "The traditional process thereby will find itself upset for a major portion of the mail." Yes and no: for as long as it is not proven that into each of our so secret, so hermetically sealed letters several senders, that is several addresses have not already infiltered themselves, the upset will not have been demonstrated. If our letters are upsetting, in return, perhaps it is that already we are several on the line, a crowd, right here, at least a consortium of senders and addressees. (*The Post Card* 105)

With the arrival of electronic mail—and its always potential dispatch to multiple senders, multiple addresses—the postal economy is indeed upset, and, with it, the spatial economy of point-to-point contact and private (inter)personal discourse as figured in Enlightenment thought.

Electronic writing's ability to allow the public to permeate the private (and vice versa) suggests the arrival of an alternate social space in which a binary relation between the two no longer makes sense. This competing virtual topography reveals that the conceptual space of a postal *fort:da* is a matter of social production, not an "essence" of writing played out in the materiality of envelopes, post offices, and delivery routes and in the lived spatial experience of letter writing, addressing, and posting. With the emergence of electronic discourse, the point-to-point can and still does exist, but only to the extent that it can perpetuate a simulation of this postal representation of space. Any analysis of the spaces of everyday life enacted by CMC will need to consider the degree to which electronic mail sustains the postal arrangement of absence made presence, along with the social spaces entailed by this representation of space. It will also need to account for the disruption of this postal map and the production of a social space that is distributive and irruptive rather than connective and partitioned. Instead of speaking of the multilinear (a favorite metaphor for hypertext theorists), perhaps it would be better to conceive of email as multi*valent* in its virtual topography, in that various situated, interpellated addresses form a cluster of network connections held together by a shared potential. As such, the "public sphere" defines a social formation no longer articulated as a *res publica*, but rather as the network itself, a virtuality of aberrant, unplanned inchoate contact, enacted and actualized in ephemeral, coalitional events of articulation. The representation of space as potential and multivalent rather than point-to-point suggests the possibility of a social space that allows the public to irrupt from within the private, and vice versa, where potentials remain humming and open and where contact is precarious and vital. But "the post" has hardly disappeared, and the lived practices of email maintain a representation of space of point-to-point contact; as such, email could also reify the social relations implicated in cybernetic spaces of control.

In his essay "Cyberdemocracy," Mark Poster argues that the "electronic geography" of CMC "pose[s] the question of new kinds of relations of power between participants" (176–77). Here, we come face to face with the concern of Ostwald and many others who have examined the social formations of networked communication: whether or not real social and political power can occur within these networked social spaces, or whether we experience the mere simulation of such things (Ostwald 142). While the concerns of Nguyen and Alexander, Knapp, and others are significant, at the same time the sorts of arrangements—and derangements—of social spaces instantiated by this multivalent, emergent network suggest the potential for a significant shift in social space, a restructuring of the global and the local, the public and the private. The structure of a network that is dynamic and enactive, rather than a map of point-to-point contact, suggests a potential social arrangement that could indeed map mediations that do not reduce to a hypermarket of point-to-point circulation and exchange. Such an alternate network structure would highlight the dynamic, emergent quality of virtual structures enacted by situated addresses caught up in this space of flows.

This alternate topography of email suggests a network that is dynamic and emergent—not simply the distributed, stable network of the post. As such, it maps a virtual topography that does not reduce to point-to-point contact, a space that is *coalescent* rather than monadic but at the same time enacted by one's own situated appearance within the network of exchange as a point of relay. If Dockwra's "invention" marked a significant moment in the production of modern urban space, it did so by articulating in form, concept, and practice the processes that were already emerging as dominant within a rising (network) culture of exchange. Email clearly takes part in that same history of the post, and, hence, history of the network. At the same time, the challenges posed by this same system to form, concept, and practice of the modern network as lived space—most notably the stable point-to-point network of private selves engaged in public exchange—suggest that email, along with Web browsing, articulates processes in an emergent network culture of altered public/private, global/local relations.

The reading I have presented of email and the WWW in the last two chapters has attempted to suggest how lived practices of CMC map fault lines in the production of space in contemporary network society. The material, conceptual, and experiential processes caught up in the production of networked social space suggest both a reification of the networks of modernity and a challenge to this dominant social structure. More specifically, the sorts of ontological categories of social space—the global and the local, the public and the private—find themselves in altered relations via CMC. What we have not addressed in detail is the ways in which one's access to these network structures positions a user within broader fields of social power. To consider how these structurings of a wired middle class provide access to social and cultural capital, I would like to turn in the final chapter to an analysis of institutional and individual practices of computer use within higher education. In the recent controversy over music file-sharing, colleges and universities have found themselves in the thick of challenges to free speech, fair use, and copyright law raised by CMC. At the same time, these same institutions of higher learning are defining their missions in relation to network technologies and are looking more and more toward CMC as a means of enhancing and extending pedagogical reach. In the final chapter, I will explore how these processes are involved in the production of interpenetrating social spaces, and, as such, how they map spaces in conflict within the spaces of everyday life in a network society. I will also examine how the body, so often abandoned in discussions of cyberspace, provides a map of discursive practices that situate users within a wired middle class.

STUDENT BODIES

IN CHAPTERS 2 AND 3, I attempted to explore how the production of on-line space provides a challenge to large, ontological categories of spatiality; namely, the global and the local, and the public and the private. In this chapter, my focus shifts to a specific instance of institutional space—the classroom—as a means of understanding how these spatial forms and structures articulate themselves in lived dispositional practices. On one hand, I am interested in the production of space as it relates to distance education. As the name implies, and as its history suggests, distance education takes the form of a "correspondence" between a teacher or an institution and a student. As such, distance education depends upon a medium to connect a remote location to a source of knowledge. Whereas institutions engaged in earlier articulations of distance education or "home learning" took for granted that one's distance from the university was an unavoidable and unfortunate condition of the student's geographic (or social) situation, online education today is marketed as a matter of convenience: a mode of study better suited to contemporary student life. The virtual university now serves as a representational space of mobile privatization, in which the classroom—*my* classroom—travels with me wherever I go.

In exploring the networked spaces of higher education, I am also interested in the position of computers in the "brick-and-mortar" university and the way in which the network has restructured the classroom as a space of flows. To some extent, *every* classroom has now become a virtual classroom. Over the last ten years, institutions at all levels have made significant expenditures to "wire" classrooms, libraries, labs, and dorm rooms. Faculty are encouraged to integrate technology into the curriculum, and students are assumed to arrive on campus possessing a familiarity with computer interfaces—along with a desire to enact that interface.[1] In providing a spatial analysis of the networked spaces of college-level instruction, within or beyond the walls of an institution, I will need to account for the lived practices of students that map these virtual topographies. If we can begin to understand how network technologies situate student bodies, we can start to understand how these technologies take part in the production of one facet of institutional social space. For it is ultimately the student and the student's body that provides the scene for the institutional event we call education.

Topographies of the Virtual Classroom

As an institutional form dating back over a century, distance education has traditionally called upon a representation of space involving a remote learner in private/solitary academic pursuit across social networks. Distance marked a student's dislocation from an institutional center—a satellite learner at the periphery, held in orbit by the pull of knowledge. Given this displacement, postal correspondence actualized a topography for the student that provided the material and conceptual conditions of possibility for citing that individual as "student."[2] This topography produces a spatial relation in which the student's dislocation from an institutional center also provides the performative context that affiliates that student with an institution, by way of postal networks. From its earliest history, correspondence courses have enacted this double articulation of affiliation and dislocation. For example, in the 1870s, Chautauqua University inaugurated a form of correspondence course, the Chautauqua Literary and Scientific Circle (CLSC), specifically to provide the late nineteenth-century cultural ideal of self-improvement through liberal education to individuals who were outside the geographic or cultural boundaries of the university

(Scott 396). During its peak years of popularity (1878–1894), the New York–based CLSC program served over 200,000 students, many of whom we would today call adult learners or nontraditional students, mostly living "in small towns of the rural Midwest" (Scott 396). While many of these students were involved in local reading circles and "independent Chautauquas" that sprang up around the country during the late nineteenth century, the correspondence program maintained a spatial relation of mediated satellite and central hub, producing a decentralized learning network that paralleled the decentralized postal and telegraph networks at the time.[3] Certainly, geographic distance was not the only measure of remoteness from institutional centrality in the nineteenth century. A year prior to Chautauqua, in 1873, Anna Eliot Ticknor instituted the Society to Encourage Studies at Home specifically to provide women (still largely excluded from institutes of higher learning) access to a formalized program of reading, tutorship, and learned exchange via the post (Bergmann 447). While the New England women who took part in this society were very much within a structure of race and class that gave them significant access to social capital, gender still positioned them beyond the margins of most colleges and universities. Although a catalyst of sorts for the growing pressure to accept women at universities,[4] Ticknor's society delineated its own peripheral relation to the institutional space of the university, maintaining, as it did, a private sphere of the home, distinct from social institutions yet negotiated by way of public social networks. In the words of one *New York Times* reporter of the time, the society "enlarges a girl's horizon without changing her sphere" (quoted in Bergmann 448). As with the CLSC for rural adult learners, correspondence learning through Ticknor's society provided the material, conceptual, and experiential context for the performative articulation of "student" for these women, defined in a satellite relation to institutes of higher learning. In effect, the lived practice of correspondence *instituted a student body* to the extent that the student subject-position found its performative context in mediated access to the social field of power mapped by "higher education." As one student in the society wrote to Ticknor:

> I do not know how else I should have ever *come into contact* with women of such character, nor have had the opportunity to receive such benefits from their hands as I have. I do not know where I should stop, if I tried to tell how much they have helped me in my isolated life. I craved so much, and there seemed *no access possible* to anything I wanted. (quoted in Bergmann 465, italics added)

Other similarly marginalized groups constructed, by way of networks of correspondence, a means of instituting subject-positions in relation to the academy—and, in some instances, using these networks to institutionalize academic subjects that were otherwise marginalized or unrecognized. In 1927, for example, the twelve-year-old Association for the Study of Negro Life and History established a Home Study Department specifically to address the lack of recognition for an emerging field of study and the individuals engaged in its development. As the announcement for the program explains: "To meet this urgent need, [founding President Carter Godwin] Woodson directed the Home Study department *to bring the school to the student*" (quoted in Janette Harris 114, italics added). In each of the preceding examples, correspondence via the postal network provides the performative context for a double articulation, marking both the student's dislocation from social and cultural centers of higher learning, and the processes that bring the periphery into a social and cultural relation.

As such, online education today replicates these late-nineteenth- and early-twentieth-century social structures, but it does so in a manner that intensifies the process of "transmission" as a spatial practice. "Access" still plays an important role in the representation of learning space for online education, promising to provide a range of services to individuals who would not otherwise have entrée to courses, thereby making remote locations less remote and the marginalized student less peripheral. By drawing parallels to the push to bring electricity and telephone lines to rural America during the first half of the twentieth century, the rhetoric surrounding the Clinton-Gore NII education initiatives were very much in keeping with this vision of network technology overcoming geography: bringing into the digital fold, so to speak, those locations that had little or no access to "advanced" classroom facilities. In the words of the 2000 report of the congressional Web-based Education Commission, "the Internet enables education to occur in places where there is none, extends resources where there are few, expands the learning day, and opens the learning place." But unlike earlier productions of social space mapped by postal correspondence, online classes conflate access and control; transmission, in other words, is figured as a performative event *in the hands of the student,* thereby repositioning the student in relation to institutional networks. To this extent, the distance-education student is anything but marginal; as both the operator that enacts the class and the target that receives course content, the student occupies a metaphorical and experiential center for the performance of the course. For advocates of online learning, the topographies of control enacted by way of online instruction serve as explicit benefits in creating "student-centered learning."[5] This representation of space is reflected in the wording of the Web-based Education Commission's three primary educational promises of the Internet:

> To center learning around the student instead of the classroom
> To focus on the strengths and needs of individual learners
> To make lifelong learning a practical reality.

The rhetoric of access and control converge in the production of a networked social space that "center[s] learning around the student instead of the classroom," or, rather, that disarticulates the classroom as a space of learning, locating it in the mobile, privatized, and irruptive spaces of control articulated in the lived practice of the "student body."

What's more, the *lack* of access to digital resources begins to appear as a significant impediment to social, cultural, and economic access. Beyond federal initiatives such as the NII or the Web-based Education Commission, grassroots providers such as Frank Odasz's Big Sky Telegraph attempted to establish community networks and to offer full Internet access for the unwired frontier, "allowing rural educators, students, and citizens opportunities for their first global collaborations" (Odasz).[6] Major state and private educational initiatives, such as Georgia Library Learning Online (GALILEO),[7] were developed to provide public libraries and public schools access to thousands of newspaper, magazine, and journal articles via full-text databases. Meanwhile, the Apple Education Grants program and the Bill and Melinda Gates Foundation were early, major charitable contributors to schools and libraries, insuring broad access to the material form of the network as a means of educating for the future.[8] In this regard, access to network structures is cast as a necessity in a society that has itself become restructured by networked spaces of flows.[9] In material form and conceptual structure, then, "access" functions as a dominant conceptual structure that shapes the lived practice of students engaged in educational computer use. In turn, as actualized practice, "access" produces a space that situates the student in an operational relation to learning—a "classroom" enacted by a student's clicks and keystrokes. As a topography of control, the virtual classroom enacts spaces of access for students, who are in turn instituted as students through their interactions with these networks. Any restructuring of the classroom by way of networked spaces of everyday life must, therefore, involve *a restructuring of the student as well.*

With the production of spaces of control via online education, student practices undergo a shift that increasingly emphasizes the ability *to make the network perform.* While earlier versions of distance education portrayed correspondence courses as a remedy for students who were disadvantaged by their spatial or social displacement from the university, online education from the 1990s onward has been described in the media and in college marketing campaigns as an improvement on the traditional classroom for a new version of "nontraditional student." For example, in a newspaper questionnaire typical of many self-tests for distance-learning readiness, readers are asked:

Feeling I am a part of a class is . . .
  (a) Not particularly necessary to me
  (b) Somewhat important to me
  (c) Very important to me (Meyers P1)

Of course, the "correct" answer for the online learner is "a." According to the questionnaire, the ideal online student also finds classroom discussion "rarely helpful" and talks with her professor "for clarification only" (P1). She can "master information just by reading it" and can "figur[e] out the instructions" independently (P1). These criteria create a radically different image of what it means to be a student in a course. In this account of the online student's pursuit of information, the primary interaction occurs not so much between the student and the teacher, or even amongst fellow students, but rather between student and *content.* This representation of the online student defines learning as a process of transmission and acquisition, and, as such, *the context of the learner*—whether or not a student is "part of a class" or situated in front of a computer—is misrecognized as *a minor, technical matter of delivery.* Instruction, in effect, translates into an instructional set operated upon by the student, in which efficiency and accuracy of delivery become a primary pedagogical concern. For those students who can "master the information" independently, the physical classroom presents nothing more than an unnecessary, inconvenient hindrance to efficient delivery. What's more, the traditional classroom itself becomes something of a remedial space for those students who cannot retrieve information efficiently and effectively on their own.

As a representation of space, such a description of online education depends upon a conduit fallacy of communication to the degree that it ultimately treats the context or medium of communication as a source of interference for transmission. Misrecognized as a technical concern (delivery), the context of learning matters only to the degree that the channel is "noisy" or "clean." For this reason, institutional assessment of online courses ultimately reduces to a comparison of channels: do online courses fare any worse than traditional classrooms in conveying course content (what gets transmitted) and achieving student outcomes (what information is received)? In practice, no matter how "student-centered" the pedagogy, the student is instituted into the position of "receiver." While the student is an active participant in this transmission, an operational relation to education casts student participation in a very distinct form, restricted as it is to the set of operations that will allow information to flow. The "course," no longer associated with a student's *path* or *way*, now describes the flow of quantifiable, measurable content from source to receiver via a *channel*. While this commodification of education—by no means limited to the virtual classroom—increasingly turns learning into an acquisition of *things* (units of instruction), ironically this same process misrecognizes learning as a mode of information retrieval, divorced from materiality and spatiality alike. Learning, then, becomes at its simplest a process of query and retrieval, and, in a more complex form, a kind of operational "application." This topography does not depend upon the student "feeling a part of a class." Rather, it necessitates a spatial practice in which the computer functions as a primary point of interaction between the body of the student and a networked body of information.

The Corporeality of Online Education

The altered social spaces of online education are very much mapped by an altered articulation of student practice. The successful student is the independent, diligent worker who requires only clarity and an instructional set in order to achieve mastery of information: a motivated, disciplined, persistent self-starter who assumes responsibility for her learning. While one might argue that the same list of adjectives equally describes the ideal student in the traditional classroom, there is a critical difference: since the student is instituted in a relation to learning through processes of transmission and delivery, whatever skills and practices insure efficient transmission and a reduction of noise serve as measures of student success. It is the difference between a practice of operation and a practice of participation. In the same newspaper survey mentioned above (Meyers), motivation and an ability to avoid procrastination top the list of desirable traits for success in an online classroom. These descriptors clearly place the student "in control" of the learning process, and, as such, present the computer interface as an improved channel for delivery to the extent that it can articulate spaces of control that supercede the traditional classroom. Positioned within these spaces of control, the student body is quite literally formalized into an operational disposition in the sense that only the student can actualize the context of learning by interacting with the computer along preconfigured, operational lines. To put it simply, in an online environment a student can never *miss* a class, although she may fail to make it *perform* by not correctly operating upon its instructional set. Discipline, active involvement, and responsibility are certainly important attributes in a traditional classroom setting, but in the online environment these traits describe performance criteria of a different order, since the "classroom" doesn't exist without the student's ability to *operate the course.*

Since transmission and exchange are foregrounded and privileged processes that produce social space, how one enacts these exchanges will structure how that social space is articulated. Although CMC is often described as a many-to-many mode of mass communication, as lived experience, reception is experienced as many-to-*one,* and transmission is experienced as *one-*to-many (or, often enough, as one-to-one). As discussed in chapter 3 in the context of email, course postings in an online class are always *addressed to me.* In the process of performing the online class, the student finds himself reading posts that each solicit a direct response. In a traditional classroom, structured around a practice of participation, each student cannot respond to the comments of every other student—such behavior would, in fact, violate and disrupt a number of dispositional cues for student participation. In contrast, the operational disposition and interface disposition elicited by online instruction encourages just this sort of relationship to a course, in which all content is targeted toward *me.* One is always prompted to respond to the course. This asymmetrical structure of exchange also restructures passive involvement in a class. The silent, "lurking" student has no presence within an ongoing exchange of students to the extent that transmission marks one's claim as a participant. Irregular posting, or posting after a long silence, occurs as an irruption of presence, and often is received as a disruption of an otherwise orderly exchange. For that lurking participant, however, his or her interface with the class marks a full-blown experience, one that is operationally directed toward *his or her* *own screen* and that is materially activated by *his or her own* reception of and response to the material. No matter how passive, the student can never assume a peripheral position in an online class, since the operational relation of the course always situates the student at its center. Such asymmetrical, monadic productions of space suggest that the classroom experience is radically transformed, and, along with it, the lived practices that produce and are produced by online instruction.

By casting the student in the role of operator, the need for access to an instructional set replaces the need for access to instructional *space.* Thus, online courses are described as the students' liberation from the physical constraints of the classroom. By separating content from context—in effect treating the classroom and the computer as mere channels for information—online education treats materiality as noise; or, rather, any material process that impedes the student-computer interface as a point of transmission becomes a measure of inefficient performance. For this reason, most online courses depend heavily upon Web pages, email, and bulletin boards for the structure of the class, with much less emphasis on chatting or other forms of synchronous communication that would require students to be at their keyboards at a specific time. In the sense that the actualization of an event of copresence ("the class") stands as an impediment to transmission, *the body itself* is treated as a form of *interference.* Freed from the "noisy" contingencies of bodies (one's own and others') in space, the online student can now take part in a course as a "clean" and efficient transmission of information.

But claiming freedom from materiality by no means eliminates the fact that student practice is still a corporeal experience, and one that is spatially situated. If we are to understand these dispositional practices as embodiments of material and conceptual spatial processes, then we will want to consider how an operational, point-and-click disposition is experienced as a zone of interaction within networked social space. When corporeality itself is articulated as a space of control, one's body becomes a kind of interface—a peripheral device that facilitates a network of flows. The use of "device" in this context should not imply an understanding of the body as a passive tool implemented by network structures but rather a figuring of embodiment itself as a schema defined by practices that actualize a field of operational relations within social space. It would be more accurate, following Judith Butler's lead, to think of bodies as processes of materialization articulated by social norms—in this instance, the normative concepts and practices of "the interface." Here we might well speak of the student body as "cyborg," precisely because it is articulated at a nexus of sorts; within the context of the online class, one's body matters/materializes only to the extent that it articulates this point-and-click disposition. While college marketing may suggest a body at rest enjoying the freedom of online instruction, as a set of dispositional practices, corporeality always materializes at a point-and-click interface. The materiality of pedagogical relations reduces to *a matter of keystrokes:* a zone of interaction measured in square inches, and a visual field of some sixty degrees. While claiming that the student is "empowered" by technology and freed from the spatiotemporal constraints of the classroom, online education necessitates a student situated within a specific materio-spatial relation with the computer itself as a corporeal materialization within a space of flows. And this change in learning space cannot occur in isolation; in other words, it assumes a ubiquity of the interface within networked social space via home computers, wired libraries, and electronic text databases. The social norm of the interface, then, provides a performative context for dispositional practices that understand the student body as a zone of operational relations—with all other measures of corporeality disarticulated as *abject noise.*

The interface can therefore treat corporeal markings of identity as immaterial precisely because of dominant social norms that define "being online" as a *transmission* of presence. In its inverse form, these dominant norms conceive of the *substantiation* of identity as costume, donned or cast off with relative ease—and at will, resulting in a form of what Lisa Nakamura calls "identity tourism."[10] Only within such a set of assumptions would it be possible to claim that a user can experience a displacement from one's relation to a normative, transparent identity (white, male, middle class, heterosexual) simply by *transmitting* an altered identity in a chat room. Social markings still signify in this context, but in a manner that reduces identity to the content of transmission—signals rather than situational marks. The claim that student bodies have somehow become literally and figuratively *immaterial* has very little to do with the corporeal experience of students' everyday lives. But the emphasis placed on the loss of material presence in online education, by supporters and detractors alike, underlines the dominating concepts of dislocation and transmission involved in the production of a distance-learning social space: fantasies of an absolute disembodiment (having your everything amputated) and an unmarked presence (raceless, classless, genderless articulations of an online self). The distance-learning Web page for Georgia Perimeter College (where I

taught), though recently redesigned, is as good an example as any.[11] The slogan, replicated on dozens of distance-learning sites in various forms, promised
students the opportunity to "earn academic credits any time, any place," accompanied by images of: a young man in repose on the ground, laptop on his
knees; a woman with a laptop at the beach; and a man with a laptop at home,
his wife embracing him. These images (and others on the Web page) presented
a diversity of students by age, race, ethnicity, and gender that are representative
of the college's student population. But for all of this diversity, the marketing of
online education depends heavily on a unifying image of a *liberated flesh:* the
mind engaged while the body basks in the sun or cuddles at home in domestic
comfort. Apparently bodies *do* matter, but only in their disarticulation from
the classroom. Once education becomes a disembodied experience, the images
promise, the body is free to wander anywhere it pleases.

Of course, student bodies are anything but unmarked by race, class, gender, and disability; yet, the production of space enacted by the dominant social space of online education insists on this disconnect between the corporeal
situation of students and the conceptual representations of cyberspace. We
need to understand, then, not only the dispositional practices involved in the
production of the virtual classroom as networked social space, but also those
"noisy" practices that signal how student bodies "never quite comply with the
norms by which their materialization is impelled" (Butler, *Bodies That Matter*
2). Bodily presence is, after all, often commented upon during online interactions, especially in real-time exchanges. While dispositional practices reduce
corporeality to a nexus of operational queries and responses marked by the
interface, the "offline" tug of corporeal situation—one's partner, roommate,
or children; the call of hunger or evacuation; the wider sensorium of other
media devices—suggests that the body, as a scene of materialization, overflows
the social norms of being online, spilling well beyond the zone of interaction
marked by the interface. The space of the body does not end at the keyboard,
nor is corporeal situatedness merely a representation of content (identity)
transmitted across a medium. Rather, one finds that the body, through dispositional practice, materializes spatial processes that map a far more complex
rendering of the lived experience of cyberspace.

If we are to understand space as relational and dynamic, and if we are to
consider how a body, in this instance a student's body, is situated in and by relational space, we need to understand how space itself is not measured by the
body but how the production of space is a production of embodiment. Failure

to perform marks a dispositional abjectness that displaces the student even further than the rhetoric of access would acknowledge; it disarticulates the user from the conditions of possibility for the materialization of the body as a *networked student body*. As with other markings of a normative identity, the more that this performative, operational disposition is connected with marks of social capital, the more "transparent" it becomes to the machinations of power. At the same time, the processes of embodiment that fail to reduce to the performative dispositions of the interface provide a penumbra of sorts that helps to make the forms, structures, and practices of this dominant social space less transparent. A spatial analysis of the virtual classroom that calls attention to online education as the lived, embodied experience of students can reveal not only the dominant forms for the production of institutional social space but also the potentials for altered spatial relations marked by "noisy" lived practice. It would need to acknowledge that learning takes place as not just a transmission of content but in the negotiation of dispositional practices that either exclude or provide entry into a field of power in social space. In doing so, such a critical analysis would help reveal what performative norms govern this field and its diffusion of power, as well as how this field enters into an exchange of cultural capital with other fields within social space.

Just-in-Time Students

Given the dominance of transmission in the production of student-centered spaces of control, it is somewhat ironic that much of the discussion of student-centered online education is cast within a larger shift in pedagogy *away from* transmission models of education, in favor of models in which "students become seekers of knowledge, not just recipients of information" (Balanko 3).[12] But "seeking" here has a closed parameter to it, since it reduces to an input-output relation in which performance becomes the ultimate measure of "outcome." The student does not really seek/explore to the extent that for an online class to *take place,* it must "go off" as planned. Students seek only as long as they arrive at the pre-appointed destination; in other words, *student input must lead to course outcomes.* The "classroom without walls" still has operational parameters to it, which ultimately restrict and delimit how the course takes place for the student. "Seeking," then, ultimately reverts to another model of control, and while the student may no longer appear as a passive receptacle in this model, she does still function as a receiver/operator. In this regard, the virtual classroom does indeed articulate a "student-centered" spatiality in that the classroom is replaced by the material form of the student-computer interface, the situated experience of keystroke command-and-control of transmission, and the personalization of mobile instruction represented on the screen as *my course(ware)*.

Rather than treating online instruction as an immaterial exchange of information, I would suggest that the flashing cursor itself serves as the material scene for a communicative event—it enacts a set of spatial relations on and with the screen that produce an irruptive opening for command-and-control operations on the student's part. And in the spacing of a course that "begins" when a student opens the courseware application or course Web site and responds to it through the solicited clicks and keystrokes, the material boundaries of the class itself shrink to that moment of interface and interaction. For example, Burkhard Lehmann and Klaus Harney point out that, rather than discouraging the procrastination that instructors and administrators admonish, this irruptive space of online learning, marked by dispositional practices of the interface, could very well reward those students who are most capable of functioning "on the fly": what they term the student habitus of "last minute learner[s]." While "cramming" certainly has always been a dominant student practice within the traditional university, in the online class, student performance, ostensively a measure of hard work, serves equally as a measure of the ability to accomplish the most superficial levels of information exchange. While student research arguably has a wider scope of available sources, the dispositional practices instituted and normalized by the network drastically limit the *actual* number of sources a student will reach. If an article is not available online, it has no ontological status. What counts as research ultimately involves performing the appropriate keyword searches, and any search that does not give the student an electronic *text in hand* remains strictly virtual. We might begin to see how what Bourdieu calls "fast thinkers," in a different context (the pundits paid to "think" on television), gain cultural capital in this highly mediated social field by being able to respond to any thread on any list, so to speak (*On Television* 28–29). While, in policy, institutions encourage diligence and perseverance from students taking online courses, the operational and interface dispositions structure and are structured by a strategy in which efficiency and performativity become misrecognized expressions of "point-and-click thinking."

The user with access to "anytime, anywhere" education is instituted as student through a contingent relation to the interface, articulated by the dispositional practices that are in turn hailed by the norms of transmission. Much as Marc Bousquet argues that the "information university" results in a form of "just in time" instruction that takes part in a wider casualization of faculty labor through part-time appointments and untenured lines, one could argue that a *casualization of the student* occurs in online education as well. Bousquet notes the degree to which students' primary complaints—better campus food and more parking—speak specifically to the primacy of bodily presence for students on campus. At the same time, a casualization of the student body—structuring its relation in a performative fashion such that the student only exists in the exchange of assignments and comments—creates a set of dispositions suited for an operationalized relation to the institution, misrecognized as the above-stated values of independent learners. Student success in such an environment speaks to an incorporation of dispositions that will serve her well in a casualized labor market in which labor is treated as a matter of data transmission and in which body matters are left outside the equation of the marketplace. The promise of a raceless, genderless, ageless agora, in the form of the MCI Anthem advertisement, for example, speaks less of a liberation from modes of social inequality than of an evacuation of all social capital from the experiences of everyday embodied life in the "work world"—at the same time that "work" itself can occur anytime and anywhere, in public or in private.

As a point of clarification, we might return once again to the parallels between online courses and correspondence courses of the early twentieth century. As David Noble notes in *Digital Diploma Mills*, today's praise for online education echoes much of the rhetoric used to describe the benefits of "home study" by mail seventy-five years ago. In fact, the words of Hervey Mallory, head of the University of Chicago's Home Study Department, might just as well appear today on a distance-learning Web site by simply replacing the word "postal" with the word "Internet":

> You receive individual personal attention; you work as rapidly as you can, or as slowly as necessary, unhampered by others as in a regular class[; and your course] may begin at any time and may be carried on according to any personal schedule and in any place where postal service is available. (quoted in Noble 10)

Noble goes on to note how most, if not all, correspondence programs failed to live up to this ideal, often setting little or no entrance requirements for students taking the courses; hiring "piecework" instructors; and maintaining a no-refund policy—the sum of which created a system in which "dropout money" became an important revenue stream for home-study programs. Then, as now, Noble argues, the distance-education model casts the classroom as an impediment to the delivery of information for the student. The very casualization of the student identity that distance education institutes is foregrounded as the primary *benefit* of online instruction. In other words, while correspondence courses overcame geographic remoteness by way of a postal network, in a network society defined as a space of flows, *remoteness itself is a desirable condition*. Whereas the ubiquitous network interface is implicated in the production of spaces of everyday life, the performative citation of a student identity within the social networks of a learning community is seen as a hailing that threatens to *disrupt* daily life if it is not operationalized. Such sentiment is reflected at the University of Phoenix Web site in a description of their students and their programs:

> University of Phoenix students are busy professionals with jobs they care about and personal lives they don't want to compromise. Our acclaimed learning model recognizes the difference between younger students without much experience and working adults with practical knowledge. You'll interact with your fellow students as you would with coworkers, working on learning teams that reflect the way things get done in the business world. The result is an education that's as efficient as it is effective.[13]

The conflation of work, productivity, and efficiency are hardly accidental, in that it correlates practical knowledge with a pragmatics of just-in-time learning. And note that, while everyday life does indeed hold a privileged place here, it is the student's corporeal relation to the classroom that poses the disruption and that forces a compromise, not the ubiquitous network.

This vision of education is far removed from what Bourdieu describes as the scholastic ideal, in which students are displaced from the concerns of everyday life in order to engage in more rarified pursuits.[14] Rather, online education enacts the inverse ideal, in which learning for its own sake is secondary to the pursuit of "relevant" knowledge. And unlike the image of the independent "seeker," the University of Phoenix's ideal student works as part of a collaborative group, but one that is defined specifically in terms of a "team" (and defined explicitly within its business context): a community of projects, so to speak, explicitly short-term in its timeframe and contingent in its arrangement. The user is situated as student by the context of the course, but that identity does not carry beyond the moment of interface. The reality of the online course may very well parallel something similar to the experience of correspondence study, in which the student finds time and space for schoolwork and then *mails it in.* But the immediacy of the event of online learning—the potential for immediate feedback and for contact with the instructor at "any time"—suggests that the spatial relation between a remote learner and the central hub of learning has been altered by the casualization of the just-in-time student.

In a similar way, the classroom as a "community of learners" becomes an expression of just-in-time exchanges. The reality of social space, as a scene of multiple, competing, interpenetrating productions, plays itself out on the college campus in the varying articulations of students' "classroom experiences." The operationalization of community via CMC, however, attempts to control "aberrant" or outlying transmissions by treating them as noise. This understanding of a learning community differs significantly from a topography of a networked "students' rhizome" to the extent that there is an emphasis on control of, rather than proliferation of, modes and forms of contact. This is not to romanticize traditional classroom encounters by any means. In fact, the mediated nature of the electronic classroom provides students with an expressive forum that at first blush appears to level the differential in authority between teacher and student present in the traditional classroom, marked as access to discourse. For example, the first time I used a MOO to communicate with students who I met with weekly face-to-face, we started off using our real names; soon, however, most students discovered how to change their names, and opted for an online pseudonym. I did the same. The expected occurred: while student commentary increased, so too did the scatological humor, the flirtations, and the general "playing around." In the midst of serious discussion and off-topic digression, a student felt compelled to ask: "Anyone remember who the teacher is?" Such a disruption in the discursive centrality of "teacher" certainly produces novel potentials for networked social spaces of learning. At the same time, however, for all the guise of a level learning field, the instructor in an online course always maintains a power differential through the very permissions that give rise to the course—the ability to remove or edit posts, to block access to the course, to silence a student, etc. It is not necessarily the *difference* in professorial authority that is marked here, but, rather, the means by which that authority is expressed—through a convenience of keystrokes, a professor can make a student disappear from a discursive community, without all the messiness of bodies in conflict.

The dominant pedagogical model for just-in-time online instruction is neither dialogic nor dialectic, but *transmissive*. "Failure" in a course is a measure of a student's inability to obtain "course outcomes." But from within a system of maximum performativity, any engagement with processes that overflow the structurings of "student-centered" spaces of control is likewise treated as noise or as a system disturbance rather than as a productive process in its own right. By allowing a greater degree of one-to-one scholarly communication, while at the same time introducing a mode of exchange that is capable of proliferation, the Internet could indeed offer a compelling forum for instruction, scholarly exchange, and collaborative research. Such an "opening," however, runs contrary to much of the institutional structuring that grants "scholarship" its social capital. And the very fact that the online class remains within an institutional structure of registration, accreditation, credit hours, etc., serves as an apparatus of capture that returns these more fluid potentialities into ordered exchanges. At the same time, the irruptive, virtual quality of these network exchanges—blurring public and private space, intimate and impersonal contact—maps topographies of the academy that alter faculty and student identities alike. How, then, might we understand the institution of student bodies and the production of networked social spaces that run contrary to institutional structures of operationality and maximum performance?

Transmissive Scholarship: A Cautionary Tale

As a virtual topography, spaces of control find expression in the student-centered digital classroom, in which material form, conceptual structure, and lived practice place the student "in charge of" the learning process. Such a model misrecognizes the degree to which control operates within parameters that define successful performance in operational terms. Drawing on John Stallabrass's analysis of "empowering technology," Jamie Daniel notes how in such a construction:

> The internet classroom would seem to provide a streamlined, late twentieth-century equivalent of the bourgeois public sphere suggested two centuries ago by Kant when he proposed the self-generation of community by discussants who saw themselves as equals collaborating in the formation of a democratic alternative to the rigidly hierarchized authoritarian institutions of church and state.

But as Daniel's analysis of online education points out, such a vision fails to account for the ways in which this empowering technology demands a specific situatedness of its students in order to make the course perform, thereby setting dispositional limits on this agora of ideas.[15] To put it succinctly, "To whom, we need to ask, is this empowering technology available? And in what contexts? Likewise, we need to ask what other prerequisites, beyond [material access] are necessary before anyone can enter into the public sphere of cyberspace" (Daniel). The digital classroom, then, defines a specific spatial arrangement that, as Daniel notes, grants access to a space of exchange, a public sphere of sorts, but one that privileges its own modes of expression. This disciplining of dispositions also expresses itself in a disciplining of modes of expression—how one can talk and the kinds of things that can be said.

Within this line of argument, "noise" or "failure to perform" marks the indisciplines of assemblages of bodies and enunciations in conflict. As such, the dispositional practices that enact the dominant topographies for online instruction also allow for the situated production of a discursive community that may not necessarily reduce to a dominant discourse of operationality and performativity. The dominant virtual topography of online education enacts and articulates community through a moment of transmission and exchange. In an academic or scholarly setting, this casualization of community, it would seem, might also provide a restructuring of how we understand "rigor." While faculty members bemoan an approach to scholarship encouraged by digital networks in which only online sources exist (and the first source retrieved is the best source retrieved), this same shift in practice maps the potential for novel spaces of learning in which the structuring concept of "flow" plays a more prominent role than "rigor." In part, as online communication becomes implicated in the articulation of social space within an academic and scholarly setting, the notion of scholarship as an ongoing conversation migrates from a truly virtual space (a potential for exchange with future scholars) to a dynamic, emergent network (peer-to-peer exchange). The material, conceptual, and lived processes that give rise to "transmission," however, alter both how we understand the spatial relation of this exchange and the means by which exchange occurs. In this regard, networked communication does indeed provide an opportunity for establishing a nonhierarchical academic environment in place of (or as supplement to) more traditional means of contact, but, in doing so, it takes part in the articulation of a space that also restructures how we conceive of and materially support the spatial practice of scholarship.

While the casualization of student engagement opposes itself to certain practices that are materially and conceptually associated with academic rigor, the irruptive spatiality of an enactive network of flows also allows for dynamic exchanges that fall well outside of the forms, structures, and practices of traditional learning spaces. My own experience within a networked scholarly community provides a relevant example. When I began logging onto PMC-MOO in 1993, this text-based virtual environment still defined itself as a real-time supplement to the online journal *Postmodern Culture:* a "place" for a community of readers to meet and exchange ideas. At first the MOO was small, but thanks to an article in *Wired,* PMC-MOO's population grew to over 2,000 active participants. Much of that popularity led to a wide range of uses that no longer fell under the institutional purview of the journal—or, for that matter, that differentiated the MOO from any other online real-time chat room: flirtations, fantasy role-playing, and identity-play in its most banal form. An interesting friction began to develop within the exchanges that took place online. On one hand, for the folks who attempted to use the space as a forum for scholarly exchange and collaborative activity, the growing number of users interested in using the MOO as a "chat space" provided a tax on digital resources and a distracting presence. On the other hand, for this growing population of nonacademic users the pursuit of "postmodern cultural studies" seemed at best boring and at worst a form of elitist infringement on their social engagements. In 1995, the administrators of the site (myself included) decided to begin actively discouraging nonscholarly use of the MOO. The "staff" shut down the site for a period of a month, announcing beforehand that the MOO would change its name to PMC2, and, in doing so, would begin to "treat themeliness as 'editorial guidelines'" for use of network resources associated with the MOO.[16] For those attempting to assert PMC-MOO/PMC2 as a space of scholarly exchange and collaborative work, the proposed enforcement of "editorial guidelines" would provide a framework of rigor while at the same time leaving open a space for creative, engaging exchange. As anticipated, however, a great number of users of the MOO protested what they saw as a draconian attack on their shared social space. Within less than a year, the apparatuses of social capital, misrecognized in this instance as scholarly rigor, had reduced the site to fewer than 400 active participants. Within another two years, PMC2, now under yet another new name and divorced from *Postmodern Culture,* had all but killed itself in an attempt to achieve its aim of becoming a rigorous forum for scholarly exchange.

This brief, cautionary tale suggests, albeit anecdotally, two morals. First, it highlights the degree to which the spatial relations of networks depend upon what is best described as, to use Austin's language, *felicity conditions*[17] in order to "go off." In this and many other instances, "the network" is an emergent spatial process that is enacted rather than simply engaged or implemented. Second, the tale reveals the degree to which "play" rather than "rigor" maps a set of dispositional practices—again, as both corporeal and conceptual orientations—that grant access to the dynamic potentials of this space as a field of social relations. In other words, in this articulation of networked social space, the dynamics of interaction replace sustained pursuit as a measure of access to social capital. The event-scene of PMC-MOO, in its original incarnation, was indeed a space of scholarly exchange, although one that often disrupted norms of rigorous academic pursuit. Over the years that I was involved in the MOO, as both participant and administrator, I took part in a number of book groups; I collaborated with a visual artist in New York City on an art and performance symposium; and I helped run online weekly poetry slams. In each instance, transmission, while still structured as a sending and a receiving, also provided a framework for the *transitory* experience that situated the user within an enactive network. The ability of the MOO to provide a kind of *irruptive engagement* added to the vitality of the social space rather than detracting from it. While critics of virtual communities fault the lack of persistent engagement for the "watered-down" quality of online community (I can shut down or sign off far more easily than I can pack up and change houses), a *transmissive community* predicated upon flow is more colloquium than seminar, in that academic projects and scholarly conversations actualize only as long as the situated participants can enact the network. While one can certainly identify the potential hazards of a "just-in-time" scholarly community or research based on quick contacts and superficial exchanges, the potential for heterogeneous, irruptive exchanges can also produce novel social spaces that are creative and critically liberating. "Contact" is refigured here in this space as *colloquy,* simultaneously intimate and impersonal. While this ephemerality may seem less rigorous in its lack of long-term engagement, the loss of formal structures of institution, replaced by structures of "transmission," has the potential of creating academic spaces predicated on dynamic, emergent forms. Whether or not entrenched institutional structures can capture or accommodate this potential is, however, another question.

Toward the tail end of my active involvement with the MOO, I organized a six-month-long real-time colloquium structured loosely around the topic of "postmodern space." A diverse group of individuals responded to my call for participants, including established scholars in Australia, France, and the United States; a Lacanian psychotherapist in Norway; a visual artist in Manhattan; a situationist serving his compulsory time in the French Marines; a couple of computer programmers; a few literature and comparative-literature graduate students; and myself. Together, the twelve of us drew up a syllabus, conducted weekly discussions of texts, and carried on an ongoing conversation using a Listserv. We webbed our discussion into an archive and began working on individual and collective writing projects. The ultimate goal: a collaborative hypermedia project that we would submit to *Postmodern Culture*.[18] We worked together at all hours in multiple time zones, following threads across several months of discussion. The difficulty we had in maintaining the project suggests a common feature of the sorts of virtual topographies enacted inside and outside of institutional structures that define a transmissive community, academic or otherwise. At no time were all participants present on the network in real time, nor did all contributors post equal volumes of material. From the perspective of individual articulations of experience, however, it became increasingly clear that the project, through its varied many-to-one receptions and one-to-many transmissions, led to a form of collaboration that resisted academic closure at the same time that it opened up a network for multiple, novel, critical endeavors. This same potential, while falling outside the dominant norms of the interface, marks a virtuality for an online academic community that positions the student and scholar alike within an irruptive, enactive space of flows.

From Periphery to Peripheral

It should be clear by now that I am not attempting to valorize the experience of the student sitting "face-to-face" with other students and a professor, nor am I attempting to demonize online instruction. Rather, I would point to the degree to which the student enacting the virtual topographies of the online classroom is instituted through dispositional practices of the interface that both reiterate social norms of "being online" and overflow its parameters. The ubiquity of these practices across contemporary networked social space "naturalizes" the interface—a metaphor I use with caution. Increasingly, one's relation to social institutions is articulated through the forms and structures of networks and a corporeality defined through the interface. As such, the student who opts for online instruction has more likely than not already been instituted into a network subject-position within a casualized community of transmission and exchange.[19] In truth, online education has for many students become a standard offering; one may very well take a combination of face-to-face classes and online classes during any given semester. In many instances, the distinction between the two forms of classes is likewise somewhat artificial, since a face-to-face class might run in tandem with a distance-learning interface, or, at the very least, offer Web-based supplements that acknowledge the network as a component of instruction.

In the case of streaming media delivery of distance education, such as the courses offered through the Harvard Extension School,[20] Web-based video archives allow for the fact that the student who sits in the classroom may very well also be the student who sits in front of her computer as a "distance learner." The virtuality of the network maps two distinct processes of materialization: one at the zone of interaction marked by the student-computer interface, "outside" class; the other "inside" class, marked by the digital camcorder recording the lecture and discussion. Yet while a spatiality of containment would correlate presence and absence with one's location inside or outside of a class, a spatiality of exchange recognizes presence in terms of transmission and reception. The corporeal presence of the instructor reduces to an image on the screen gesturing toward a space that the instructor *inhabits* but that the student only *receives*. "Body" undergoes a translation in the sense that what might seem naturalized gestures—pacing, hand movements, etc.—become denatured in a spatiality of exchange and transmission. The student's own body likewise materializes at the interface as an articulating schema for a space of control, one that naturalizes the student's contingent relation to a social structure centered on network access. The "irrelevancies" of the course—students' laughter off-camera, an instructor's comments about tired faces and late-night parties—are communicated to the online student, but unlike the naturalized interface, these corporeal asides caught in real time and transmitted through an archival space of flows have a denatured quality, reduced to noise. This denatured quality is even more apparent for the student watching the stream at lower speeds, since body movements quite literally transmit as noise: jumpy, blurred data streaks, discontinuous with the flow of the professor's voice.[21] What's more, the "student-centered" course delivery means that the student can freeze the course, rewind it, or skim through it in fast-forward.

As such, the *scroll bar* replaces the lectern as the spatial marker of corporeal centrality and discursive control.

In this exemplary instance of a student's operational relation to the *course* as a flow of information, literalized in the form of *streaming media,* the student's body encounters a secondary dislocation to the degree that it is now free to move away from the monitor and still "receive" the lecture, controlled through the click of a pause button. While the demands of lecture halls and seminar rooms elicit a disposition of quiet seating and studious attention, or a displacement of attention onto another corollary task (crossword puzzles in the back row—or, more likely today, text messaging), with the online class, "anytime, anywhere" not only necessitates dispositional practices that institute the student body as a network interface, it also marks the potential to break off this spatial relation without "disrupting" the class. I can pick up a crying child or leave the room to get a snack or answer a phone call requiring my attention, all the while "attending" to my course. Such enactions of embodiment suggest a student's situated experience exceeds the interface's zone of interaction and highlight both the penetration of institutional forms of the network into a private space (so much for Ticknor's domestic sphere) and the ephemeral, irruptive form and structure of these enactive networks in lived experience. While correspondence courses of the late nineteenth and the early twentieth centuries mapped a double articulation of dislocation and affiliation, the network structures of online classes define a lived space of student bodies that is dynamic and enactive, transmissive and ephemeral. It is not simply a matter of fragmenting my attention between different tasks, as the buzzword "multitasking" suggests, but, rather, of producing a novel space for learning, one that does not fit at all within a scholastic ideal nor that corresponds to the efficiency models of commodified, casualized education. One might best describe this virtual topography as an articulation of "spaces of distraction."[22] Likening the experience of movie watching to one's lived experience within architecture, Walter Benjamin comments that, in contrast to the concentration demanded by painting, distraction marks a "social conduct" that does not focus upon the object but, rather, that provides the structuring focus for one's continued range of actions. He writes:

> Distraction and concentration form polar opposites which can be stated as follows: A man who concentrates before a work of art is absorbed by it. He enters into this

work of art the way legend tells of the Chinese painter when he viewed his finished
painting. In contrast, the distracted mass absorbs the work of art. (241)

If the traditional correspondence model created a social network that both
concentrated institutional centrality and mediated its authority to its dislo-
cated students, online courses allow for a space of distracted relations to institutional structures, virtually absorbed, as it were, by the dispositional practices that situate students at an operational center, yet actualized through
casualized, transmissive articulations. In contrast to the traditional classroom,
in which successful student habitus embodies the signs and behaviors of a
studied concentration, the online student gains social capital by incorporating the corporeal and conceptual orientations that afford her a *distracted* focus beyond the hailing of the screen while still being spatially *contracted* by the
interface.

(Inter)face Time

As previously noted, in the same manner that the student participating in an
online course most likely will also find himself in a traditional classroom at
some point, the spatial relations enacted by the virtual classroom are by no
means limited to the experience of distance education. For most students, the
spaces of everyday life produced by the material, conceptual, and experiential
processes of networked social space have much more to do with the computers at home, in libraries, and in computer labs than with online learning. The
spatiality of the network is very much caught up in the material, conceptual,
and experiential processes that articulate everyday life at all levels of the university. And these articulations are heavily invested with social capital. At many
institutions, it has become conventional wisdom that it is far easier to obtain
a classroom full of computers than to secure an assistant-professor line. And,
as a majority of instructor/assistant-professor job announcements at teaching
colleges will attest to, the ability to integrate computer skills into the classroom
has increasingly become a primary measure of student-teacher interaction and
effective classroom performance. As with the rhetoric surrounding Internet-
based distance education, the material presence of—or access to—computers
is seen as a student-centered restructuring of classroom space on campus. And,
once again, a logic of maximum performance dominates, such that the "stu-
dent-empowering" network interface is described as a more efficient mode of

delivery. And this altered institutional space is reflected in both student and faculty habitus.

The student dispositions that command and control the flow of information via CMC provide an altered sense of what it means to be in a classroom *even when students' bodies are in the classroom.* Traditionally, the university has marked a zone of social distinction and differentiation. On campuses today, one's dispositional comfort at and with a computer increasingly marks one's role as a student. It is not the case that one must show certain computer literacies in the process of becoming a student (although many institutions do require some demonstration of computer skills as part of a general education program); rather, these digital dispositions increasingly serve as marks of distinction that articulate a student's place within a college or university. Student bodies are cyborg to the extent that the performance of a student subject-position increasingly depends upon a fluidity with a point-and-click interface; one's lack of mental and corporeal comfort conversely speaks of a form of disability approaching abjectness. The hailing of a student into a subject-position increasingly calls upon a set of assumptions that a student not only has convenient access to email, a Web browser, and word processing software, but that she has already incorporated a relation to these computer technologies that amounts to a second nature or second skin. This is very much at the heart (so to speak) of an understanding of what Theresa Senft (citing Barbara Browning) calls "prosthetic identity," in that the machinic network of informatic exchanges replicates or runs parallel to organic systems in a way that attempts to undermine distinctions between the two. Senft writes, "We once knew—or we thought we did—who were the able-bodied, what was machine-assisted, and which stories were true. Now we cannot be sure." In a similar fashion, it has become increasingly difficult to determine what courses should count as "computer-assisted," when the student subject-position already assumes an integration of networks into the spaces of everyday life.

As marks of institutional distinction, these dispositional practices extend well beyond the classroom and the library. For many institutions, the student-computer interface now serves as the first point of material contact with the college or university. The State University of New York (SUNY) at Buffalo's "iConnect@UB" portal provides a good example of this integration of network technology into lived spaces: what have come to be branded as "click-and-mortar" institutions.[23] The implementers of the portal describe it as a tool that makes the large university setting more personal for the student by integrating resources and by facilitating student contact with professors and other university officials. As the term "portal" implies, the Web site is conceptually structured as a point of entry into the institution, but with the difference of privatization (I take it with me wherever I interface) and personalization (*iConnect* to *MyUB*). In fact, what a user sees on the screen differs based on institutional affiliation (student, faculty, or staff), class level, and major, such that the world of SUNY Buffalo's MyUB mirrors back the same parameters that situate the student within the institutional structure—all portrayed as a means of facilitating "learner communities" and a sense of integration (Bernstein, Gorman, and Wright). Driven by a cybernetic principle of information management, MyUB provides focused information distribution to students and guides information queries through a "cyberian" application:

> to mine deeper for the right sites: not just the top pages, but also the hidden gems that can match the needs of our students. Links that personally and actively reach out to students act as a system of online coaching and mentoring to make sure that students have access to the resources they need when they need them. (Bernstein, Gorman, and Wright)

While claiming to serve as an orientation to the university, a university portal such as MyUB assumes that the student is *already oriented toward and by* network technology. While designed as a retention feature, it also distinguishes those students who can best integrate network technology, who can best make networked spaces of control personalized points of entry. Contact and community, then, become features of communication and a point-and-click interface. As a result, institutional and informal collectivization—what counts as a *student body* in the abstract sense—is increasingly articulated in the personal by way of network interface. On- or off-campus *matters less* in the production of social space than a student's ability to establish a networked interface with the institution.

The student's body enunciates a situatedness within the network: not a noncorporeal self but a material presence that is articulated by network structures, in which interactions become a matter of informational exchange and the ability to integrate network technologies into everyday life. One's relation with fellow classmates, either within the classroom or outside of class, is expressed in "prosthetic" or cyborg form to the extent that corporeal articulations are caught up in a materiality of network exchange. "Face time" signifies because communication in all forms has become colloquialized as a kind of interface: *contact* as a mode of spatial contraction. To some degree, the more traditional the student, the more likely that the student is already situated within a virtual middle class, and therefore already entrenched within these networks of mediation. For example, the mediation of contact between student in dorm and parent at home now takes place as much by email as by phone, and with webcam-synched instant messaging (IM),[24] the prostheses of networks become all the more integrated in everyday life. The casualized quality of this spatial contraction, in which contact occurs as an ephemeral transmission, translates presence into an enunciation of exchange, such that one's corporeal relation to the interface precedes and precludes material copresence with one's interlocutor. Unlike the double articulation of the student subject-position in earlier modes of distance learning, "remote" now marks a spatial relation of controlled, mediated contact (quite literally a spatiality of *remote control*), rather than a spatial displacement from a locus of institutional centrality.

The digitization of instruction transforms social space in its material, conceptual, and experiential processes—not because instruction is now without bodies, space, tables, and chairs, but because the technological point of interface situates dispositional practices that then establish new social norms and new social systems of value. The casualization of the student, while encouraged by institutional arrangements of social space, also results in gaps and fissures in this same dominant social space. Computers in the classroom, for example, not only aid instruction; they also provide an interface that pulls the student beyond the interpellations of the institution. While in a traditional classroom, students are on task to the degree to which they are *attending* to their instructor, as a material interface, the students in a "computer lab" classroom are "on task" as long as they are engaged with the computer. What's more, the arrangement of most standard labs creates a material distance between student and faculty by way of the computer itself—in other words, what the faculty member sees is the back of the monitor rather than the student's face. What has been introduced into the class as an opening onto instructional possibilities, in effect restructures teacher-student spatial relations. In any given class, a student might well have a Web browser pointed to a site that has nothing to do with classroom instruction. But here's the biggest point, one that again calls attention to the dispositions that are socially reinforced in these environments. Within an institutional field of power mapped by networks of exchange, the "best" student is not the one involved in browsing for a new car during a class lecture or the one who ignores the monitor and holds the faculty member in rapt attention; rather, it is the *distracted* student whose dispositional practices engage both modes of attention, who can "toggle" between two modes of corporeal and cognitive orientation. The computer interface marks a double articulation here: between spaces of *attentive distraction* and spaces of *oriented contraction*.

To some degree, the networked student within the face-to-face classroom provides a mirror situation of the student in an online class receiving streaming video, in which the mediated presence of others "out there" is signaled by the structure of the class itself, while at the same time maintaining a material distinction between articulations of "face time" and "screen time." The student who browses online in class is materially present in the class but, at the same time, materializes in a dispositional practice that contracts to a spatial relation with the interface. To this extent, then, the networked computer also marks a noisy, material interface that maps a virtuality that is (abjectly) beyond the potentials of the classroom. The operational imperative of the university demands an efficiency and a performativity that makes information flow; the student who interacts with a computer in class is involved in a process that actualizes the network as a kind of opening "beyond" the class, always holding the potential of enacting networks that distort the conceptual structuring of the class, regardless of the faculty member's intentions. This is not a matter of "good" or "bad" student practices; from an account of dispositional practices, there is little difference between shopping for used cars online and researching a term paper (or, for that matter, shopping for a used research paper). In each instance, the student is enacting a relation to the network that enunciates the normative demands of a point-and-click student habitus. Such gaps and fissures in lived practice suggest ways in which the interpellations of the network never fully reduce to the normative, institutional demands of the student subject-position.

But is there any difference between the distracted student, networked to the Web, and the student slumped in the back of the class, reading a novel or doing crossword puzzles? I would argue that the foregrounding of the network in the class by dominant institutional structures of the virtual university (student-operated, casualized, driven by principles of efficient transmission) is what provides for this distinction. In other words, since the network pointed "outward" already functions as a dominant conceptual structuring, material formation, and lived practice of the classroom, a habitus of distracted browsing holds significant relevance in the production of social space. The network stands at the very heart of social and cultural processes. In this regard, we might think again about parallels with the position of newsprint in the eighteenth century, in its relation to postal delivery routes and international trade routes. The newspaper could function as a ubiquitous material articulation of conceptual structures of community precisely because daily use placed it in a relation to larger social processes involved in the production of space. A similar argument can be made today for the dispositional practices that situate social actors at the point of network interface. One can identify spaces in conflict articulated by the lived practice of the student-computer interface precisely because it enunciates dominant processes within the production of social space in a network society. If the classroom still marks a significant scene in the structuring of subject-positions, it does so because it implicitly or explicitly acknowledges the network as a central material, conceptual, and lived process in the production of spaces of everyday life.

From Virtual Students to Student Virtualities

As email suggests a shift in spatial articulations in which enfoldings and irruptions perform effectively as social forms, so too does the position of networks of exchange place the classroom in an altered space more prone to irruptions and enfoldings. The student whose phone goes off during class is doing nothing more than taking part in a performative act that very much "goes off" within the conditions of possibility for network processes that are increasingly involved in the production of social space. The dominant norms of a network society, in this instance as instituted by the university, cannot entirely capture these material, conceptual, and experiential processes. While a student's casualized relation to the network allows for just-in-time instruction, it also situates the student at a moment of irruptive possibility that may well overflow institutional norms of "being online." The relation of scholarly pursuit to ludic linkages, banalities, and transgressive material provides a structuring in which the situation of the student at the interface—as both a material and a conceptual orientation—is foremost in providing the network with its conditions of possibility. Critical thinking in the classroom now involves *filtering* above all else—an attempt to distinguish signal from noise in such a way that one can sketch out a domain of scholarly pursuit from an entropic field of information. This operational relation is heavily institutionalized within the university to the extent that "student-centered" instruction remains within the structures of course *outcomes* and *programs* of study. At the same time, ephemeral material-izations of both the student subject-position and the enactive communities of exchange that result from networked social space allow for social formations that refuse to reduce to expressions of efficiency and maximum performance.

To be a student, then, takes on a novel position within institutional social space in a network society. On one hand, a dominant spatial practice suggests that the network articulates spaces of control while encouraging a habitus that speaks very much of a just-in-time world of casual labor and casual thought. At the same time, one can find signs that novel network structures do occur, often in ways that step outside of the control/out-of-control binarism while appearing to dominant social structures as system errors, perversions, or corruptions of otherwise clear channels. While the online course and the correspondence course share a conduit model of instruction in which "content" is delivered to the student/receiver, the potential for the student to share or distribute content by way of the same medium presents some interesting consequences for the production of networked social space. The ability of the student to pull a discussion off tangent has significant consequences for the production of space, to the extent that an irruptive potential exists with each situated articulation of a student subject-position, no matter how casualized or how controlled.

What's more, as scenes of citation, the network interface not only articulates the technologically able-bodied and the normatively centered but also allows for the situation and articulation of a range of student subject-positions. In the same way that a site like Hipmama.com can allow for the situated corporealities of pregnant women to speak—including pregnant women of color and of various class structures and sexualities—one might imagine how a network of student situatedness could function to give space to enactive networks and communities of exchange that make normative online identity less transparent. The point-and-click interface of Web sites can quite literally formalize normative identities—resulting in what Lisa Nakamura notes as the "suppression of the unclickable, hyphenated, hybrid, 'messy' kinds of racial, gendered, and sexual identity" (120); yet the potential exists for enactive network structures that disrupt or dissipate these normative hailings, as articulated through the singularities of situated student bodies in networked social space. Network structures can allow for articulations that do not reduce to a kind of digital cross-dressing or to the banalities of "celebrating" diversity, but instead speak to a materiality predicated upon the interface but attentive to a range of bodily dispositions and suppositions. Within the irruptive potentials of these virtual student topographies, "minority" maps a Deleuzian minor that overflows institutional categories of difference and diversity.

Whatever potential exists for network processes to give rise to social spaces that do not reduce to a matter of just-in-time learning would find itself specifically in this terrain in which spaces of control fail to account for productive networks implemented by students. What I have in mind, then, would be spaces of learning that cut across institutionality—not simply run contrary to but, rather, emerge from within the zones in which institutional space exerts its greatest control. If we were to take into account how Web-based information has altered doctor-patient relations—for example, the challenge to medical authority one often finds even on commercial pregnancy sites such as Babycenter.com—we might have an important point of contrast. As the amount of information on the Web concerning medical conditions increases, it becomes increasingly easy for an individual to construct a network of information that would map a form of casualized expertise for him- or herself. The same kind of impetus does not exist for students to become emergent experts in *American Literature I* or *Intro to Psychology.* For the most part, the relation between student and coursework remains institutional in that it maintains a commodified form as "course content." As an alternate structure, however, one might imagine how the dynamic, enactive networks of a community of exchange, regardless of how ephemeral, might give rise to productive relations of what it means to be a situated, enactive node within a global space of flows.

Noble's book is worth commenting on in this context. In the introduction, he reveals the difficulty he had in getting his initial article, "The Coming of the Online University," published; it was rejected by both the *Nation* (for which it had been originally written) and by *Lingua Franca.* "Happily," he writes, "the article was ultimately published on the Internet, through which it was enthusiastically received as a 'manifesto' of resistance, distributed worldwide, and repeatedly republished, as were the subsequent articles in this series" (xi).[25] The technological distribution afforded by the Internet allowed Noble (and countless others) to restructure a network of circulation, to appropriate material form and conceptual structure in such a way that alternate modes of expression become actualized. Noble specifically sees in the corporatization and commodification of online education (and higher education in general) a training model that restricts learning to a skill acquisition process, measured in terms of query/stimulus and response. But the network structures that allow for this conduit model of education, encouraging operational and point-

and-click dispositions, are at the same time available for a "hack" on the order of Noble's "manifesto"—or the countless aberrant, "noisy" sites that situate spaces of flow in a minor relation to a dominant field of social power. Such appropriations never "take over" the network; rather, they map indisciplines that allow for articulations of unforeseen social relations.

Perhaps, then, an additional disposition is available to bodies online, one that is very much both a cognitive and a corporeal orientation. One can never "hijack" the network without falling back into a model of spaces of control. But one can operate by way of an "experimental" disposition, "experimental" here defined specifically as a Deleuzian mode of empirical embrace, an attempt to articulate relations that parallel philosophy's pursuit of concept-building. The structuring of network interactions would involve access to a kind of drift, not only as a consumption-driven "browsing" but also as a deterritorializing opening of spaces of flow. In other words, Noble's "manifesto," once placed within an ephemeral community of exchange, articulates a social space that could not have taken form within traditional modes of publication and distribution, or within a traditional university seminar room or lecture hall. What allows for this opening of flow is very much an experiential practice of placing "oneself" into spaces of flows, or, more accurately, of understanding "being online" not within an operational input-output relation to the network but as produced by and producing a cognitive and corporeal orientation toward the relational processes of dissipation and flow. Such a set of dispositional practices would mark the human-computer interface as a nexus of experimentation rather than of control, an opening toward corporeal and semiotic potentialities rather than an ordering and disciplining of performative actualities. As such, "messy" identities, "noisy" exchanges, and "aberrant" practices enact situated relations that—in their very articulation—map altered virtual topographies within the dominant orderings and institutionalizations of networked social space.

Here, then, is an interesting shift worth noting, as a generation of students arrives in college classrooms with an interface disposition incorporated from their youngest years. The students in American colleges and universities today literally grew up with "cyberspace" in popular parlance. As spaces of control present themselves as a dominant social space, students find their own interface with the computer as a locus for a monadic world of "my university." Access to computer technology, then, allows for a shift in structure such that the student is positioned in a relation of autonomy to channels of communication. At the same time, the same technology that is touted as increasing student learning by creating a "student-centered" environment now provides a locus for a student to redirect attention and orientation. As faculty find themselves positioned within institutional structures that still demand an "official" relation, the shift speaks to a restructuring not only of attention but of bodily engagement. This is not to romanticize the passive, attentive, "docile body" of the student, but, rather, to note the differential way in which network technology positions student bodies, while at the same time noting the challenges to institutional structures opened up by this relation. The networks that promise a "classroom without walls" also allow for forms, structures, and practices that disarticulate the centrality of the classroom and the dynamics of a teacher-driven student relation, and do so in a way that overwhelms the institution's dominant norms of efficiency and maximum performance.

In Noble's introduction to the second edition of *Digital Diploma Mills,* he speaks of how the events following 9/11, coupled with the sobering of profit expectations from online learning, have taken much of the wind out of the push toward the virtualization of the classroom. In contrast, I would argue that much of what seemed a profound challenge to the structure of the classroom has already found a home in most "face-to-face" classrooms, in that much of how students understand the pursuit of knowledge is dictated by operational dispositions that attempt to make information perform. In my afterword, I would like to turn to the paired events of 2000 and 2001—the Internet "bubble burst" and 9/11—to assess how networks function "after" these events. On one hand, the deflation of a technologically driven euphoria, coupled with the profound, global impact of the 9/11 attacks and the subsequent U.S. military response, has had a significant effect on what virtual topographies still map as spaces of everyday life. At the same time, however, I would argue that much of what had been articulated as productions of social space in the 1990s has found its home in a dominant social space of network society. What had seemed a struggle between a "the real" and "the virtual" a decade earlier has become a banality of the network in everyday life. What's more, while spaces of control remain the dominant articulation of networked social space, that control increasingly takes the form of the distributed, emergent processes of the network itself.

AFTERWORD

DIGITAL DIS-STROPHE

T RUTH BE TOLD, the "Y2K bug" was quite a disappointment. While the technopundits wooed us with visions of network failures worthy of millennial fervor, January 1, 2000, came and went without even a glimmer of the catastrophic. Yet the Y2K "bug" did reveal the degree to which the American apocalypse took the form of the network itself.

As I suggest throughout this book, the dominant topographies of a network society produce spaces of control—lived spaces in which the network interface marks a set of material and conceptual relations that place a "world of information" at a user's fingertips. Yet these spaces of flow enact network relations that are emergent and dynamic, not static. While spaces of control articulate forms and practices associated with point-to-point contact and stable lines of transmission, these same spaces of flow map a topography of contingent, enactive relations. In such a representation of space, networks do not *go down;* they dissipate. As such, topographies of control are not continuously on the brink of "crisis" in any traditional Marxist sense; rather, the potential for dissipation is at once the condition of possibility for the production of network social space and its deterritorializing indiscipline. Y2K was simply the wrong millennial event—a computational error that, in a society dominated by flows, seemed as outmoded as the old mainframes it threatened to seize. *Catastrophe* today is marked more by dispersion and dissipation than by breakdown or failure—a *dis-strophe* of social forms, structures, and experience. Within two years of January 1, 2000, however, two events occurred—gateposts of sorts on either end of the new millennium—that indeed signaled critical moments for a network society: moments in which enactive, distributed networks serve as both the victims and the agents of ironic revenge.

After several years of phenomenal growth and delirious investment in dot-com companies, in mid-March 2000, the Internet stock "bubble" burst, leading to an overall market correction, a slew of bankruptcies, and the evaporation of billions of dollars in capital. Much as the growth period of 1998 and 1999 was accompanied by a media saturation of "new economy" rhetoric, in the months following the bubble burst, financial pundits declared an end of the virtual and a return of the real, measured in economic terms as a return to *fundamentals*. Eight months later, in the closest and most disputed presidential election in U.S. history, Al Gore, the "inventor of the Internet," was defeated by George W. Bush, whose personal, business, and political connections speak to decidedly "old-economy" global interests (most notably petrochemical) and whose first-term administrative appointments spoke to a resuscitation of pre-informational economy Ford-administration politicians. Within a year we took for granted that the new economy was over (or, to borrow from Baudrillard, that it never took place). Yet for all of the discussion of the collapse of the new economy, the spaces of everyday life "post-bubble" are no less caught up in topographies of the network. The "grounding" of stock prices did not, for example, impact the degree to which the economy now depends unquestioningly on the spaces of flow defined by just-in-time manufacturing and electronic transfer of funds (ETFs). Networks still provide the material, conceptual, and lived processes that allow corporations to rely heavily on distributed labor and professional work alike, be that through around-the-corner telecommuting or through overseas outsourcing. And while chat rooms have not turned out to be the digital replacement for disappearing town commons, social structures today are all the more implicated in networks of flows, from the banality of private text messaging to the public uptake of Web-based grassroots movements. Without question, the March 2000 bubble burst marked a significant political, economic, and cultural moment. Yet by no means did the virtual topographies articulated by network technology disappear in the evaporation of investment capital.

Eighteen months after the bubble burst, the United States experienced its worst act of foreign aggression on domestic soil, in the form of terrorist attacks on the World Trade Center in New York City and on the Pentagon in Washington, D.C. While not meaning to diminish the significance of an attack on the primary architectural symbol of American military might, it is the collapse of the World Trade Center towers that serves as the second millennial event for our network society. As the bubble burst signaled an instance of digital *dis-strophe,* the 9/11 attacks on the World Trade Center marked a similar dissipative moment, articulated in the material terror of over 1,300 feet of skyscraper steel and human bodies turned to wreckage and dust. Much as the market crash of 2000 represented a collapse from within of the same network processes that enabled the market's phenomenal growth, the attacks themselves, rather than emerging from "outside" or "beyond" a network society, were articulations of a global space of flows. Only within the conditions of possibility of networked social space (coordinated flight schedules, ETFs) could such attacks occur. For all its embrace of premodern religious *fundamentals,* al-Qaeda as an organization appeared decidedly at home in the globalized network society that it threatened to destroy. In an instance of Baudrillardian "ironic revenge," terrorism appropriated all the trappings of a global space of flows in the name of subverting that same social structure (Baudrillard, *The Spirit of Terrorism* 17–19). Terror had taken the form of a horrifying distributed network, a human articulation of a space of flows gone *out of control.*

It should be no surprise that within weeks of 9/11, the U.S. Congress approved (unread) the Patriot Act, which not only "streamlined" due process but also introduced interventions into distributed networks that, in effect, allowed for more state-based control. In an era of a global space of flows, the Patriot Act reestablished *the homeland* as both a representation of space and a delimited space of practice, articulated through those very same global network structures. While President Bush declared a "war on terror," the Patriot Act declared a war on nomadic articulations of a global space of flows, introducing state-based apparatuses of capture. Much as the market collapse of March 2000 left the global flow of network capital well in place, the catastrophic collapse of the Twin Towers by no means marked the "end" of transnational networks. While the ensuing U.S. military and legislative acts may well have signaled a shift from "transnational globalist" to "international hegemonist" policies and practices of capitalist power,[1] these actions would by no means return us to the social spaces of a pre-network society. Rather, these military, political, and economic controls marked an active attempt to capture the forms, structures, and practices of a space of flows within state-initiated spaces of control.

With both the bubble burst of 2000 and the 9/11 World Trade Center attacks, the catastrophic arose from within the successful functioning of the same system it threatened to collapse. As such, each event could only have taken place within a social space produced by and productive of the material, conceptual, and lived processes of the network. These events did indeed have an impact on the networked spaces of everyday life, but in a way that left dispositional practices largely untouched. We have seen, in the years following the end of the Cyberspace Decade, the growing dominance of topographies in which the network functions as an apparatus of capture that attempts to order the indisciplines of digital dis-strophe. We still live the network; increasingly, however, spaces of everyday life are enacted by the forms and structures of *distributed control*.

Bubbles and Cubicles

In mid-March 2000, PSInet, a leading provider of Internet backbone, announced it would pay nearly $2 billion to acquire Metamor Worldwide, an information technology (IT) consulting firm. It was the last, and largest, of a long string of corporate acquisitions, one that sent its stock teetering, down 15 percent, days before the markets began their March tumble. A little over a year later, the company filed for bankruptcy. While it would be overly simplistic to claim that the collapse of PSInet caused, or even signaled, the dot-com bubble burst, the company does provide a convenient marker of sorts for the material investment in, conceptual restructuring of, and dispositional practices for a network economy during the late 1990s, and the way in which this network created an ephemerality of flows that is still very much in place, although many of the dot-com miracle companies have long since disappeared. PSInet was one of the earliest ISPs and was a major provider of and investor in fiber-optic cables for global networks in Asia, South America, and Europe. By the start of 2000, PSInet was purchasing companies (not to mention a football stadium) at a staggering rate. When the opportunity arose to purchase Metamor, it was touted as the next logical step in the company's attempt to become a "full-service provider" (FSP), bringing distributed business structures within the compass of the corporation's emphasis on IP/ISP infrastructure. In the words of PSInet CEO Bill Schrader at the time of the purchase, "This deal is a real no-brainer.... The acquisition of Metamor Worldwide furthers our plans to move into the applications outsourcing arena" (Fusco). Instead, in a little over a year, the multibillion dollar corporation was "de-listed" from NASDAQ, filed for bankruptcy, and replaced Schrader with a new CEO. What happened to PSInet in a matter of months became emblematic of (if not a catalyst for) the market collapse during the second quarter of 2000.

The question we should ask is: What exactly collapsed with the economic shift marked by the bubble burst? The impact of the evaporation of billions of dollars from the U.S. stock market certainly had real-life effects, measured most directly for many Americans in shrinking pension funds, IRAs, and personal investments; and certainly the economic downturn had a major impact in all sectors, domestically and worldwide. Yet the collapse in stock prices did not necessarily mark a shift in the production of networked social space. In fact, one could argue that the bubble burst reaffirmed the dominance of the spatiality of the network in a wired world. Certainly, the material form of PSInet's backbone outlived the company, and as a representation of space, the virtual topographies of global exchanges still situate a virtual class in networked spaces of everyday life. In part, what collapsed (or rather imploded) with the bubble burst was the all too familiar dualist separation of information from materiality. While the euphoria of dot-com investment celebrated a liberation of informatic exchanges from material context, the bubble burst, as ironic revenge, exposed the degree to which all processes—material, conceptual, and experiential—are defined by the ephemerality of flows. In 1998 and 1999, the indicators of profitability, connected with the buying, selling, or trading of *things,* became less and less important compared to market capitalization as a measure of a company's ability to enact a relational space of exchange, be that through capital investment, media hype, or Web-site hits. The marketplace as a social space became a relational space of *marketability.*[2] Perhaps more than the crash itself, the ensuing "return to fundamentals" during the second half of 2000 revealed that the material forms of the economy still remained entirely predicated upon a network of flows. While tech bubbles come and go, the ephemerality of the market as an enactive, dynamic network continues to assert itself as the fundamental material form and conceptual structure for the economy.

As Eli Ofek and Matthew Richardson note, the precipitous rise in stock prices in the late 1990s paralleled an increasing number of individual investors in the marketplace, many of whom were attracted by the promise of easy profits through dot-com stocks. At the close of the 1990s, individual investors outpaced institutional investors across the market, many of whom were buying and selling through online accounts. Individual/retail investors accounted for nearly 75 percent of all Internet stocks—roughly $53.9 billion in market capitalization (Ofek and Richardson). Much as online classes institute students in a subject identity through an interface disposition, the hailing of online trading situates users in an operational relation to global markets. Once interpellated as "investor," the market becomes *my* market, the bubble burst appearing very much as a personalized and privatized event, reported on cookie-reading Web-site tickers and daily email portfolio updates. The bubble burst, then, was not an "outlier" or system failure but rather an extreme event within the same virtual topography that allows for the calling forth or liquidation of capital with the stroke of a key. While the dominant social space of a network society produces spaces of control for its users, the casualized articulation of the user within this enactive network implies that these distributed structures configure or disperse as emergent spaces well beyond the individual user's operational relation to the network. When the personalized, privatized user finds himself disarticulated from this operational disposition, the result is an experience of flow as abject, chaotic dispersal: dis-strophe. The bubble burst, then, marked less a crisis for the market as a space of exchange (since its ephemerality is also a measure of the robustness of an enactive network) than a dispositional crisis for the user, mapped as a shift in virtual topographies from spaces of control to spaces of dissipation.

While a phenomenal amount of capital disappeared when the bubble burst, the network forms and structures that allowed individual users "direct access" to the flows of capital are still very much in place for the dispositional practices of everyday life for a normative virtual class. In fact, by many measures they are more dominant today than five years ago, though rarely foregrounded as the practices of *cyberspace*. True, the number of online investors decreased in 2001, according to Nielson/NetRatings, but less than two years after the bubble burst, financial sites were attracting over 50 million users per month—particularly those sites that gave users the ability to transfer funds, pay bills, or trade stock. According to a senior analyst at NetRatings, "We are seeing the true adoption of the Internet as a resource consumers turn to in order to move money and monitor their financial holdings. . . . As markets have matured, new features and services such as interactive planning tools and extended online bill payment have been integrated into consumers' lives" (Nielsen/NetRatings). Likewise, Jupiter Research anticipates a steady growth in households making use of online banking, particularly for everyday functions such as transfers and payments (Haley). The solid popularity of financial sites provides a mapping of cyberspace not merely as a tool or resource but rather as an enunciation of the processes of network exchange that make up everyday life, articulated as personalized and privatized spaces of control.[3] The proprietary nature of commerce—that it is *my* funds that I transfer, and no other—demands an increasingly reified understanding of "being in control," and commercial Web sites have responded accordingly. The operationalized relation of the user to the interface allows for enactive, ephemeral articulations of the network; yet, increasingly, this zone of interaction demands *authentication* as a precursor to the hailing of "being online."

The growing number of individuals involved in financial and commercial transactions online certainly speaks to an increasing number of individuals who have incorporated the normative dispositions of a virtual class. But the corporeal and cognitive orientations that mark a network habitus extend well beyond economic transactions, most notably in the workplace. By no means did the bubble burst signal the end of the dispositional practices of organizational, distributed functions that provide a major underpinning for everyday corporate life through email, intranets, and various modes of outsourcing. In the workplace of the "post–new" economy, productive relations are still very much articulated by the forms, structures, and practices of the network. The casualization of professional and blue-collar workers alike, in which an interface disposition defines one's relation to corporate structure, is, if anything, all the more dominant, now misrecognized as a measure of cost-saving efficiency. Perhaps, then, it is ironic revenge par excellence that the very business structure that signaled PSInet's collapse—namely, its attempt to acquire an "applications outsourcing" company—would remain one of the most deeply entrenched restructurings of daily corporate life, as business functions increasingly become a matter of just-in-time network exchanges, often thousands of miles away. The collapse of PSInet, then, by no means sounded a death knell for distributed network functions. Rather, it marked a moment in which the everyday experiences of these business network functions became all the more invisible. Spaces of control serve as corporate models for managing distributed networks of employees, such that "access" now defines an apparatus of capture in the workplace, not individual empowerment. Increasingly, the "digital divide" describes a dynamic rather than a static condition—not a line between the "haves" and "have nots" but an operational measure of one's valence within a network of flows. Distributed networks demand distributed control, such that one's location within a material matrix of human-computer interaction provides the conditions of possibility for *employment*, in the broadest sense of the term.

As such, it is not the ephemerality of this enactive network that presents a threat to the dominant forms and structures of social space, but a *lack of control*. As Deleuze notes in his essay on "societies of control," in a world of flows, "capture" occurs as a *modulation*, not as an enclosure ("Postscript on the Societies of Control" 4). The ability to articulate corporate work relations through a network of immaterial flows does not make the realities of corporate outsourcing any less real; rather, it suggests a relation between the actual and the virtual that is articulated through an interface disposition of keystroke control. In the same way, the suggestion that the network had somehow lost its economic significance after the crash of 2000 merely misrecognizes the centrality of the network to social, cultural, and economic practices that made the crash the economic disruption that it was. Modulation, then, speaks to a system of distributed control that is itself expressed in flows. And it is precisely this structure of modulated flows that survived the dot-com collapse, articulated through the dispositional practices that situate users in spaces of control while at the same time allowing for a casualized and operationalized relation to that same network. As long as telecommuting appeared as a liberation of the white-collar worker from the corporate cubicle, the network appeared as a space of possessive individualism and cyber-libertarianism. Yet it is these same systems of distributed control that allow for an increase in outsourcing of IT, technical, and customer-support positions, in which the spatial relations of the network define the terms and parameters for corporate *flow charts*. In the rearticulation of the corporate subject-position through network relations, it becomes increasingly clear that one can only gain access to networked spaces of control by submitting oneself to the ephemeral modulations of a space of flows.

So while "virtual reality" has lost its cultural cachet (only seventy articles mentioning "cyberspace" appeared in the *New York Times* in 2004, compared with 410 in 1999), the virtualities of the network very much define and delimit the conditions of possibility for everyday life in a network society. The degree to which network dispositions are misrecognized as forms of social capital suggests the degree to which the rhythms and patterns of lived practice are implicated in the production of networked social space. While chat rooms have not taken over as the coffeehouses of a wired generation, one finds more and more that the coffee shops in local neighborhoods in U.S. urban centers now provide some form of wireless or wired Internet connection, and, internationally, the number of Internet cafés is directly proportional to the population of tourists, students, refugees, and immigrants who find themselves caught up in global flows. The global and the local find themselves increasingly co-situated in irruptive relations, as are the public and the private: neither evacuated of meaning, nor returned to the stabilizing oppositions of modernity. Likewise, while corporations are interested once again in price-earnings (P/E) ratios and production, the emphasis on marketing to and through spaces of flows suggests a more fundamental change has already taken place. Although an era of delirious investment has ended, and, along with it, the euphoric predictions of a radically altered economy, the economy has in fact already been restructured by flows, and everyday life has already integrated the dispositional practices that situate individuals in relation to these flows. As billions of dollars of capital evaporated, the very digital nature of the economy was confirmed—that capital could increase tenfold[4] or disappear entirely through the stroke of a key. The crash, then, did not necessarily indicate a system failure, in the way that the "Black Monday" crash required the development of systems interventions to curtail automated trades. Rather, it marked a moment of increased misrecognition of the forms, structures, and practices that were the conditions of possibility for the event itself, as an ideology of authentication eclipsed a rhetoric of emergence and flow. Billions in capital disappeared in a matter of weeks, but the network forms and structures that allowed individual users "direct access" to the flows of capital remained in place for a normative virtual class, articulated as personalized and privatized spaces of control. The very "failure" of the economy spoke to its success as an articulation of a space of flows.

Certainly much more can be said about the impact of globalizing networks on the distribution of human resources via contract outsourcing. What is worth noting here, in short, is simply that many accounts of the post-bubble economic restructuring overlook the ways in which representations of space remain notably *unchanged* in the degree to which distributed networks define business processes. What has changed is the degree to which spaces of distributed control have emerged, and emerged in loci that function primarily as apparatuses of capture. While distributed networks articulate spaces of flows, authority finds its expression in *authentication protocols* that delimit who has access to or control over situated articulations of the network. The virtual topographies of distributed business processes continue to exist, but the virtualities of noise, dissemination, and drift are all the more modulated within spaces of distributed control.

Distributed Terror

The vast majority of individuals worldwide experienced 9/11 as a mediated event, watching the towers collapse on television, expressing a collective horror by declaring it "just like a movie" (as a number of my students—and countless others—would claim) as a way of handling the scale of the catastrophe. But for the individuals caught up in the event itself—what even Baudrillard has called "the absolute event, the 'mother' of all events"—distributed networks mediated the lived horror of this event in a singular form (Baudrillard, *The Spirit of Terrorism* 4). In the hours following the attacks on the World Trade Center and the Pentagon, the television began to carry reports of the cell-phone calls that came directly from the towers after the impacts of the two planes. Networks did not merely distribute news of the event as it was taking place; rather, the place of the event itself was distributed to friends and loved ones in real-time communication. The *place* of CMC during the events in Tiananmen Square (occurring at a moment when the Internet had just entered the popular imagination) provides a notable point of contrast. Throughout the student protests, the computer network figured as a representation of space that *bridged* distance, overcoming state-based apparatuses of censorship: a mode of transmission from a remote location to a wider world. The lists and bulletin-board services that allowed individuals to report on the events "on the ground" provided a service not unlike the traditional newswire, in which student protestors and engaged onlookers filed communiqués to a world beyond the site of conflict. But on the morning of 9/11, a different order of networking occurred during the time period between the impact on the towers (or the hijacking of Flight 93) and the catastrophic collapse. Individuals made connections to family and friends via mobile communication networks in ways that allowed the personal and the intimate to irrupt within an event of global, political consequence. While not to blur the line between the practices of cell-phone use and the practices of CMC, it is relevant here to note the degree to which everyday life, even in the midst of the extraordinary and the catastrophic, involves itself in network processes that have altered the topographies of public and private, global and local. Four days after the 9/11 attacks, Ian McEwan commented in the *Guardian:* "The mobile phone has inserted itself into every crevice of our daily lives. Now, in catastrophe, if there is time enough, it is there in our dying moments." For McEwan, these expressions of love made over cell phones provide a narrative of the personal and the emotional that ruptures the narratives of antiglobalism, anti-imperialism, and fundamentalism expressed in terrorism. As a mapping of social space, I would argue, it also speaks to the manner in which the network itself has become the terrain in which all scales of life find their expression.

As material form, representation of space, and space of dispositional practice, the World Trade Center was very much caught up in articulations of "the global" as a network of flows, expressed in economic, political, and cultural terms. While attempting to disrupt this network society, the attack on the Twin Towers could only have taken place within the conditions of possibility articulated by a global space of flows. Given my own critical trajectory over the last ten years, perhaps it is only fitting to turn briefly to Baudrillard's comments on this relation between terrorism and globalization. In *The Spirit of Terrorism,* he writes:

> There is, indeed, a fundamental antagonism here, but one which points past the spectre of America (which is, perhaps, the epicentre, but in no sense the sole embodiment, of globalization) and the spectre of Islam (which is not the embodiment of terrorism either), to *triumphant globalization battling against itself.* (11)

As Baudrillard notes, globalization provides the conditions of possibility for terrorist attacks, but in a manner that refuses to reduce to a binary opposition. Rather, terrorism appears within Baudrillard's critical framework as globalization's ironic revenge. For Baudrillard, terrorism can occupy a "symbolic sphere" precisely because it does not oppose globalization but, rather, appropriates all the trappings of a global space of flows in the name of subverting that social structure (*The Spirit of Terrorism* 17–19). He writes: "it is the combination of two mechanisms—an operational structure and a symbolic pact ['unto death'] that made an act of such excessiveness possible" (22). Thus, the "realness" of the event becomes a measure of the attacks themselves as structured by these very processes of globalization, not by its annihilation. The virtuality that allowed for the attacks, in other words, exists within the virtuality of networked social space.

As with the bubble burst, the catastrophic event of the Twin Towers collapse signals an *ending* (an end of irony, an end of the virtual) that in many ways marks a moment of increased misrecognition of the forms, structures, and practices that were the conditions of possibility for the event itself. The 9/11 attacks and the subsequent "war on terror" initiated by the United States mark both a restructuring of social space and an affirmation of the networked nature of contemporary life. As Baudrillard suggests, the shift in cultural attention from the virtual referent of simulacra to the symbolic referent of ground zero suggests a shift in rhetoric away from "virtual reality" to the realness of lived space.[5] While the Internet suggested the dangers of distributed networks in the form of identity theft, predatory masquerading, and allusive viruses, worms, and hacks, terrorist networks represented a "return of the real," as the American media made the connection between the action of distributed, autonomous cells and the coordinated attacks on the symbolic center of a global economy. Thus, an "end of irony" and the "postmodern" was declared at the moment at which the dominance of a postmodern networked social space was perhaps most clear. Shortly after the attacks, the columnists and commentators began to appear on the news programs and call-in shows, discussing the altered nature of terrorism in the twenty-first century, defined now as a distributed network. As Laura Trippi noted on her Netvironments weblog within days after the attacks, the popular press was quick to exhibit a "sudden ramping up of distributed systems and heightening awareness of them following the September 11 events." The enemy, it seemed, was not some reclusive *organization*, but, rather, the spatiality of the network itself, enacted by distributed, autonomous agents. In an article by Joel Garreau that appeared in the *Washington Post*[6] on September 17, Garreau asks, "In the Information Age . . . how do you attack, degrade, or destroy a small, shadowy, globally distributed, stateless network of intensely loyal partisans with few fixed assets or addresses?" Garreau and other cultural theorists were quick to note that the Internet—after a decade of cyberspace—provided a resonant model for a shift that had occurred in contemporary political and social forms, one that allowed for a "shadowy, globally distributed" form of agency to actualize in political, social, and economic arenas.

While, in the years leading up to the market collapse of March 2000, a growing number of an emerging virtual middle class (from cyberhippy to daytrader manqué) began to understand distributed networks as material expressions of a social revolution, the image of a distributed network changed after 9/11, becoming a global spatiality of fear and danger. As independent scholar Sam Smith notes in his weblog:

> I expect the organizing principle of the coming age—the era that began on September 12 . . . —will be the *distributed network,* and we already have some early indications of what this period might look like. The decentralized potency of the Internet is a perfect metaphor in so many ways, and *al Qaeda* itself provides an apt demonstration of the character and power of the distributed network. . . . As our ill-prepared military has discovered, it's hard to kill something you can't find. Thank goodness for the Taliban, eh?[7]

Although figured as an antimodern fundamentalism, the terrorist networks associated with 9/11 served as an image of contemporary network structures themselves. While, in the 1990s, critics of "virtual reality" blamed CMC for producing simulacrum worlds that threatened to replace the real world of politics and social relations, 9/11 revealed the degree to which the political and the social have taken on the forms, structures, and practices of the network, enacted as a very real attack on a steel-and-mortar world. Carl Conetta, writing on the nature of al-Qaeda as a distributed network, notes in particular the organization's ability to "[link] subnational elements together in a transnational web," to thrive in nation-states that have collapsed or are about to collapse, and to operate "in the interstices" of modern global space. If governments and transnational corporations are capable of exploiting spaces of flows, distributed networks of terror provide a measure of abject (t)error within these global spaces of control, error that appropriates the social forms and structures that it threatens to destroy.[8] Whereas al-Qaeda proclaimed an antimodern fundamentalism, its terror operates in an interstitial space of hypermodern distributed networks.

While it is not the intent of this short afterword to address the complicated issues of U.S. global political positioning prior to and following the events of 9/11, it is relevant to note the degree to which the "war on terror" has attempted to introduce modes of control into distributed networks and to place them at the fingertips of state-based agencies. In effect, much as business practices have developed modes of distributed control to modulate the dissipative processes of a space of flows, the government's response to the threat of distributed terror has been to accelerate its attempts to capture network flows of information, people, and capital within the forms and structures of the state. In an era of global flows, the U.S. government reestablished *the homeland* as both a concept of social space and a delimited space of practice. The Patriot Act declared war on the dispersive and dissipative nature of distributed networks by introducing state-based apparatuses of capture. But rather than "shutting down" global network structures, the Patriot Act acknowledges networks themselves as modes of agency (noted in its frequent reference to an "intelligence service or network of a foreign power"), and, as such, it institutes a legislative structure to "trap and trace" emergent network structures. In effect, the Patriot Act marks a modulation of networked social space that affirms the primacy of global flows in contemporary life at the same time that it initiates state-based systems of distributed control.

Apparatuses of capture modulate flows by eliminating the interstitial and *regulating* transmission as a mode of order. The "homeland security" measures, then, are precisely this sort of effort to modulate the forms, structures, and practices of a space of flows. As the U.S. military force mounted, one heard less and less talk of the distributed-network form of terror, as an uncontrollable threat coalesced in the modulated image of a handful of figureheads: a "line up," in its most literal sense, connecting bin Laden, Zakawi, and Hussein. The infamous "Most Wanted" card deck shifted our imagination from the shuffling networks of global terror to a linear ranking of Ba'ath Party players—a chain of command in a "rogue nation," from ace of spades to the two of clubs. The topology of fear had changed. Within months, the U.S. government's rhetoric swayed our attention from terrorist networks to an "Axis of Evil." Gone were the references to the complex webbings of distributed systems, and in its place were found the reassuringly linear, gravitational orientations of good and evil. The "axis" not only revived the relatively clear lines of geopolitics of the Second World War; it also attempted to reestablish a representation of space predicated upon unidirectional movements and centralized control.

Meanwhile, back in the homeland, DARPA's[9] Total Information Awareness (TIA) Program (renamed the Terrorist Information Awareness Program, for better public relations) promised a means of capturing flows of information through distributed control over the network. Whereas terrorist organizations exploit the interstitial spaces of a global network society, TIA as a state-based apparatus of capture promised to utilize these same networks to modulate a space of flows and extract orderly patterns of information. "In short, DoD's aim in TIA is to seek to make a significant leap in technology to help those working to 'connect the dots' of terrorist-related activity" (Defense Advanced Research Projects Agency, Executive Summary 1).[10] The agent of the state doesn't necessarily control the flow of these networks but, rather, extracts mappings of emergent connections enacted by the network itself. Patterns of informatic exchange and transmission, then, provide distributed control over a network environment that can be defined only by virtualities and flows.

In contrast to the data mining that has become common practice in a commercial setting—in which patterns of aggregate data give rise to "meaningful" market analysis—distributed control systems focus on "rare but significant connections" mapped by the relational structures of a situated subject (Defense Advanced Research Projects Agency A14). Spaces of control are repositioned such that the network itself provides the emergent ordering, not the agent at the keyboard. In fact, such systems capture much of what has been foregrounded as the network's challenge to the autonomy, homogeneity, and singularity of the modern subject, modulating a subjectivity of flows into an emergent "subject profile." For example, TIA's Evidence Extraction and Link Discovery (EELD) program, which aimed to "automatically extract evidence about relationships among people, organizations, places, and things from unstructured textual data," explicitly understands *individuals* in relational terms, a virtuality of data transactions in networked social space that can be actualized only through emergent, relational patterns (Defense Advanced Research Projects Agency 7). The distributed network remains a potent articulation of global flows of information, but through systems of distributed control, enactive networks now increasingly speak to a social space in which the interpellations of a subject-position are formulated through one's relation to patterns of information. *Lines of contact* emerge as pattern recognition allows authorized agents to "connect the dots" (a favored expression throughout DARPA's report to Congress) within an undifferentiated network of data flow. Distributed control creates a means for modulating what would otherwise appear as abject noise or aberrant links; the very fact that terrorist networks are represented as abject, interstitial social formations (and vice versa) becomes the condition of possibility for their recognition and capture.

Less than two years after the Patriot Act was signed into law, DARPA lost Congressional funding for TIA, in part over fears of the potential for abuse of such a large body of data by governmental agencies.[11] Again, it was the potential for success that induced our visions of digital catastrophe—that such a large body of data subjected to distributed control presented the potential for the network's ironic revenge. Yet while TIA (as a domestic program, at least) has ceased to exist, in many ways the modes of distributed control enacted by networks of pattern recognition are already matters of everyday life, misrecognized as "conveniences" in a network society. While spam filters and software agents hardly equate with the sophistication of TIA programs, the goal of each is the same—to modulate flows and to cast off or capture the interstitial within programs of order. We willingly, and often unwittingly, submit ourselves to systems of distributed control that "connect the dots" of legitimacy, relevancy, and authenticity. But rather than dispersing the subject-position in a space of flows, our self-enacted distributed controls increasingly reify normative constellations that define identity as a "profile" that queries for and responds to specific fields of information. While information may want to be free, the forms, structures, and practices of everyday life reveal the degree to which a normative virtual class exerts a *will to control*, and an ironic willingness to distribute that control to the network itself.

In a world in which spaces of flows shape both state structures of power and the attempts to destroy those same structures, distributed controls are all the more implicated in everyday life, and all the more misrecognized as such by a citizenry terrified by terrorist networks and placated by lines in the sand.

Misrecognizing Everydayness

When I first began writing on the social and cultural implications of CMC, there were just under 3 million servers making up the Internet. At the time, it seemed like a phenomenal number, given that a decade earlier there had been fewer than 1,000 hosts. As I write these sentences, a decade after my first article, the number of hosts has reached over 300 million. In fact, at present there are twice as many "mistake" servers listed on the Internet Systems Consortium (ISC) host count as there were total number of hosts online in 1994.[12] The worldwide distribution of servers still reflects a dominance of the original G7 countries, but, at the same time, mappings at a global level increasingly suggest that being "wired" is as much a condition of domination as of dominance (while the United States still ranks first in host count, Brazil and Mexico now both rank in the top twenty). Certainly, much has changed in what we might, still somewhat tentatively, call a network society. Whereas "cyberspace" as a term of reference has lost much of its cultural capital, it still has a place in popular speech, to describe the forms, structures, and practices of networked social space. The Cyberspace Decade may have come to a close, and, along with it, many of the anxious visions of simulacrum worlds and a death of "real space"; however, the spaces of everyday life are still articulated as spaces of flow, and "the network"—as concept, material form, and lived practice—still defines and delimits the dominant processes in the production of social space.

As contemporary life post-bubble and post-9/11 unfold, the pace and texture of daily life have undoubtedly been altered. A range of technologies has become matters of everyday life that increasingly place networks at the fore of daily practice. As an attempt to theorize the spatiality of CMC, I have in part attempted to call attention to what had either been ablated in the hyperbole in the 1990s, or what has become all the more obscured behind the veneer of banality that takes for granted the network processes that underpin everyday life. Spam, in other words, is discussed in Congress as a violation of privacy and a trespass on network efficiency, but it is not recognized as a mapping of shifting virtualities, in which social contact is increasingly irruptive and ephemeral. Web sites such as Meetup.com or MoveOn.org are heralded as new arenas of civic space, without really exploring the ways in which it is not the Web sites themselves that situate civic discourse, but a network of flows, as enacted by individual users. The challenge of a critical spatial analysis, then, is not only to provide a depiction of the processes that give rise to the production of social space, but to do so in a way that reveals the ways in which the very everydayness of these processes keeps them from being recognized.

It has been my purpose throughout this book to call attention to the ways in which spatial relations have been restructured by network technology. The attempt to understand the Internet in terms of cyberspace forces us to reconsider not only how we understand space but how we understand the relationship between material processes, conceptual structures, and lived practice. To some degree, the less noticeable "cyberspace" is in the media, the more it has become a matter of everyday life. The public and the private as concept, form, and experience maintain a place in contemporary life, but in a dynamic engagement that is specifically enactive and irruptive, suggesting the potential for novel social arrangements. In a similar fashion, the restructuring of the global and the local by way of CMC suggests a radical potential for understanding how situated, local existence materializes and enacts global structures, and, vice versa, by way of networks and flows. Most important, these processes are not merely theoretical abstractions, but are quite literally lived out in the embodied experience of users, who enact, through dispositional practices, the forms and structures of everyday life.

Toward the end of his essay "Everyday (Virtual) Life," Mark Poster writes:

> The everyday life emerging in information society is a battleground over the nature of human identity. If the old order has its way, identities will be stabilized and information machines will become as invisible as they will be ubiquitous. But if alternatives are developed, a global space of cyborgs may emerge whose life task becomes precisely the exploration of identity, the discovery of genders, ethnicities, sexual identities, and personality types that may be enjoyed, experienced, but also transgressed. (758–59)

Along a similar line of argument, I would claim that spatiality, as with identity, marks a critical domain within network society. Critical interventions such as this current book allow for greater attention to the material, conceptual, and lived processes that take part in the production of network social space. Misrecognized as mere technical concerns, or abstracted out of everyday life entirely, the network dissolves into the unseen fabric of the contemporary. But a spatial analysis of the network, and particularly one that attempts to analyze the spaces of everyday life, allows us to become increasingly aware of the dominant forms, structures, and practices of social space, and the openings that exist for altered social formations.

NOTES

Introduction

1. According to the Internet Systems Consortium's July 2004 domain survey, there were over 285 million host sites making up the Internet. While the material growth of networked domains has slowed since 2000, there was a steady increase by about 40 million hosts each year for four years. That rate of growth has recently increased. The January 2006 domain survey reports nearly 395 million host sites.

2. By the end of 1998, Internet stocks were the hottest investment in a volatile stock year. According to the NASDAQ report on January 1, 1999, sector leaders such as the Web portal company Yahoo and the Internet venture capital group CMGI closed out the year 800 percent above their fifty-two week lows. In addition, more than 10 percent of all initial public offerings in 1998 were Internet companies—greater than 25 percent in the last quarter alone. See "Lift from Internet." Although by March 2000 the delirious investment in dot-com companies came to an abrupt end in what would amount to a multibillion dollar evaporation of capital, Internet stocks throughout 1999 increased at unbelievable rates. The ongoing success of those companies that managed to survive the "bubble burst," most notably Amazon.com and eBay, speaks less to the revolutionary arrival of a "new economy" than to an integration of everyday consumer functions into the forms and structures of global networks.

3. Note that in popular representations of home computers (as opposed to govern-

ment and corporate "supercomputers"), processing speed is most often associated with a computer's ability to send or to receive information, not to perform complex operations. In *Life on the Screen,* Sherry Turkle describes this change as a fundamental shift in our relation to computers, from "modern" machines, used as number-crunching tools, to "postmodern" media that simulate environments of communication and interaction (18–21).

4. See Tom Standage's *The Victorian Internet* for more on the parallels between the telegraph and the Internet. Also see James Carey, *Communication as Culture,* especially "Technology and Ideology," 201–30.

5. For a more complete history of interface design and the impact of Engelbart's work of CMC, see Steven Johnson's *Interface Culture* (11–41). See also Jean Trumbo, "Describing Multimedia."

6. As might be expected, estimates for "Internet population" range considerably. Matthew Zook, in "Geography of Internet Users," sets the 2004 population at 843 million. Computer Industry Almanac estimates 1.08 billion users for 2005. See also ClickZ Stats, "Population Explosion!"

7. In my recollection, the first significant instance of mass media commercial use of a Web address came in 1995, when Universal Pictures ran a full-page advertisement for its science fiction film *12 Monkeys* in the Sunday *New York Times,* featuring nothing more than a large graphical image (an icon in its broadest sense) and a Web address.

8. As Marie-Laure Ryan notes in "Immersion vs. Interactivity: Virtual Reality and Literary Theory," immersion and interaction serve as two measures of what gives virtual reality (in various forms) its "reality effect": one feels a *world* around oneself, a world in which the user *takes part.*

9. In May 2001, CNN cancelled "The Spin Room," a political debate show that incorporated viewer's email and chat-room comments into the on-air discussion. In fact, by 2001, CNN had already cut back significantly on its CMC-based interactive features, such as chat rooms and message boards. For the most part, viewers can now just email comments to specific shows: the digital equivalent of "calling in." For more discussion on the implications of this restructuring of CNN, see chapter 2, "Virtual Worlds and Situated Spaces."

10. The term "network society" occurs in a range of writing on the impact of network technology on social, political, and cultural forms, most notably in Manuel Castells's *The Rise of the Network Society.* In speaking of a network society, I am drawing attention to the ways in which "the network" now serves as a dominant material form, conceptual structure, and dispositional orientation for a growing number of individuals in the developed world. In fact, one might go as far as to say that it now makes more sense to speak of the networked and unnetworked world, as opposed to the developed and the developing world.

11. Mark Poster engages in a similar autoethnographic method is his own attempt to discuss Henri Lefebvre's concept of the "everyday" within the everyday experiences of media ("Everyday (Virtual) Life").

12. Although Baudrillard first uses the term "hyperreal" in 1976 in *Symbolic Exchange and Death,* even his 1968 *The System of Objects* shows traces of this idea in a protean form. In his first book, Baudrillard calls attention to a slippage in the relation between subject and object in contemporary society. The object, once invested with a portion of the imaginary, now only exists as part of a functional system, a system of signs. As

the object becomes a sign, anything that does not signify falls away. The result is a system of objects organized as a cybernetic system and defined by operationality. He elaborates on this theme in *Symbolic Exchange and Death* through a discussion of a "metaphysics of the code" that places the object itself secondary to its operational definition—from DNA to digital bits. The hyperreal serves as his term for this moment when "the real" presents itself as entirely and completely operationalized in the form of a "more real than real" model and code.

13. This concept of "ironic revenge" presents itself in varying forms throughout Baudrillard's writing, from his early interest in the anagrams of Saussure, up through his most recent fascination with cloning.

14. Prior to the translation of *The Production of Space*, only a handful of Lefebvre's books had been translated into English, most notably *Critique of Everyday Life*. Much of Lefebvre's spatial analysis made it to an English-speaking audience in the 1980s through the critical geography of David Harvey and Edward Soja, culminating in works such as Harvey's *The Condition of Postmodernity* and Soja's *Postmodern Geographies*.

15. Einstein's introduction of a space-time continuum marks a rupture in this tradition, suggesting in its place a more relational, relativistic, and dynamic understanding of space. See Max Jammer's *Concepts of Space* for an overview of Einstein's impact on twentieth-century scientific understandings of space.

16. One can identify a similar project at work in the early writings of the Situationist International (SI), but in a more radicalized form. As with Lefebvre's own call for a "new urbanism," the SI called into high relief a dialectic triad of conceptual/semiotic processes, material processes, and the experience of everyday life. With the "psychogeography" of Debord and others in the SI, we see a double-mapping of the conceptual and the material by way of everyday experience. Likewise, the wandering (often drunken) experiments of the *dérive* attempt to dis-arrange the city so as to produce other material, conceptual, and experiential mappings of space. As Simon Sadler ably describes in *The Situationist City*, the relation between the spatial analysis of Lefebvre and the spatial experiments of the SI hinges on this emphasis on the embodied spaces of the city at the intersection of concept and materiality; their division had less to do with an understanding of space than in their understandings of praxis and revolutionary fervor (44–47).

1. The Problem of Cyberspace

1. In spring 2004, as I was working on a final revision of this chapter, I invited Deborah Barndt to my college to give a lecture on globalization and its local articulations, both in the tomato fields of Mexico and in the supermarkets and fast food chains of Canada and the United States. Her book *Tangled Routes: Women, Work, and Globalization on the Tomato Trail* opens with a "seemingly simple question. . . . [that] raises many other questions," namely, "Where does our food come from?" (1). Inspired by her ability to ground complex matters of theory in the most everyday contexts, both in print and in the lecture hall, it struck me that my own project stemmed from a similar simple question that raised a range of questions.

2. In fact, the city of Wilmington, Delaware, did declare the '90s the ".com decade," or, in the words of Paul Levinson of Fordham University, "the information decade. . . . It's only been in the '90s that we've paid

attention to information as a commodity" (quoted in Vejnoska).

3. See Gretchen Barbatsis's visual field analysis of the "sensory world" of hypermedia, "Hypermediated Telepresence."

4. For popular film depictions of this violation, consider the characters of Mike Teavee in *Willie Wonka and the Chocolate Factory,* Chauncey Gardner in *Being There,* and the eponymous *Cable Guy.*

5. Michael Ostwald has made a similar argument about the evolution of spatial metaphors for the computer screen in the late 1980s and early 1990s: from a door/window onto a potentially dangerous otherworld to a mall-like networked community hub and virtual urban center. See his essay "Virtual Urban Futures."

6. In *The Ecstasy of Communication,* Jean Baudrillard discusses how communications technologies "implode" real space by creating a "hyperpotential point. . . . Where all trips have already taken place; where the vaguest desire for dispersion, evasion and movement are concentrated in a fixed point, in an immobility that has ceased to be one of non-movement and has become that of a potential ubiquity, of an absolute mobility, which voids its own space by crossing it ceaselessly and without effort" (39).

7. For example, Paul Virilio has argued that telecommunication not only allows users to "inhabit" a metaphorical space, in which the computer becomes the "last vehicle" that threatens to resolve all geographical concerns into a media interface; it in turn treats geographic space as equally metaphorical ("The Last Vehicle"). According to Virilio, the speed of telegraphy, along with the accelerating media that follow it, allows for the emergence of a "teletopology" in place of the world (*The Vision Machine* 63–64). Here is always here and now; real-

time replaces real space. In a similar line of argument, Baudrillard (following Barthes) notes how easily automobiles can transform motion into a visual experience in which the driver/viewer interacts with images, rather than with the physical world (*The Ecstasy of Communication* 13). Unlike this metaphorical transformation of the physical world into images "on" a windshield, cyberspace blurs the real and the metaphorical as it becomes its own simulation of "beyond the screen." The real no longer serves as a referent for this postmodern version of Alberti's Window, in which a logic of the simulacrum serves as the screen's only reality principle.

8. For example, much of George Lakoff and Mark Johnson's work on "spatial relation concepts" suggests that metaphors based on a spatiality of volume (containers) or path (conduits) not only make complex concepts manageable, they structure and limit how we think about, talk about, and make use of complexes of everyday life. See Lakoff and Johnson's *Philosophy in the Flesh.* These spatial metaphors have a real impact on everyday life by creating inferences and expectations in (and about) the user involved in HCI, even if they do not denote spatiality per se. See Raymond Gozzi, "The Cyberspace Metaphor," along with Jean Trumbo, "Describing Multimedia," for an elaboration on the impact of metaphor on user expectations of the medium.

9. Raymond Williams uses the term "mobile privatization" to describe the bubble-like existence increasingly common in developed nations, an alienation experienced equally behind the wheel and in front of the television screen (*Television*).

10. In his review of the literature on cyberspace, Lance Strate constructs a taxonomy in which he identifies three levels of discussion of cyberspace: "zero order cyber-

space," in which ontological considerations are foregrounded; "first order cyberspace," which addresses the physical, conceptual, and perceptual "elements" of cyberspace; and a "second order cyberspace," which synthesizes those elements. He argues that first-order conceptual cyberspace creates a metaphorical space that in turn shapes human interactions and experiences of the medium. For all its emphasis on the multiplicities of cyberspaces, Strate's taxonomy threatens to collapse to a conceptually generated space that stands in an interface relation to the physical structurings of CMC and HCI. Thus he notes that metaphor (and thus conceptual space) shapes the physical space that provides the interface for perceptual space. It also provides the conceptual structure that provides cyberspace with a leg-up beyond zero-order ontological concerns and a foundation for second-order syntheses. See Strate's "The Varieties of Cyberspace."

11. For another reading on "conduits" of communication, see also Hillis, 60–89.

12. See also Poster, "The Being of Technologies," in *What's the Matter with the Internet?* 21–38, for a more general discussion of Western, metaphysical anxieties over technologies of presence.

13. Certainly there are also aspects of electronic writing that challenge and subvert this history of logocentrism and its metaphysics of presence, to which I will return later, especially in chapter 3. Mark Poster has written a number of pieces on the impact of digital writing on the construction of the subject-position and author-function in contemporary society. See, in particular, Poster, "The Digital Subject and Cultural Theory," in *What's the Matter with the Internet?* 60–77.

14. According to Poster in *The Mode of Information*, first-time computer users often will claim that "writing is now very much like speaking" (111). Perhaps, for this reason, email allows spelling errors and grammatical mistakes to a degree that parallels spoken communication rather than written correspondence. One could make a similar argument to explain why email tends toward short, informal statements rather than long treatises. As a written form of discourse, one might expect to find on discussion lists and other email "forums" long, developed arguments. While such epistles do exist, they are far outnumbered by shorter off-the-cuff comments. Likewise, a long, involved communiqué is likely to be met with a quick response, or a silent "delete."

15. As noted in Peter Steiner's oft-cited *New Yorker* cartoon: "On the Internet, nobody knows you're a dog."

16. Barlow, along with Howard Rheingold, was perhaps one of the most utopian (and ubiquitous) advocates for a "new world" vision of cyberspace in the 1990s. Typical of his idealist—in every sense—rhetoric, Barlow's 1994 manifesto from the Electronic Freedom Foundation archive, titled "Jack In, Young Pioneer!" declares cyberspace a realm apart from physical space: "unmappable, infinitely expansible cerebral space. Cyberspace. And we are going there whether we want to or not."

17. As McLuhan himself notes, his vision of an electronic globe presents a version of Teilhard de Chardin's noosphere, an evolutionary advance in human society that places us *above and beyond* the materiality of geography (*The Gutenberg Galaxy*). Within a decade after McLuhan's *The Gutenberg Galaxy*, it was more than apparent that sitcoms and the nightly news had not brought about the global village, and the changed world of electronic communication appeared closer to Paddy Chayefsky's *Network* than McLuhan's

"cosmic membrane" (*The Gutenberg Galaxy* 32). With the popular emergence of the Internet, however, this vision began to recirculate. CMC, by networking the world, held utopian promise, specifically to the extent that these emerging virtual communities took place in a space distinct from real space.

18. Rheingold, perhaps the most vocal advocate of virtual communities, became synonymous with the hopes and dreams of cyberspace in the 1990s. In his own version of the transcendent geography of cyberspace, Rheingold describes virtual communities as modern agorae, offering the possibility of becoming "informal public places where people can rebuild the aspects of community that were lost when the malt shop became a mall" (26).

19. Central to Pierre Lévy's discussion of "knowledge space" in *Collective Intelligence* is an analogy between cyberspace and the angelic realms of Jewish mysticism, in which virtual subjects ("angelic bodies") carry and receive messages that provide "dynamic descriptions of *the world below*, moving images of the events and situations into which human communities are plunged" (98, italics added). Lévy provides a more nuanced understanding of a relation between a knowledge space and a space of social processes, but even this description of a "virtual world [that] is no more than a substrate for cognitive, social, and affective processes that take place among actual individuals" tends to divide off a mental cyberspace from a material "world below" (112).

20. One of the earliest attempts to describe the fluid virtuality of cyberspace occurs in Marcos Novak's contribution to the Cyberspace Conference, in which he describes the "liquid architecture" of cyberspace as "poetry inhabited" ("Liquid Architectures in Cyberspace" 229). For Novak, the status of cyberspace as "a world of our creation" provides an opportunity to challenge the assumptions of "the real" in everyday life ("Liquid Architectures in Cyberspace" 243).

21. Sherry Turkle's influential book *Life on the Screen* makes a similar point about the construction of the self and its relation to "the real" and "the imaginary." While cyberspace is an imaginary space that allows for role-playing and multiple selves, so too is the mental space in which we construct our "real" identities, mediated by a wide array of social and material structures.

22. In his essay "Community and Identity in the Electronic Village," Derek Foster develops this line of argument with specific reference to Benedict Anderson. Certainly imagined communities exist online as well as "offline" in the mediated experiences of everyday life; what differentiates the two is the grounding that structures the form in which community relations take place. Foster argues that online, community is communication, thus grounded in symbolic exchange, not materiality.

23. For an excellent overview of how cyberspace gives place to the fantasy of Western metaphysics (*finally* thought is free of the flesh), see Robert Markley, "Introduction."

24. For an alternate reading of "pure" communication channels as Neoplatonic conduits of "light," see Hillis, 137–50.

25. In the issuing of an utterance, Austin identifies a locutionary act: the uttering of *meaningful* words. But in addition to conveying meaning, the successful performance of a speech act also involves a conventional effect within and upon a given speech situation—what Austin terms the "illocutionary" act. The illocution has a force to it: a measure of how a statement is to be taken, given the speech situation. Not directly connected with the semantics of a statement, the force

measures its (pragmatic) significance within a given context or situation. See Austin, *How to Do Things with Words*.

26. Austin makes a point of separating this sort of infelicity from an abuse, in which the performative does in fact occur but without the party's intent to follow through on the act (*How to Do Things with Words* 15). This distinction between misfires and abuses is important for Austin because it allows him to characterize more explicitly the performative not on internal conditions of truthfulness, but on the successful performance of specific conventional speech acts within a conventional speech situation.

27. As Jonathan Culler notes in "Convention and Meaning: Derrida and Austin": "What the indissociability of performative and performance puts in question is not the determination of illocutionary force by context but the possibility of mastering the domain of speech acts by exhaustively specifying the contextual determinants of illocutionary force" (24). This point also frames the debate between Searle and Derrida over speech act theory. See: Derrida, "Limited Inc."; Derrida, "Signature Event Context"; and Searle, "Reiterating the Differences."

28. For Deleuze and Guattari, performatives call attention to the structuring quality of speech acts: their role in marking power within a given context. While they make explicit mention of "performatives" early in *A Thousand Plateaus*, they quickly rename these utterances "order-words" to emphasize the role of performatives in shaping social relations and social contexts. While order-words constrain social relations, Deleuze and Guattari identify within this power a potential for mutability within social orders. In their rendering of the performative as a site marking both virtual and actual "assemblages of bodies," Deleuze and Guattari also

transform Austin's performative speech act theory into a theory of social relations.

29. For further clarification of Deleuze and Guattari's discussion of performatives and incorporeal transformation, see "November 20, 1923—Postulates of Linguistics" in Deleuze and Guattari, 75–110. See also Massumi, "Force," in *A User's Guide to Capitalism and Schizophrenia*, 10–46.

30. For this reason, Deleuze and Guattari focus on the second axis of discipline/indiscipline as a means of exploring the political ramifications of order-words. Social orderings depend upon a "major" language, one that would recognize the conventional illocutionary force of an utterance. But Deleuze and Guattari also recognize the existence of "minor" languages that make the major language "stammer" (98). The major territorializes by determining and regulating expression; in contrast, the deterritorializing effects of the minor "send the major language racing" by deregulating the constants of the order-words (105).

31. Deleuze and Guattari specifically use mapping in this context to distinguish between tracing (a repetition of the same) and a creative, experimental process of calling into actuality from the virtual possibles (12–15).

32. For further discussion of this aspect of cyberspace, see Nunes, "Virtual Topographies."

33. Topographies do not merely name a space; they simultaneously create and reveal a relation between metaphor and metonym. In *Topographies*, J. Hillis Miller notes: "'Topography' originally meant the creation of a metaphorical equivalent in words of a landscape. Then, by another transfer, it came to mean representation of a landscape according to the conventional signs of some system of mapping. Finally, by a third transfer,

the name of the map was carried over to name what is mapped" (3). This blurring of metaphor and metonym describes the current process by which "cyberspace" comes into being.

34. Lefebvre identifies the modernist "model of the ideal city" as an agora of circulations that places human relations into a system of "traffic" rather than encounter (*Writings on Cities* 97–98). The ideology of planning "claim[s] that the city is defined as a network of circulation and communication, as a centre of information and decision-making" (98). This is the materialization of the technological utopia, the space of the technocrat that Lefebvre argued against as early as the 1960s. See, in particular, Lefebvre, *Position: contre les technocrates*.

35. In contrasting smooth and striated space, Deleuze and Guattari write: "In striated space, one closes off a surface and 'allocates' it according to determinate intervals, assigned breaks; in the smooth, one 'distributes' oneself in an open space, according to frequencies and in the course of one's crossings" (481).

36. By the mid-1990s, a number of theorists had begun to make explicit reference to Deleuze and Guattari to describe cyberspace as a "rhizomatic" space in which the network functions as a structure within which any one point could connect to the other. In one of its earliest figurations, Hakim Bey's *T.A.Z.* draws a specific contrast between the striated, grid-like structures of "the Net" and the "piratic" and nomadic smooth spaces of "the Web," which constantly erupts from within the striated space of legitimated government and business activities, like Mandelbrot peninsulas "hidden within the map" (112). Likewise, in "Physics and Hypertext: Liberation and Complicity in Art and Pedagogy," Martin Rosenberg remains suspicious of the "geo-metric ideological construct" of the network, deriving as it does from principles of cybernetics and post–World War II Department of Defense. Rosenberg's concept of a writing space that would break from these structures takes the form of a Deleuzian smooth space, as suggested by his RHIZOME writing application, which he co-designed (287). See also Shaviro, "12.Bill Gates," for an analysis of hypertext as rhizome.

37. The phrase "connect the dots" appears repeatedly in DARPA's May 20, 2003 "Report to Congress Regarding the Terrorism Information Awareness Program" as an image of how cybernetic control can convert chaotic raw data of network transmissions into fields of "useful" information.

38. The earliest years of the Advanced Research Projects Agency Network (ARPANET) provide a good example of what Deleuze and Guattari call "apparatuses of capture," and one that has become part of the creation myths of Internet folklore. As the story goes, the Department of Defense had to find a means of allocating a growing volume of nongovernmental network communication (mostly discussions about science fiction and interactive fantasy games) within the function of its Advanced Research Projects Agency (ARPA); rather than clamping down on communication, ARPANET administrators permitted (captured) this flow, seeing it as one mode of information exchange within a larger system of productivity. See Rheingold, 179–80, for a more complete account. See also Rheingold's chapter "Telematique and Messageries Roses," 220–40, for an account of France's struggle to capture the flows of Minitel.

39. In "Of Other Spaces," Foucault describes this current "epoch of space" as an "experience of the world ... less that of a long life developing through time than that of a

network that connects points and intersects with its own skein" (22).

40. For a more thorough account, see Jammer, *Concepts of Space*, 53–126.

41. For another reading of a history of "space," and its challenges to and reaffirmations of Enlightenment constructs, with a particular focus on lived, embodied space, see Grosz, "Space, Time, and Bodies," in *Space, Time, and Perversion*, 83–101.

42. See Albert Einstein's discussion of "box space" in the forward to Jammer, especially xv–xvi.

43. In other words, one can maintain a concept of abstract space, which would function as the basis for classical physics from Newton to Einstein, while at the same time acknowledging that in fact we are still dealing with a *concept* of space, integrated in its function by way of a materiality of objects and the varied practices of spatial use.

44. See, in particular, Hillis, "The Sensation of Ritual Space," 60–89.

45. For another account of Leibniz's monadology and the metaphysics of cyberspace, see Heim, *The Metaphysics of Virtual Reality*, 83–108.

46. This triad of terms presents the crux of Lefebvre's spatial analysis. "Spatial practice" refers to those material processes that "secrete society's space" (*The Production of Space* 38). It is a production of relations between objects and products and corresponds to the potential to be "perceived." "Representations of space" refer to relations (ideological, linguistic, symbolic) between lived space and a conceptual framework. Representational space refers to a "lived" space, emerging through a passive, daily social interaction with objects, images, and symbols.

47. This logic is hardly something that is new to computer use. As Katie Hafner and Matthew Lyon note in *Where Wizards Stay Up Late*, even in its earliest implementation, developers of email protocols saw a high importance in the use of time stamps in headers, both as a point of pride for those who were up late on the system and as a measure of temporal and spatial proximity of responses to one another (214).

48. The growing popularity of Web-ready cell phones and text messaging devices suggests an alternate emergent material form not entirely separate from the spaces of laptops and desktops but distinct enough to warrant further consideration. Such devices may well point to a convergence of media, much as Friedrich Kittler describes in *Literature, Media, Information Systems*, that will significantly alter the spaces of everyday life.

49. See Unsworth, "Living Inside the (Operating) System," for a similar line of argument on the interpenetration of work and play with the rise of telecommuting.

50. Likewise, the Weather Channel's Web site does not make geography irrelevant by giving the remote individual access to "local" weather around the world; rather, it reveals a terrain where global access to local weather has significance in everyday life.

51. See also Beniger, *The Control Revolution*, which informs Shapiro's work.

52. See, in particular, Poster, "The Culture of Underdetermination," in *What's the Matter with the Internet?* 1–20.

53. In a similar manner, Kevin Kelly, executive editor of *Wired* magazine, redefines network structures as "swarm systems" that are self-regulating and adaptive but, by definition, "out of control." Drawing on complexity theory, Kelly's book *Out of Control* describes the Internet not as a network of controlled circulations from node to node, but as an emergent system: "Every day authors all over the word [sic] add millions of

words to an uncountable number of overlapping conversations. They daily build an immense distributed document, one that is under eternal construction, constant flux, and fleeting permanence" (464). See, in particular, "Wholes, Holes, and Spaces," 450–67.

54. The oft-cited "Anthem" advertisement for MCI explicitly suggests that the Internet is that long-awaited utopia of the mind where bodies cease to matter. The text for this television spot reads: "There is no race. There is no gender. There is no age. There are no infirmities. There are only minds. Utopia? No, Internet." See Silver, "Margins in the Wires," for a quotation and analysis of the "Anthem" advertisement.

55. I am reminded, in particular, of the early stages of "cleaning up" Times Square in Manhattan, when barricades were erected at various street corners to impede pedestrian crossing and augment traffic flow.

56. In *Postmodernism*, Jameson identifies a contemporary form of capitalism structured by "the multinational network" that gives rise to a social space that "involves the suppression of distance . . . and the relentless saturation of any remaining voids and empty places, to the point where the postmodern body . . . is now exposed to a perceptual barrage of immediacy from which all sheltering layers and intervening mediations have been removed" (410–13).

57. In *The Rise of the Network Society*, Castells argues that radical changes in technology lead to restructurings of material arrangements as well as processes of interaction. Castells describes the rise of an "information technology paradigm" from the 1970s into the 1990s, in which "networking logic" and the technologies based upon (and reinforcing) this logic became of primary economic and social importance (60). He writes: "The information technology paradigm does not evolve towards its closure as a system, but towards its openness as a multiedged network. It is powerful and imposing in its materiality, but adaptive and openended in its historical development. Comprehensiveness, complexity, and networking are its decisive qualities" (65). The result is a radical restructuring of social space by way of restructured information flows.

58. For Castells, "global" need not imply "worldwide." More specifically, Castells defines a global economy as "an economy with the capacity to work as a unit in real time on a planetary scale" (*The Rise of the Network Society* 92).

59. This space of flows is expressed materially by the actual "circuit of electronic impulses" that present the bursts of data, a structure of "nodes" and "hubs" that organizes these bursts, and a social structure of "informational elites" who direct and interact with these flows in terms of their select interests (Castells, *The Rise of the Network Society* 412–18).

60. See, in particular, Castells, *The Power of Identity*, 68–109.

61. In his contribution to the collection of essays *Race in Cyberspace*, for example, Sterne points to how the history of computing technology's place in the classroom maps issues of race and privilege in online discourse, often presented through a rhetoric "racelessness" online. He notes: "The social space of schooling and the imagined space of cyberspace are not nearly so far apart as technophilic pundits would have it. The politics of region return as the repressed: the topology of cyberspace mimics the racial and economic topology of housing and schooling" ("The Computer Race Goes to Class" 193).

62. In his 1956 "Theory of the Dérive," reprinted in *Situationist International Anthology*, Debord explains : "In a dérive one or

more persons during a certain period drop their usual motives for movement and action, their relations, their work and leisure activities, and let themselves be drawn by the attractions of the terrain and the encounters they find there" (50). As Sadler notes in *The Situationist City*, situationist psychogeography holds certain resonances with Kevin Lynch's concept of the "cognitive city," mapped out in the daily lives of its inhabitants (92). For another rendering of how an "aesthetic of cognitive mapping" relates to reconfigurations of both global and urban space, see Jameson, 51–54.

63. Lefebvre defines the ludic as "a fundamental desire of which play, sexuality, physical activities such as sport, creative activity, art and knowledge are particular expressions and *moments*, which can more or less overcome the fragmentary division of tasks" (*Writings on Cities* 146).

64. Communities.com was one of many dot-com ventures to disappear post-bubble. Interestingly, the Palace survived, or rather, a distributed network of Palace servers survived on multiple hosts worldwide. The result is a form, structure, and practice of space having more in common with peer-to-peer distributed systems than controlled "channels" of communication.

65. The missing third term in this triad is the city in its projected or imaginary form—the city as utopia. For Lefebvre, these three points stand in dialectical tension: a sort of "grid" for understanding the contradictory relation between spaces. This conceptual framework "distinguishes between types of oppositions and contrasts in space: *isotopias*, or analogous spaces; *heterotopias*, or mutually repellent spaces; and *utopias*, or spaces occupied by the symbolic or the imaginary—by 'idealities' such as nature, absolute knowledge, or absolute power" (Lefebvre, *The Production of Space* 366).

66. In "Of Other Spaces," where Foucault describes his own version of heterotopias, he speculates that: "Our epoch is one in which space takes for us the form of relations among sites" (23). The heterotopic site, Foucault argues, stands in a peculiar relation to these other sites in that they "suspect, neutralize, or invert the set of relations that they happen to designate, mirror, or reflect" (24). With his discussion of "sites," written well before the proliferation of networked computer servers, Foucault cannily finds a home in Internet discourse. In addition to Deleuze and Guattari, Foucault (in particular his discussion of heterotopias) has been used as a common critical lens to discuss cyberspace. Shaviro's "13.Pavel Curtis," for example, references Foucault to define networked heterotopias as "other-spaces, or spaces of otherness, in contrast to utopian non-spaces. . . . [T]hey are never exempt from the power relations and constraints of the societies that spawn them. Indeed, heterotopias express these relations and constraints even to excess."

67. See, for example, Hipmama.com or Indymedia.org, discussed at length in chapter 2.

68. In discussing the dominant abstract space of modernity, Lefebvre draws a distinction between "produced differences" and "induced differences" (*The Production of Space* 370–74). Produced differences "[emerge] from the chasm opened up when a closed universe ruptures" (372); in contrast, "induced differences" maintain localization and anomaly within a functional system. For a complete discussion, see Lefebvre, *The Production of Space*, 370–74. See also note 30 above for a discussion of the major and the minor in Deleuze and Guattari.

2. Virtual Worlds and Situated Spaces

1. Note that this materiality also maps geographies of inequality, not global distribution. For most of the 1990s, an overwhelming majority of servers that housed Web pages in various user accounts were located in the United States; by 2000, only 50 percent were U.S.-based. While the numbers suggest a shift away from a material form dominated by U.S. servers, the distribution of domains still structures what is primarily a network linking servers in the G8 countries (with Russia marking only a nominal presence). See Matthew Zook, "Percentage of the World's Domains in the Top Twenty-five Countries, January 2000."

2. The phrase "links of association" derives from Steven Johnson's work on hypertext, presented in *Interface Culture*. Johnson calls upon Dickens's novel *Great Expectations*, in which the phrase "links of association" originates, to describe the process whereby ideas are held together through these associative links (112–16).

3. For example, according to media relations manager Bill Avington, anecdotal accounts of students having problems accessing the Beaver College Web site played a part in the college's decision to change its name to Arcadia when it became a university in 2001. See Noah Adams, "Beaver College."

4. In some regards, Berners-Lee's conception of the Web as a version of Newtonian space derives from his understanding of information as a *thing*, which then resides within a state of affairs. In *Weaving the Web*, he writes: "The web was not a physical 'thing' that existed in a certain 'place.' It was a 'space' in which information could exist" (36). By thinking of information as a thing, rather than as the product of an event, Berners-Lee falls within a cybernetic tradition that abstracts information as an entity separate from the context in which it occurs. See N. Katherine Hayles, *How We Became Posthuman*, 50–83.

5. As the Semantic Web learns significance through hypercomplex linkages between sites, Berners-Lee believes an organic structure begins to emerge from the Web as a whole, with the potential for ideas—and social forms—to evolve out of its structures of connectivity (187). Berners-Lee approaches statements similar to Pierre Lévy's discussion of collective intelligence, but backs away from a strong embrace of emergent structures. For his discussion of the Web as "Global Brain," see Berners-Lee, 204–5.

6. Much of Nelson's thinking about hypertext involves an attempt to parallel cognitive structures in a computer medium. Influenced by the work of Marvin Minsky, in particular, Nelson imagines thought as a *structangle*, which he describes in *Literary Machines* as "an interwoven system of ideas" (1.14). The medium of hypertext, then, would serve as a tool to materialize the "structangle" of thought.

7. As with Berners-Lee and his Semantic Web, Nelson sees an emergent order in the complex interconnectivity of hypertext, but one that is more contingent than organic. In *Computer Lib*, Nelson explains: "I hold that all structures must be treated as totally arbitrary, and any hierarchies we find are interesting accidents" (DM32).

8. Holland, France, and England offered similar rewards over the next two centuries. For more on the quest for the *punto fijo*, see Howse, 10–18.

9. Umberto Eco's novel *The Island of the Day Before* plays out this history in fictional form. At one point, Jean-Baptiste Colbert, soon to be Louis XIV's secretary of state and head of finance, explains to the main char-

acter that the "unknown southern lands" have to exist where Europe has failed to map because the balance of the globe demands such a space: "This expanse of waters is not empty because of a grudging Nature; it is empty because we know all too little of Nature's generosity" (187). Eco's novel goes on to emphasize that this period during the seventeenth century marks not only an attempt to determine the unknown world, but also to determine and define the boundaries of European states.

10. See, for example, Berland, "Mapping Space."

11. See also Dodge, "An Atlas of Cyberspaces."

12. According to Matthew Zook's count, the United States accounted for about 60 percent of the .com, .net, .edu, and .org domains in 2001 ("Growth of Domains in US and the World").

13. With the United States at approximately 50 percent, the countries with the next two highest percentages of domains in January 2000 were Germany and the United Kingdom, at approximately 9 percent each. Canada ranked fourth, at approximately 4 percent. France, Japan, and Italy accounted for another 5 percent of the world total. South Korea, while not a G7 nation, ranked fifth after Canada and ahead of France, at 2.5 percent. By Zook's count, the only G7 country not to make the top-ten list in January 2000 was Italy, which ranked eleventh ("Percentage of the World's Domains in the Top Twenty-Five Countries, January 2000,"). For data as of January 2006, see Internet Systems Consortium, "Distribution of Top-Level Domain Names by Host Count, January 2006."

14. As cited earlier, more recent estimates place the worldwide Internet population at around a billion. See ClickZ Stats, "Population Explosion!" See also Zook, "Geography of Internet Users."

15. Consider also the instance of Eva's Cafe, discussed in chapter 3, in which Internet access in a bar in Belize mapped very different global relations for ecotourists, academic researchers, and locals. See Koeppel, "Jungle Outpost Offers Beer, Mayan Ruins and the Net."

16. Manuel Castells addresses the space of flows of a global economy in relation to these three regions, and the local specificity of each network structure within a larger global flow, in *The End of Millennium*, especially in chapters 4 and 5. See also Castells, *The Rise of the Network Society*, 92–106.

17. I should note that mobile telephones produce their own sense of which geographies are on or off the map, by way of service areas.

18. Town Online and its various editions of eastern Massachusetts local newspapers are still online. The site, however, no longer posts this publishing philosophy.

19. The *Northern Pen* Web site no longer records hits, but as of summer 2004, the site still claimed a print circulation of 6,000.

20. While Robertson is often associated with the term "glocalization," he himself points to the early 1990s marketing term "glocalize" as a precursor, with particular reference to the Japanese *dochakuka*, or "global localization" (*Globalization* 173–74).

21. In an attempt to classify "globe-oriented ideologies" in terms of the sociological concepts of *Gemeinschaft* (community) and *Gesellschaft* (society), Robertson identifies two versions of a "global *Gemeinschaft*" and two versions of a "global *Gesellschaft*" (*Globalization* 78–83).

22. While emphasizing the interplay between the local and the global, Robertson

is at the same time unapologetically universalizing in some instances. He defines the four features of the global human condition, which operate within a field of interaction, as: "societies, individuals, the system of societies, and [hu]mankind. . . . which draws attention to both the world in its contemporary concreteness and to humanity as a species" (*Globalization* 77–78).

23. This need not always be the case. By 2001, CNN.com had discontinued its open news chat and now only hosts moderated chats. It has also made bulletin-board lists a sporadic feature of the Web site.

24. According to the "About Indymedia" page, the Independent Media Center was established in 1999 to disseminate on-the-street coverage of the WTO protests in Seattle. Their mission statement declares: "We work out of a love and inspiration for people who continue to work for a better world, despite corporate media's distortions and unwillingness to cover the efforts to free humanity."

25. In a similar fashion, but with a less overtly political purpose, Slashdot provides readers with an opportunity to add stories, but states that its criteria has more to do with providing readers "interesting" content. In a rather poor analogy provided in their editorial FAQ, the editors describe the Slashdot site as an omelet with varying ingredients: "Over the years, we've figured out what ingredients are best on Slashdot. The ultimate goal is, of course, to create an omelette that I enjoy eating: by 8pm, I want to see a dozen interesting stories on Slashdot. I hope you enjoy them too."

26. See, for example, Independent Media Center, "Indymedia Ireland Editorial Guidelines."

27. In an attempt to decrease abuse of its resources, in May 2002, Indymedia.org altered its open publishing format by making its main page an automatic "feed" from the dozen or so local IMC Web pages. Open publishing would remain at the core of the local IMC pages, but the main IMC page would now only carry articles that had already made it through an editorial filter. Indymedia.org continues to revise its editorial policies. See Independent Media Center, "Trend toward More Editorial Control."

28. For an analysis of the relation between the virtual class and possessive individualism, see Kroker and Weinstein, *Data Trash*, 4–26. See also Kroker, *The Possessed Individual*.

29. For another discussion of the relationship between personalization and cybernetic control, see Shapiro, *The Control Revolution*, 44–52 and 105–14.

30. For a discussion of "fluidity" in community, on- and offline, see Willson, "Community in the Abstract."

31. The structure of exchange I am describing here, while allowing for indisciplines that can escape from the normative structurings of a virtual class, need not be entirely antithetical to corporate interests. According to a now-defunct Web site FAQ, posted shortly after Johnson and Johnson purchased BabyCenter.com from the soon-to-be-bankrupt eToys.com, the company chose to purchase the site because it was "deeply impressed with how the site has grown and evolved. . . . [and] attracted to BabyCenter's unique ability to create strong, personal relationships with parents through its Web sites."

32. This feature of BabyCenter.com is not uniform. The "Ask the Experts" pages do not offer parents a place to add their own words. These pages reinforce the position of "experts" in hierarchical relation to the voices of parents themselves, although the site offers

many loci where parents express dissenting, minority, or contrarian versions of "responsible parenting."

33. While topics seem to pigeonhole discussions, it is quite common for discussions to head in directions that have only tangential relations to the subject heading, if any connection whatsoever.

34. For a discussion of the limitations of what Lisa Nakamura calls "menu-driven identities," see Nakamura, *Cybertypes*, 101–35.

35. In no way can a site that explicitly addresses the embodied experiences of pregnancy and motherhood declare that somehow its members "leave their bodies behind" to engage in an agora of ideas. For specific discussion of the spatiality and corporeality of the pregnant body, see Young, "Pregnant Embodiment," in *Throwing Like a Girl and Other Essays in Feminist Philosophy and Social Theory*, 160–74.

36. In 2003, Hipmama.com changed the design of its Web site. It now requires site membership as a means of registering as a "friend of hipmama." While the mission statement is no longer posted on the site, and to some degree the site is less open, it still maintains itself as a highly situated site that attempts to establish a space of coalitional politics and feminist mothering for a range of situated identities.

37. Shapiro addresses a similar point in his chapter "In Defense of Accidents," 197–207.

38. In fact, Wiener goes as far as to associate the resistance of entropy with a principle of evil. In most information systems, this is an Augustinian evil, a *lack* of perfect order—in contrast to the Manichaean evil that actively works *against* the forces of order in the world (Wiener 35).

3. Email, the Letter, and the Post

1. By 2008, the USPS expects to lose approximately 27 percent of its first-class mail to CMC, both through a decline in personal correspondence by letter and through an increase in electronic payment of bills (NUA Internet Surveys, "End of an Era for the National Postal Service").

2. After the Glorious Revolution, Dockwra petitioned Parliament for losses he suffered since 1682. Parliament agreed that he deserved payment for his invention and granted him a pension, which would last him ten years (Robinson 83). The Penny Post, however, remained a part of the Post Office.

3. I am indebted to Robinson's wonderful and comprehensive monograph for most of my information on the history of the postal system in Britain and in Europe.

4. This service ended in 1637, amidst growing political tensions, but it was revived again first under Cromwell in 1657, and then permanently in 1660 by an act of Parliament (Robinson 33–48).

5. By midcentury, the conveyance of "by and cross road" posts for the Post Office had become an increasingly profitable venture, reflecting a large increase in letters from provincial town to provincial town (Robinson 100–109).

6. In the second half of the nineteenth century, telegraphy mapped a similar network of everyday practice. This "Victorian Internet," to use Tom Standage's phrase, functioned as a decentralized network of telegraph operators meshed into the urban fabric through a distributed network of door-to-door "telegraph boys."

7. In *The Letters of the Republic*, Michael Warner makes a similar point about the network of printers that existed in colonial America (34–72).

8. It was, in fact (and coincidentally enough), the son of a British post-office worker, Donald Davies, who introduced the concept and the term "packet-switching" to describe the process by which a message divides; travels by way of multiple, often circuitous routes; and then reconvenes at the point of delivery (Hafner and Lyon 67–77).

9. This potential multiplicity differs from postal mass-mailings in significant ways. First, email arrives without a "bulk rate" stamp to reveal its status as mass reproduction. Furthermore, and more significantly, mass mailings lack that quality of potential dissemination; while a single electronic dispatch can disseminate to multiple points of arrival, a mass mailing always maintains a strict space of point-to-point contact. Perhaps chain letters, which transgress postal space by circulating rather than arriving, come closest to the virtuality of email.

10. A number of analyses of Listserv and USENET correspondences have emphasized the role of the personal in these exchanges— the lived practice of email as a "social technology." See, for example, Sproull and Faraj, "Atheism, Sex, and Databases."

11. See also Poster, "Authors Analogue and Digital," in *What's the Matter with the Internet?* 78–100.

12. See, in particular, Baudrillard, *Simulations.*

13. Robinson tells tale of an invention by Samuel Morland, who had created a machine of legendary ability that would open and re-seal letters without betraying the violation. The machine also was "capable of reproducing handwriting in facsimile so exactly that the writer himself could not distinguish the original letter" (54). This marvelous "fax" machine of the seventeenth century was destroyed in the fire of 1666 (54).

14. For a discussion of fragmentation,

abstract space, and the social forms of capitalism, see Lefebvre, *The Production of Space,* 352–67.

15. See, in particular, Warner, 11–17.

16. This increase in volume led to a number of problems (delayed deliveries, clandestine postings hidden in bundles, wet papers damaging other correspondences), leading the Post Office to establish a separate newspaper office in 1787. In the following decade, the number of newspapers heading out of London on the post nearly tripled, from 3.2 million to 8.6 million. (Robinson 148)

17. For example, Stuart Sherman describes the *Spectator* as a public medium that consciously calls attention to these converging processes through the publication of a newspaper that emulates the diary form (113–14).

18. Clearly "membership" in this community involves some measure of class membership. It is worth noting, however, as Bob Harris suggests in *Politics and the Rise of the Press,* that access to the networks of modernity as material, conceptual, and lived space provides an important index of position within the social spaces of modernity, and one that does not entirely overlay the social structurings of class (28). Similar issues of access, and what it means to be "on" or "off" the network, are of course very relevant to a discussion of the Internet and the spaces of everyday life.

19. As Ian Watt notes in *The Rise of the Novel,* our author/narrator "pauses only to listen with wild surmise to footsteps in some other part of the house, and who communicates the intolerable sense of strain which arises when an opening door threatens some new violation of a cherished privacy" (189).

20. In *The Wired Neighborhood,* Stephen Doheny-Farina refers to these self-same communities as "lifestyle enclaves," as op-

posed to social collectives "in which the public and private lives of its members are moving toward interdependency regardless of the significant differences among those members" (50).

21. In addition, spaces of control delimit access in terms that are ultimately proprietary, in that the "public" is structured by subscription, both to a list and to a service provider.

22. As in other instances of virtual topographies, these produced spaces involve conflicting articulations: the "About" page also cites Andrew Shapiro's *The Control Revolution* as an inspiration for Meetup.com, suggesting articulations of social space in keeping with the dominant topographies associated with spaces of control.

23. MoveOn.org provides a similar instance of emergent networks produced by viral processes of dispersal. What had begun as an email petition on September 18, 1998, to "Censure President Clinton and Move On to Pressing Issues Facing the Country" became, in a matter of days, a coalition numbering in the thousands. While Joan Blades and Wes Boyd were able to "capture" this space of flows into a political action committee of sorts, the dynamic, emergent elements of this topography of a networked "public" are inseparable from its dissipative, ephemeral qualities. See MoveOn.org, "About the MoveOn Family of Organizations."

24. Note that the "digital divide" is not marked by access to networks but, rather, to how those networks situate individuals within social fields of power and a global space of flows.

25. This quote, and all previous quotes in this paragraph, were drawn from "Reduction in Distribution of Spam Act of 2003 Hearing Before the Subcommittee on Crime, Terrorism, and Homeland Security of the Committee on the Judiciary House of Representatives." July 8, 2003. http://commdocs.house.gov/committees/judiciary/hju88203.000/hju88203_0f.htm.

26. "Public phones" have undergone a similar shift. Once, booths provided an enclosure: a telephone closet for private-in-public communication. With the shift from booth to phone stand, enclosure disappeared, although the phone itself did not change in function. With cell phones, this same condition is taken to extremes: no longer enclosed, private space now irrupts from within the midst of the public.

27. For a discussion of "fractional dimensions" in this context, see Deleuze and Guattari, 482–88.

4. Student Bodies

1. The use of the passive voice here is intentional because it reveals the trickiness of attribution when discussing the processes involved in the production of social space. Certainly one could say that it is college administrators who are encouraging faculty to use network technology, while making assumptions about students' desire and need for access. But college administrators themselves are enacting dispositions within a field of power, not creating them.

2. Here, I am specifically making use of citationality as a reiterative performance that produces material form and conceptual structure associated with subject-formation. For a reading of citationality and performativity, see Butler, *Bodies That Matter*, 12–16.

3. For a complete discussion of Chautauqua's role as a founding correspondence program, along with its influence on adult education in general, see Scott, "The Chautauqua Movement."

4. Harriet Bergmann's article "'The

Silent University'" provides a general history of Ticknor's society, with a specific interest in its relation to changing attitudes toward women in higher education.

5. In his "Ten Ways Online Education Matches, or Surpasses, Face-to-Face Learning," Mark Kassop's number one reason is student-centered learning: "Students are empowered to learn on their own and even to teach one another." This rhetoric of empowerment is common to most accounts of how online learning provides students with educational space of control.

6. Odasz's article "Big Skies and Lone Eagles" provides a personal history of the inspiration for and development of the Big Sky Telegraph bulletin-board system and network, along with its eventual demise in 1998. His article also offers an interesting reflection on the community networking movement in the context of the rise of affordable ISPs in the mid-1990s. For a snapshot of the community networking movement at this critical moment in Internet history, see also Schuler, "Community Networking."

7. GALILEO provides public schools, public libraries, and University System of Georgia schools access to dozens of full-text and bibliographic databases. It was established in 1995, the first such state-based system in the nation. For an overview of the GALILEO initiative, see GALILEO, "About the Initiative."

8. Although Apple was very early in its grant and donation programs (starting practically at the company's inception), including its Apple Libraries of Tomorrow and Apple Classrooms of Tomorrow research programs, Gates Foundation contributions have since far outpaced Apple's efforts. As of the start of 2005, the Gates Foundation had given $2.28 billion in education grants (Bill and Melinda Gates Foundation).

9. This is the vision of groups, such as the League for Innovation in the Community College, who see in computer-aided instruction and online learning a remedy for the outmoded spatial and temporal structures that define and restrict the traditional classroom. See, for example, Terry O'Banion, *A Learning College for the Twenty-first Century.*

10. See Nakamura, 31–60.

11. See Georgia Perimeter College, "Center for Distance Learning."

12. In "Review and Resources," written for the University of Washington's Office of Educational Assessment, Balanko pairs issues of access and issues of student control in a description of online education as a valuable, student-centered pedagogical form.

13. The University of Phoenix Web site no longer contains this text; however, the text does still appear at www.colleges.com/colleges/phoenix/students.html.

14. In *Pascalian Meditations,* Bourdieu maintains that the constituting rule of "the scholastic" is that one can only encounter universal, transcendent truths by removing oneself from the tangles of social life. He points to the root *skhole* (leisure) as key to understanding scholasticism as learning "liberated from practical occupations and preoccupations," in an environment of "studious leisure" (13).

15. Following in the tradition of Oskar Negt and Alexander Kluge's *Public Sphere and Experience,* Daniel argues for an understanding of multiple public spheres, which often "operate outside the usual parameters of institutional legitimation, responding to the contingent needs of all of those groups whose self-expression is excluded or 'blocked.'" Such an understanding accounts for the ways in which a dominant discourse can structure participation within the public

sphere, while leaving open the potential for alternate discursive formations. See Daniel, "Virtual Communities?"

16. To read the announcement posted in the MOO, see Brawley et al., "PMC MOO."

17. While conditions of felicity and infelicity are critical elements of Austin's analysis of performative speech acts within given speech situations, the phrase "felicity condition" actually originates in Umberto Eco's rendering of speech act theory in *The Role of the Reader.*

18. The project was published as Mark Nunes et al., "Postmodern Spacings." Appropriately enough, the journal described the collaborative piece as a "colloquy."

19. Perhaps this is a secondary lesson to be learned from the phenomenal spread of Napster in colleges during the tail end of the 1990s: peer-to-peer networks for music exchange caught on so rapidly because, for students already instituted into communities of exchange, "P2P" practices had already been "naturalized" as a dominant habitus.

20. As of 2003, Harvard offered online courses at two of its schools—Public Health and Harvard Extension. The Extension School offers a number of distance-education courses as adjuncts to traditional undergraduate and graduate degree programs. As a version of adult education, then, distance education serves an aligned purpose of *extending* (spatially and culturally) the Harvard classroom to students anywhere in the (networked) world. Samples of its online lectures are available at www.extension.harvard.edu/2003-04/programs/DistanceEd/lectures/. Students have the option of viewing lectures in a multiwindow high-speed-access media player, or, at lower speeds, as a choppier video or an audio-only stream.

21. At the slowest audio-only transmission, online Harvard Extension students see only a static, generic image of a silhouetted instructor standing before a lectern.

22. For an alternate reading of the virtualities of distraction, see Morse, "An Ontology of Everyday Distraction," in *Virtualities,* 99–124.

23. For an overview of iConnect@UB, see Bernstein, Gorman, and Wright, "MyUB."

24. See, for example, an online product review of an IM-ready webcam: "The results were good enough to convince me that this is finally a viable way to steal some face time, in real time, with that child who's left the nest" (Buechner).

25. In *Digital Diploma Mills,* Noble notes that some will see the success of this Internet distribution as ironic, "but such a perspective merely reflects the Manichean worldview of the ideology of technological programs which, like other dogmatic belief systems, allows for only orthodoxy or heresy" (xii). One might speak instead, to use Baudrillard's term, of an ironic revenge, in that the very strengths of the network provide the conditions of possibility for appropriations that run contrary to a system's own dominant norms.

Afterword

1. Jerry Harris uses these two terms, "transnational globalist" and "international hegemonist," to discuss a fracture in a transnational capitalist class, mapped specifically in terms of the military industrial complex ("The Conflict for Power in Transnational Class Theory").

2. According to Eli Ofek and Matthew Richardson's account of the collapse of Internet stock prices, in the month preceding the dot-com crash "the largely profitless Internet sector equaled 6% of the market

capitalization of all U.S. public companies, and 20% of all publicly trade[d] equity volume" ("DotCom Mania").

3. Recent marketing data suggest that a majority of Internet users now feel that financial and consumer online transactions are safe; in one survey, half of all users had used the Internet to access bank accounts, and roughly one-third had transferred funds electronically (Greenspan). The data also suggest that the number of years online and one's household income correlate with one's comfort engaging in these sorts of transactions, speaking again to a kind of dispositional ease. The incorporation of these corporeal and cognitive orientations is also measured by an age differential, with the under-thirty-four age group noticeably more integrated than users over age fifty-five.

4. According to Ofek and Richardson, from 1998 until the start of March 2000, the "Internet sector" increased by 1,000 percent, only to ultimately return to its overall 1998 value.

5. For Baudrillard, the "excess of reality" marked by the World Trade Center attacks marks the degree to which "the real" has become an aftereffect of mediated images within global networks. In an extended passage in *The Spirit of Terrorism*, he writes: "How do things stand with the real event, then, if reality is everywhere infiltrated by images, virtuality and fiction? In the present case, we thought we had seen (perhaps with a certain relief) a resurgence of the real, and of the violence of the real in an allegedly virtual universe. 'There's an end to all your talk about the virtual—this is something real!' Similarly, it was possible to see this as a resurrection of history beyond its proclaimed end. But does reality actually outstrip fiction? If it seems to do so, this is because it has absorbed fiction's energy, and has itself become fiction. We might almost say that reality is jealous of fiction, that the real is jealous of the image. . . . It is a kind of duel between them, a contest to see which can be the most unimaginable" (28). It is the symbolic for Baudrillard that provides the terror of the terrorists' attack—the fact that through a collapse of the World Trade Center towers, the "unimaginable" event maps the processes of globalization at the same time that it attempts to bring about the destruction of these same global processes.

6. Trippi's blog "More Signs of 911's Complex Effects" points to Garreau's article in the *Washington Post* and to McEwan's September 15 piece in the *Guardian* as two early attempts to understand the relationship between an everyday life of distributed networks and the terrorist attacks of 9/11. I am grateful to Trippi for calling these two articles to my attention.

7. See also Sam Smith, "Postmodernism Is Dead."

8. Conetta's memo goes on to note that such a structure makes it difficult to find a "center" to attack, suggesting instead measures to control the flow of capital, armaments, and people that enact its network.

9. In yet another instance of ironic revenge, DARPA—the same agency that spawned the first distributed network—would be given a project that would attempt to create effective apparatuses of capture for extracting information from redundant, distributed networks and modulating its flows.

10. DARPA's "Report to Congress Regarding the Terrorism Information Awareness Program" goes on to state, much as Norbert Wiener did some half a century earlier, that today the volume of information "far exceeds the capacity of the unaided humans

in the system," who are best assisted by "machines guided by human users" (Executive Summary 2). The spaces of control that provide the form, structure, and practices of a dominant social space are foregrounded here, and in a fashion that specifically addresses the overload of information as an Augustinian evil in Wiener's sense—a resistance to the ordering of "connecting the dots" necessary to combat the Manichean evil of terrorism that exploits the interstitial gaps of the system.

11. See Electronic Frontier Foundation, "Conference Report on H.R. 2658, Department of Defense Appropriations Act, 2004."

12. The ISC defines "ARPA" mistake domains as hosts that, during setup, the system administrator "left off the trailing dot in their zone files. These are hosts that probably exist, but have an invalid host name." For more information on mistake hosts, "unknowns," and other anomalies in the host survey, see Internet Systems Consortium, "ISC Internet Domain Survey Background."

WORKS CITED

All Web-site addresses are valid as of April 2006, except where noted as "defunct."

Aarseth, Espen. *Cybertext*. Baltimore: Johns Hopkins University Press, 1997.

Adams, Noah. "Beaver College." *All Things Considered*, March 1, 2001. http://www.npr.org/ramfiles/atc/20000301.atc.07.ram.

Adams, Paul. "Cyberspace and Virtual Places." *Geographical Review* 87, no. 2 (April 1997): 155–71.

Adrian, Robert. "Infobahn Blues." *CTHEORY*, 1995. http://www.ctheory.net/text_file.asp?pick =63.

"Agenda for Action." 1994. http://www.ibiblio.org/nii/NII-Agenda-for-Action.html.

Albuquerque, Luis de. "Portuguese Navigation: Its Historical Development." In *Circa 1492: Art in the Age of Exploration*, ed. Jay Levenson, 35–39. New Haven: Yale University Press, 1991.

Althusser, Louis. "Ideology and Ideological State Apparatuses." In *Lenin and Philosophy and Other Essays*, trans. Ben Brewster, 127–86. New York: Monthly Review Press, 1971.

Amazon.com. "Amazon.com Help: Friends & Interesting People." http://www.amazon.com/exec/obidos/tg/browse/-/468600/ref=br_bx_c_1_3/.

———. "Amazon.com Help: Listmania Lists." http://www.amazon.com/exec/obidos/tg/browse/-/14279651/ref=br_bx_c_1_4/.

———. "Friends & Favorites." http://

www.amazon.com/exec/obidos/subst/ community/community-home.html. [defunct]

———. "Listmania Lists." http://www. amazon.com/exec/obidos/tg/browse/- /542566. [defunct]

Anderson, Benedict. *Imagined Communities*. New York: Verso, 1991.

Argyle, Katie. "Life after Death." In *Cultures of Internet: Virtual Spaces, Real Histories, Living Bodies*, 133–42. Thousand Oaks, Calif.: Sage, 1996.

Augé, Marc. *Non-Places*. Trans. John Howe. New York: Verso, 1995.

Austin, J. L. *How to Do Things with Words*. Cambridge: Harvard University Press, 1975.

———. "Performative Utterances." In *Philosophical Papers*. Cambridge: Harvard University Press, 1962.

BabyCenter.com. "Bulletin Boards." http:// bbs.babycenter.com/bbs/.

Balanko, Shelley. "Review and Resources: On-line Education Implementation and Evaluation." 2002. http://www.washington. edu/oea/pdfs/reports/OEAReport0211. pdf.

Barbatsis, Gretchen. "Hypermediated Telepresence: Sensemaking Aesthetics of the Newest Communication Art." *Journal of Broadcasting & Electronic Media* 43, no. 2 (Spring 1999): 280–98.

Barker, Francis. *The Tremulous Private Body*. New York: Methuen, 1984.

Barlow, John Perry. "Jack In, Young Pioneer!" 1994. http://www.eff.org/Misc/ Publications/John_Perry_Barlow/ HTML/jack_in_young_pioneer.html.

Barndt, Deborah. *Tangled Routes: Women, Work, and Globalization on the Tomato Trail*. Lanham, Md.: Rowman & Littlefield, 2002.

Baudrillard, Jean. *Baudrillard Live*. Ed. Mike Gane. New York: Routledge, 1993.

———. *The Ecstasy of Communication*. Trans. Bernard and Caroline Schutze. New York: Semiotext(e), 1988.

———. *Simulation and Simulacra*. Trans. Sheila Faria Glaser. Ann Arbor: University of Michigan Press, 1994.

———. *Simulations*. Trans. Paul Foss et al. New York: Semiotext(e), 1983.

———. *The Spirit of Terrorism*. Trans. Chris Turner. New York: Verso, 2003.

———. *Symbolic Exchange and Death*. Trans. Iain Hamilton Grant. Thousand Oaks, Calif.: Sage, 1993.

———. *The System of Objects*. Trans. James Benedict. New York: Verso, 1996.

———. *The Transparency of Evil*. Trans. James Benedict. New York: Verso, 1993.

———. *The Vital Illusion*. New York: Columbia University Press, 2000.

Benedikt, Michael, ed. *Cyberspace: First Steps*. Cambridge: MIT Press, 1992.

———. "Cyberspace: Some Proposals." In *Cyberspace: First Steps*, 119–224. Cambridge: MIT Press, 1992.

Beniger, James. *The Control Revolution*. Cambridge: Harvard University Press, 1989.

Benjamin, Walter. *Illuminations*. Trans. Harry Zohn. New York: Harcourt, 1968.

Bergmann, Harriet. "'The Silent University': The Society to Encourage Studies at Home, 1873–1897." *New England Quarterly* 74, no. 3 (2001): 447–77.

Bergson, Henri. *Essai sur les donneés immédiates de la conscience*. Paris: Quadrige, 1997.

———. *Matter and Memory*. Trans. Nancy Margaret Paul and W. Scott Palmer. New York: Zone Books, 1991.

Berland, Jody. "Mapping Space: Imaging Technologies and the Planetary Body." In

Technoscience and Cyberculture, 123–37. New York: Routledge, 1996.

Berners-Lee, Tim. *Weaving the Web*. New York: HarperCollins, 1999.

Bernstein, Rebecca, James Gorman, and Robert Wright. "MyUB: The University at Buffalo's Personalized Service Portal." *The Technology Source*, November–December 2002. http://technologysource.org/article/myub/.

Bey, Hakim. *T.A.Z.* Brooklyn: Autonomedia, 1991.

Bill and Melinda Gates Foundation. "Grants: Bill and Melinda Gates Foundation." http://www.glf.org/Grants/.

Boal, Mark. "Malling the Cybercafe." *Village Voice*, November 26, 1996: 29.

Bolter, Jay David. *Writing Space*. Hillsdale, N.J.: Lawrence Erlbaum, 1991.

Bolter, Jay David, and Richard Grusin. *Remediation*. Cambridge: MIT Press, 2000.

Bourdieu, Pierre. *On Television*. Trans. Priscilla Parkhurst Ferguson. New York: New Press, 1998.

———. *Outline of a Theory of Practice*. Trans. Richard Nice. New York: Cambridge University Press, 1977.

———. *Pascalian Meditations*. Trans. Richard Nice. Stanford: Stanford University Press, 1996.

———. *The State Nobility*. Trans. Lauretta C. Clough. Stanford: Stanford University Press, 1996.

Bousquet, Marc. "The Information University." *Electronic Book Review*, October 4, 2003. http://www.electronicbookreview.com/v3/servlet/ebr?command=view_essay&essay_id=bousquetfivealtx.

Brawley, Lisa et al. "PMC MOO: A Change of Direction." August 29, 1995. http://jefferson.village.virginia.edu/pmc/moonews.html.

Brooks, James, and Iain Boal, eds. *Resisting the Virtual Life*. San Francisco: City Lights, 1995.

Buechner, Maryanne Murray. "Face Time." *Time Online Edition*, August 2003. http://www.time.com/time/techtime/200308/story.html.

Burnett, Kathleen. "The Scholar's Rhizome." *Arachnet: The Electronic Journal on Virtual Culture* 1, no. 2 (1993). http://www.infomotions.com/serials/aejvc/aejvc-v1n02-burnett-scholars.txt.

Bush, Vannevar. "As We May Think." *Atlantic Monthly* (July 1945): 101–8.

Butler, Judith. *Bodies That Matter*. New York: Routledge, 1993.

———. *Gender Trouble*. New York: Routledge, 1990.

Carey, James. *Communication as Culture*. New York: Routledge, 1992.

Castells, Manuel. *The Rise of the Network Society*. Malden, Mass.: Blackwell, 1996.

———. *The Power of Identity*. Malden, Mass.: Blackwell, 1997.

———. *The End of Millennium*. Malden, Mass.: Blackwell, 1998.

Chadwick, Alex. "Dot-T.V." *Morning Edition*. National Public Radio, October 16, 1998. http://www.npr.org/ramfiles/981016.me.07.ram.

ClickZ Stats. "Finance Sites the Stickiest Online." *ClickZ Network*, February 28, 2002. http://www.clickz.com/stats/markets/finance/article.php/983221.

———. "Population Explosion!" *ClickZ Network*, November 3, 2005. http://www.clickz.com/stats/sectors/geographics/article.php/5911_151151.

Cobb, Jennifer. *Cybergrace*. New York: Crown, 1998.

Communities.com. "About the Company." 1999. http://www.thepalace.com/corporate/about/index.html. [Defunct]

Computer Industry Almanac. "Worldwide

Internet Users Top 1 Billion in 2005." 2005. http://www.c-i-a.com/pr0106.htm.

Conetta, Carl. "Dislocating Alcyoneus: How to Combat al-Qaeda and the New Terrorism." *Project on Defense Alternatives,* June 25, 2002. http://www.comw.org/pda/0206dislocate.html.

Connery, Brian. "IMHO: Authority and Egalitarian Rhetoric in the Virtual Coffeehouse." In *Internet Culture,* ed. David Porter, 161–79. New York: Routledge, 1997.

Crang, Mike. "Public Space, Urban Space, and Electronic Space: Would the Real City Please Stand Up." In *Virtual Globalization: Virtual Spaces/Tourist Spaces,* ed. David Holmes, 76–94. New York: Routledge, 2001.

Culler, Jonathan. "Convention and Meaning: Derrida and Austin." *New Literary History* 13 (1981): 15–30.

Curtis, Pavel. "MUDding: Social Phenomena in Text-Based Virtual Realities." In *Culture of the Internet,* ed. Sara Kiesler, 121–42. Mahwah, N.J.: Lawrence Erlbaum, 1997.

Daniel, Jamie Owen. "Virtual Communities? Public Spheres and Public Intellectuals on the Internet." *Electronic Book Review,* April 1, 1996. http://www.altx.com/ebr/ebr2/2daniel.htm.

Davis, Erik. *Techgnosis.* New York: Three Rivers Press, 1998.

Dawkins, Richard. *The Selfish Gene.* New York: Oxford University Press, 1976.

de Certeau, Michel. *The Practice of Everyday Life.* Trans. Steven Rendall. Berkeley: University of California Press, 1984.

Debord, Guy. "Theory of the Dérive." *Situationist International Anthology,* ed. K. Knabb, 50–54. Berkeley: Bureau of Public Secrets, 1981.

Defense Advanced Research Projects Agency. "Report to Congress Regarding the Terrorism Information Awareness Program." May 20, 2003. http://www.eff.org/Privacy/TIA/TIA-report.pdf.

Deleuze, Gilles. *Difference and Repetition.* Trans. Paul Patton. New York: Columbia University Press, 1994.

———. *The Fold: Leibniz and the Baroque.* Trans. Tom Conley. Minneapolis: University of Minnesota Press, 1993.

———. "Postscript on the Societies of Control." *October* 59 (Winter 1992): 3–7.

Deleuze, Gilles, and Félix Guattari. *A Thousand Plateaus.* Trans. Brian Massumi. Minneapolis: University of Minnesota Press, 1987.

Delio, Michelle. "Klez: Don't Believe 'From' Line." *Wired News,* April 30, 2002. http://www.wired.com/news/technology/0,1282,52174,00.html.

Derrida, Jacques. *Acts of Literature.* New York: Routledge, 1992.

———. *Archive Fever.* Trans. Eric Prenowitz. Chicago: University of Chicago Press, 1996.

———. *Dissemination.* Trans. Barbara Johnson. Chicago: University of Chicago Press, 1981.

———. "Limited Inc." *Glyph* 2 (1977): 162–254.

———. *Of Grammatology.* Trans. Gayatri Chakravorty Spivak. Baltimore: Johns Hopkins University Press, 1976.

———. *The Post Card.* Trans. Alan Bass. Chicago: University of Chicago Press, 1987.

———. "Signature Event Context." *Margins of Philosophy.* Trans. Alan Bass. Chicago: University of Chicago Press, 1982. 307–30.

Dibbell, Julian. "A Rape in Cyberspace." *The Village Voice,* December 21, 1993: 36–42.

Dodge, Martin. "An Atlas of Cyberspaces." 2004. http://www.geog.ucl.ac.uk/casa/martin/atlas/atlas.html.

Dodge, Martin, and Rob Kitchin. *Mapping Cyberspace.* New York: Routledge, 2001.

Dodge, Martin, Andy Smith, and Simon Doyle. "Virtual Cities on the World Wide Web." 1997. http://www.casa.ucl.ac.uk/martin/virtual_cities.html.

Doheny-Farina, Stephen. *The Wired Neighborhood.* New Haven: Yale University Press, 1996.

Dyson, Esther. "If You Don't Love It, Leave It." *New York Times Magazine,* July 16, 1995: 26–27.

Eco, Umberto. *The Island of the Day Before.* New York: Penguin, 1996.

———. *The Open Work.* Cambridge: Harvard University Press, 1989.

———. *The Role of the Reader.* Bloomington: Indiana University Press, 1984.

Einstein, Albert. Forward to *Concepts of Space,* xii–xvii. New York: Dover, 1993.

Electronic Frontier Foundation, ed. "Conference Report on H.R. 2658, Department of Defense Appropriations Act, 2004." Excerpted from *108th Congressional Record,* September 24, 2003: H8500-H8550. http://www.eff.org/Privacy/TIA/20031003_conf_report.php.

Evenson, Laura. "Coffeehouse Patrons Get Wired: Cybercafés Offer E-mail, Web Access." *San Francisco Chronicle,* September 2, 1996: E1.

Everard, Jerry. *Virtual States: The Internet and the Boundaries of the Nation-State.* New York: Routledge, 1999.

Fanderclai, Tari Lin. "Like Magic, Only Real." In *Wired Women: Gender and New Realities in Cyberspace,* 224–41. Seattle: Seal, 1996.

Fink, Jeri. *Cyberseduction: Reality in the Age of Psychotechnology.* New York: Prometheus Books, 1999.

Foster, Derek. "Community and Identity in the Electronic Village." In *Internet Culture,* ed. David Porter, 23–37. New York: Routledge, 1997.

Foucault, Michel. *Discipline and Punish.* Trans. Alan Sheridan. New York: Vintage, 1995.

———. "Of Other Spaces." *Diacritics* 16 (1986): 22–27.

———. "Questions on Geography." In *Power/Knowledge,* ed. Colin Gordon, 63–77. New York: Pantheon, 1980.

———. "Space, Knowledge, and Power." *The Foucault Reader,* ed. Paul Rabinow, 239–56. New York: Pantheon, 1984.

Friedman, Ken. "Restructuring the City: Thoughts on Urban Patterns in the Information Society." 1996. http://www.anu.edu.au/caul/cities.htm.

Fusco, Patricia. "PSInet Aims to Join ASP Giants." *ASPNews,* March 22, 2000. http://www.aspnews.com/news/print.php/374661.

GALILEO. "About the Initiative." http://www.usg.edu/galileo/about.

Garreau, Joel. "Disconnecting the Dots." *Washington Post,* September 17, 2001: C1. http://www.washingtonpost.com/ac2/wp-dyn?pagename=article&contentId=A41015-2001Sep16.

Georgia Perimeter College. "Center for Distance Learning." Home Page. http://www.gpc.edu/~dl/.

Gibbs, Mark, and Richard Smith. *Navigating the Internet.* Carmel, Ind.: Sams, 1993.

Gibson, William. *Neuromancer.* New York: Ace, 1984.

Gozzi, Raymond. "The Cyberspace Metaphor." *et Cetera* 51 (1994): 218–23.

Greenspan, Robyn. "Income, Tenure, Age Spurs Online Banking." *Click Z Network.* http://www.clickz.com/stats/markets/finance/article.php/3344111.

Gregory, Derek. "Areal Differentiation and Post-Modern Human Geography."

Human Geography, ed. J. Agnew et al., 211–32. Malden, Mass.: Blackwell, 1996.

Grosz, Elizabeth. *Architecture from the Outside*. Cambridge: MIT Press, 2001.

———. *Space, Time, and Perversion*. New York: Routledge, 1995.

Grusin, Richard. "What Is an Electronic Author? Theory and the Technological Fallacy." In *Virtual Realities and Their Discontents*, 39–53. Baltimore: Johns Hopkins University Press, 1996.

Guattari, Félix. "Regimes, Pathways, Subjects." In *Incorporations*, 16–37. New York: Zone, 1992.

Gunkel, David, and Ann Gunkel. "Virtual Geographies: The New Worlds of Cyberspace." *Critical Studies in Mass Communication* 14 (1997): 123–37.

Habermas, Jürgen. *The Structural Transformation of the Public Sphere*. Trans. Thomas Burger. Cambridge: MIT Press, 1989.

Hafner, Katie, and Matthew Lyon. *Where Wizards Stay Up Late: The Origins of the Internet*. New York: Touchtone, 1996.

Haley, Colin. "Interest in Online Banking Grows." *ClickZ Stats*, December 30, 2003. http://www.clickz.com/stats/markets/finance/article.php/3292041.

Haraway, Donna. *Simians, Cyborgs, and Women*. New York: Routledge, 1991.

———. *Modest Witness@Second Millennium*. New York: Routledge, 1996.

Harmon, Amy. "Redefining Cafe Society, Online." *New York Times*, August 25, 1997: D7.

Harris, Bob. *Politics and the Rise of the Press*. New York: Routledge, 1996.

Harris, Janette Hoston. "Woodson and Wesley: A Partnership in Building the Association for the Study of Afro-American Life and History." *Journal of Negro History* 83, no. 2 (Spring 1998): 109–19.

Harris, Jerry. "The Conflict for Power in Transnational Class Theory." *Science & Society* 67 (2003): 329–39.

Harvard Extension School. "Distance Ed: Sample Lectures." August 18, 2004. http://www.extension.harvard.edu/2003-04/programs/DistanceEd/lectures/.

Harvey, David. *The Condition of Postmodernity*. Malden, Mass.: Blackwell, 1989.

———. *Justice, Nature, and the Geography of Difference*. Malden, Mass.: Blackwell, 1996.

Hayden, Dolores. *The Power of Place*. Cambridge: MIT Press, 1997.

Hayles, N. Katherine. *How We Became Posthuman*. Chicago: University of Chicago Press, 1999.

Heidegger, Martin. "The Question Concerning Technology." In *The Question Concerning Technology and Other Essays*, trans. William Lovitt, 3–35. New York: Harper, 1977.

Heim, Michael. *The Metaphysics of Virtual Reality*. New York: Oxford, 1993.

Hillis, Ken. *Digital Sensations: Space, Identity, and Embodiment in Virtual Reality*. Minneapolis: University of Minnesota Press, 1999.

Hipmama.com. "Mission Statement of Hipmama.com." http://www.hipmama.com/phpBB/viewforum.php?forum=15&18. [Defunct]

Holmes, David. "Virtual Identity: Communities of Broadcast, Communities of Interactivity." In *Virtual Politics*, ed. David Holmes, 26–45. London: Sage, 1997.

Holmes, Michael. "Naming Virtual Space in Computer-Mediated Conversation." *et Cetera* 52 (1995): 212–21.

Holtman, Steven. *Digital Mosaics: The Aesthetics of Cyberspace*. New York: Simon & Schuster, 1997.

hooks, bell. *Talking Back*. Boston: South End, 1989.

Howse, Derek. *Greenwich Time*. Oxford: Oxford University Press, 1980.

Hunt, Kevin. "Establishing a Presence on the World Wide Web: A Rhetorical Approach." *Technical Communication* 43, no. 4 (November 1996): 376–88.

IDC. "Email Usage to Exceed 60 Billion by 2006, According to IDC." September 26, 2002. http://www.idc.com/getdoc.jhtml?containerId=pr2002_09_23_113035. [Defunct]

Ihde, Don. *Bodies in Technology*. Minneapolis: University of Minnesota Press, 2002.

Independent Media Center. "About Indymedia." http://www.indymedia.org/en/static/about.shtml.

———. "Indymedia Ireland Editorial Guidelines." 2004. http://docs.indymedia.org/view/Local/IndymediaIrelandEditorialPolicy.

———. "Trend toward More Editorial Control." 2004. http://docs.indymedia.org/view/Global/TrendTowardMoreEditorialControl.

Internet Systems Consortium. "Distribution of Top-Level Domain Names by Host Count, January 2001." http://www.isc.org/ops/ds/reports/2001-01/dist-byname.html.

———. "Distribution of Top-Level Domain Names by Host Count, Jan 2006." http://www.isc.org/ops/ds/reports/2006-01/dist-bynum.php.

———. "Internet Domain Survey, January 2000." http://www.isc.org/ops/ds/reports/2000-01/report.html.

———. "Internet Domain Survey, Jul 2004." http://www.isc.org/ops/ds/reports/2004-07/.

———. "Internet Domain Survey, Jan 2006." 2006. http://www.isc.org/ops/ds/reports/2006-01/.

———. "ISC Internet Domain Survey Background." 2004. http://www.isc.org/ds/new-survey.php.

Jameson, Fredric. *Postmodernism*. Durham: Duke University Press, 1991.

Jammer, Max. *Concepts of Space*. New York: Dover, 1993.

Johnson, Steven. *Interface Culture*. New York: Harper Collins, 1997.

Jordan, Tim. *Cyberpower*. New York: Routledge, 1999.

Jupiter Media Metrix. "Rapid Media Consolidation Dramatically Narrows Number of Companies Controlling Time Spent Online, Reports Jupiter Media Metrix." June 4, 2001. http://www.jup.com/company/pressrelease.jsp?doc=pr010604. [Defunct]

Kapor, Mitch. "Where Is the Digital Highway Really Heading?" *Wired*, July–August 1993: 53–59, 94.

Kassop, Mark. "Ten Ways Online Education Matches, or Surpasses, Face-to-Face Learning." *The Technology Source*, May–June 2003. http://technologysource.org/article/ten_ways_online_education_matches_or_surpasses_facetoface_learning/.

Kelly, Kevin. *Out of Control*. Reading, Mass.: Addison-Wesley, 1994.

Kelly, Kevin, and Howard Rheingold. "The Dragon Ate My Homework." *Wired*, July–August 1993. http://www.wired.com/wired/archive/1.03/muds.html.

Kendall, Lori. "Recontextualizing 'Cyberspace.'" In *Doing Internet Research*, ed. Steve Jones, 57–74. Thousand Oaks, Calif.: Sage, 1998.

Kendrick, Michelle. "Cyberspace and the Technological Real." In *Virtual Realities and Their Discontents*, ed. Robert

Markley, 143–60. Baltimore: Johns Hopkins University Press, 1996.

Kittler, Friedrich. *Literature, Media, Information Systems.* Amsterdam: G+B Arts International, 1997.

Klein, Naomi. "Old Hates Fuelled by Fear." *Globe and Mail* [Toronto], April 24, 2002: A17.

Knapp, James. "Essayistic Messages: Internet Newsgroups as Electronic Public Sphere." In *Internet Culture,* ed. David Porter, 181–97. New York: Routledge, 1997.

Koeppel, Dan. "Jungle Outpost Offers Beer, Mayan Ruins and the Net." *New York Times,* July 16, 1998: G8.

Koerber, Amy. "Postmodernism, Resistance, and Cyberspace: Making Rhetorical Spaces for Feminist Mothers on the Web." *Women's Studies in Communication* 24 (2001): 219–40.

Kotkin, Joel. *The New Geography.* New York: Random House, 2000.

Kroker, Arthur. *The Possessed Individual.* New York: St. Martin's, 1992.

Kroker, Arthur, and Michael Weinstein. *Data Trash.* New York: St. Martin's, 1994.

Lacan, Jacques. "Seminar on 'The Purloined Letter.'" In *The Purloined Poe,* trans. Jeffrey Mehlman, 28–54. Baltimore: Johns Hopkins University Press, 1987.

Lakoff, George. "Body, Brain, and Communication." Interview. In *Resisting the Virtual Life,* eds. James Brooks and Iain Boal, 115–29. San Francisco: City Lights, 1995.

Lakoff, George, and Johnson, Mark. *Philosophy in the Flesh.* New York: Basic Books, 1999.

Landow, George. *Hypertext.* Baltimore: Johns Hopkins University Press, 1992.

Lefebvre, Henri. *Critique of Everyday Life.* Trans. John Moore. 2 vols. New York: Verso, 1991.

———. *Le droit à la ville.* Paris: Anthropos, 1968. *Right to the City.* In *Writings on Cities,* ed. and trans. Eleonore Kofman and Elizabeth Lebas, 61–181. Malden, Mass.: Blackwell, 1996.

———. *Position: Contre les technocrates.* Paris: Editions Gonthier, 1967.

———. *The Production of Space.* Trans. Donald Nicholson-Smith. Malden, Mass.: Blackwell, 1994.

———. *La revolution urbaine.* Paris: Editions Gallimard, 1970. *The Urban Revolution.* Trans. Robert Bononno. Foreword by Neil Smith. Minneapolis: University of Minnesota Press, 2003.

———. *Writings on Cities.* Trans. Eleonore Kofman and Elizabeth Lebas. Malden, Mass.: Blackwell, 1996.

Lehmann, Burkhard, and Klaus Harney. "Theories and Learning on the Datahighway: An Example of Network-Based Information and Communication." Trans. Systran, http://babelfish.altavista.com. *Rundbrief* 22 (March 1999). http://www.uni-essen.de/~kte0b0/Harney.htm.

Lestringant, Frank. *Mapping the Renaissance World.* Berkeley: University of California Press, 1994.

Lévy, Pierre. *Collective Intelligence: Mankind's Emerging World in Cyberspace.* Trans. Robert Bononno. New York: Plenum, 1997.

"Lift from Internet," *New York Times,* January 2, 1999: B1.

Lynch, Kevin. *The Image of the City.* Cambridge: MIT Press, 1960.

Lyotard, Jean-François. *The Inhuman.* Trans. Geoffrey Bennington and Rachel Bowlby. Stanford: Stanford University Press, 1991.

———. *The Postmodern Condition.* Trans. Geoffrey Bennington and Brian Massumi. Minneapolis: University of Minnesota Press, 1984.

Markley, Robert. "Introduction: History, Theory, and Virtual Reality." In *Virtual Realities and Their Discontents*, ed. Robert Markley, 1–10. Baltimore: Johns Hopkins University Press, 1996.

Marriott, Michel. "The Ballad of the Cybercafe." *New York Times*, April 16, 1998: G1.

Massumi, Brian. *A User's Guide to Capitalism and Schizophrenia*. Cambridge: MIT Press, 1992.

McEwan, Ian. "Only Love and Then Oblivion." *Guardian*, September 15, 2001. http://www.guardian.co.uk/wtccrash/story/0,1300,552408,00.html.

McKenzie, Alan. *Sent as a Gift*. Athens: University of Georgia Press, 1993.

McLuhan, Marshall. *The Gutenberg Galaxy*. Toronto: University of Toronto Press, 1962.

———. *Understanding Media*. Cambridge: MIT Press, 1994.

McLuhan, Marshall, and Quentin Fiore. *The Medium is the Massage*. New York: Touchstone, 1989.

Meetup.com. "About Meetup." http://www.meetup.com/about/.

Menser, Michael. "Becoming Heterarch: On Technocultural Theory, Minor Science, and the Production of Space." In *Technoscience and Cyberculture*, 293–316. New York: Routledge, 1996.

Meyers, Anne. "Worldwide College." *Atlanta Journal-Constitution*, September 10, 2000: P1, P10.

Miller, J. Hillis. *Topographies*. Stanford: Stanford University Press, 1995.

Miller, Laura. "Women and Children First: Gender and the Settling of the Electronic Frontier." In *Resisting the Virtual Life*, 49–57. San Francisco: City Lights, 1995.

Mitchell, William J. *City of Bits*. Cambridge: MIT Press, 1995.

"More on D+G+Internet." Edited and compiled by Mark Nunes. 1995. http://www.gpc.edu/~mnunes/d2.html.

Morse, Margaret. *Virtualities*. Bloomington: Indiana University Press, 1999.

MoveOn.org. "About the MoveOn Family of Organizations." http://www.moveon.org/about/.

Nakamura, Lisa. *Cybertypes*. New York: Routledge, 2002.

Negt, Oskar, and Alexander Kluge. *Public Sphere and Experience: Toward an Analysis of the Bourgeois and Proletarian Public Sphere*. Trans. Peter Labanyi, Jamie Owen Daniel, and Assenka Oksiloff. Minneapolis: University of Minnesota Press, 1993.

Nelson, Ted. *Computer Lib*. Redmond, Wash.: Tempus, 1987.

———. *Literary Machines*. Edition 87.1. Published by the author, 1987.

Nguyen, Dan Thu, and Jon Alexander. "The Coming of Cyberspacetime and the End of Polity." In *Cultures of Internet: Virtual Spaces, Real Histories, Living Bodies*, 99–124. Thousand Oaks, Calif.: Sage, 1996.

Nielsen/NetRatings. "Finance and Investment Web Sites Secure the No. 1 Spot as the Most Addictive Online Web Destinations, According to Nielsen/NetRatings." February 27, 2002. http://www.nielsen-netratings.com/pr/pr_020227.pdf.

Noble, David. *Digital Diploma Mills*. New York: Monthly Review Press, 2002.

Novak, Marcos. "Liquid Architectures in Cyberspace." In *Cyberspace: First Steps*, 225–54. Cambridge: MIT Press, 1992.

———. "Transmitting Architecture: The Transphysical City." *CTHEORY*, 1995. http://www.ctheory.net/text_file.asp?pick=76.

———. "TransUrban Optimism after the Maul of America." *CTHEORY*,

1996. http://www.ctheory.net/text_file. asp?pick=258.

NUA Internet Surveys. "End of an Era for the National Postal Service." October 21, 1999. http://www.nua.com/surveys/ ?f=VS&art_id=905355356. [defunct]

———. "How Many Online." 2002. http:// www.nua.com/surveys/how_many_ online/index.html. [defunct]

Nunes, Mark. "What Space Is Cyberspace? The Internet and Virtuality." In *Virtual Politics,* ed. David Holmes, 163–78. London: Sage, 1997.

———. "Virtual Topographies: Smooth and Striated Cyberspace." In *Cyberspace Textuality,* ed. Marie.-Laure Ryan, 61–77. Bloomington: Indiana University Press, 1999.

Nunes, Mark et al. "Postmodern Spacings." *Postmodern Culture* 8, no. 3 (May 1998). http://muse.jhu.edu/journals/ postmodern_culture/v008/8.3spacings. html.

O'Banion, Terry. *A Learning College for the Twenty-first Century.* Phoenix: Oryx Press, 1997.

O'Byrne, Darren. "Working Class Culture: Local Community and Global Conditions." In *Living the Global City,* 73–89. New York: Routledge, 1997.

Odasz, Frank. "Big Skies and Lone Eagles: Lending Wings to Others, Online—A Rural Perspective." http://lone-eagles.com/ history.htm.

Ofek, Eli, and Matthew Richardson. "Dot-Com Mania." *Stern Business,* Spring–Summer 2002. http://www.stern.nyu. edu/Sternbusiness/spring_summer_ 2002/dotcom.html.

Oldenburg, Ray. *The Great Good Place.* New York: Marlowe, 1999.

O'Leary, Stephen. "Cyberspace as Sacred Space: Communicating Religion on Computer Networks." *Journal of the American Academy of Religion* 64 (1996): 781–808.

Ortiz, Maegan "la Mala." "Slip." 2002. http:// mamitamala.blogspot.com/2005_02_01_ mamitamala_archive.html.

Ostwald, Michael. "Virtual Urban Futures." In *Virtual Politics,* ed. David Holmes, 125–44. London: Sage, 1997.

Poster, Mark. "Cyberdemocracy." In *Virtual Politics,* ed. David Holmes, 212–28. London: Sage, 1997.

———. "Everyday (Virtual) Life." *New Literary History* 33 (2002): 743–60.

———. *The Mode of Information.* Chicago: University of Chicago Press, 1990.

———. "Theorizing Virtual Reality." In *Cyberspace Textuality,* ed. Marie-Laure Ryan, 42–60. Bloomington: Indiana University Press, 1999.

———. *What's the Matter with the Internet?* Minneapolis: University of Minnesota Press, 2001.

Project Xanadu. "Misson Statement." http:// www.xanadu.com.

Proulx, Annie. *The Shipping News.* New York: Scribner, 1994.

"Reduction in Distribution of Spam Act of 2003 Hearing Before the Subcommittee on Crime, Terrorism, and Homeland Security of the Committee on the Judiciary House of Representatives." July 8, 2003. http://commdocs.house.gov/ committees/judiciary/hju88203.000/ hju88203_0f.htm.

Reid, Elizabeth. "Virtual Worlds: Culture and Imagination." In *Cybersociety: Computer-Mediated Communication and Society,* ed. Steven Jones, 164–83. Thousand Oaks, Calif.: Sage, 1995.

Rheingold, Howard. *The Virtual Community.* Reading, Mass.: Addison-Wesley, 1993.

Robertson, Roland. *Globalization: Social*

Theory and Global Culture. Newbury Park, Calif.: Sage, 1992.

———. "Glocalization." In *Global Modernities*, ed. Mike Featherstone, 25–44. Thousand Oaks, Calif.: Sage, 1995.

Robinson, Howard. *The British Post Office*. Princeton: Princeton University Press, 1948.

Rosenberg, Martin E. "Physics and Hypertext: Liberation and Complicity in Art and Pedagogy." In *Hyper/Text/Theory*, ed. George P. Landow, 268–98. Baltimore: Johns Hopkins University Press, 1994.

Ryan, Marie-Laure. "Immersion vs. Interactivity: Virtual Reality and Literary Theory". *Postmodern Culture*. 5, no. 1 (September 1994): 39 pars. http://jefferson.village.virginia.edu/pmc/text-only/issue.994/ryan.994.

Sadler, Simon. *The Situationist City*. Cambridge: MIT Press, 1998.

Sansbury, Jen. "Library Buying Computers for Shelter." *Atlanta Constitution*, July 28, 2001: H1, H6.

Schmich, Mary. "Vonnegut? Schmich? Who Can Tell in Cyberspace?" *Chicago Tribune*, August 3, 1997.

Schuler, Doug. "Community Networking: Building a New Participatory Medium." *Communications of the ACM* 37, no. 1 (January 1994): 38–51.

Scott, John. "The Chautauqua Movement: Revolution in Popular Higher Education." *Journal of Higher Education* 70 (1999): 389–412.

Searle, John. "Reiterating the Differences: A Reply to Derrida." *Glyph* 1(1977): 198–208.

Senft, Theresa. "Introduction: Performing the Digital Body—A Ghost Story." *Women & Performance* 9, no. 1 (1996). http://www.terrisenft.net/wp17/introduction.html.

Shannon, Claude, and Warren Weaver. *The Mathematical Theory of Communication*. Urbana: University of Illinois Press, 1949.

Shapiro, Andrew. *The Control Revolution*. New York: Public Affairs, 1999.

Shaviro, Steven. "12.Bill Gates." *Doom Patrols*, 1995–1997. http://www.dhalgren.com/Doom/ch12.html.

———. "13.Pavel Curtis." *Doom Patrols*, 1995–1997. http://www.dhalgren.com/Doom/ch13.html.

Sherman, Stuart. *Telling Time*. Chicago: University of Chicago Press, 1996.

Shields, Rob. Introduction to *Cultures of Internet*, 1–10. Thousand Oaks, Calif.: Sage, 1996.

Silver, David. "Margins in the Wires: Looking for Race, Gender, and Sexuality in the Blacksburg Electronic Village." In *Race in Cyberspace*, eds. Beth Kolko, Lisa Nakamura, and Gilbert Rodman, 133–50. New York: Routledge, 2000.

Slashdot. "FAQ: Editorial." http://brak.slashdot.org/faq/editorial.shtml.

Slouka, Mark. *War of the Worlds: Cyberspace and the High-Tech Assault on Reality*. New York: Basic Books, 1995.

Smith, Sam. "Postmodernism Is Dead. Now What? Distributed Culture and the Rise of the Network Age." *Intelligent Agent* 3, no. 1 (Winter–Spring 2003). http://www.intelligentagent.com/archive/v03[1].01.polisci.smith.PDF.

———. "Weblog: July/August 2002." http://www.lullabypit.com/blog/02.jul_aug.html.

"Smooth/Striated Cyberspace." Edited and compiled by Mark Nunes. 1995. http://www.gpc.edu/~mnunes/smooth.html.

Soja, Edward. *Postmodern Geographies*. New York: Verso, 1989.

Sproull, Lee, and Samer Faraj. "Atheism, Sex,

and Databases: The Net as a Social Technology." In *Culture of the Internet*, ed. Sara Kiesler, 35–51. Mahwah, N.J.: Lawrence Erlbaum, 1997.

Stallabrass, Julian. "Empowering Technology: The Exploration of Cyberspace." *New Left Review* 211 (May–June 1995): 3–32.

Standage, Tom. *The Victorian Internet*. New York: Walker, 1998.

Steiner, Peter. "On the Internet, Nobody Knows You're a Dog." Cartoon. *New Yorker*, July 5, 1993: 61.

Steinglass, Matt. "Amsterdam's Brave New World." *New York Times*, February 7, 1999: 12, 22.

Sterne, Jonathan. "The Computer Race Goes to Class: How Computers in Schools Helped Shape the Racial Topography of the Internet." In *Race in Cyberspace*, eds. Beth Kolko, Lisa Nakamura, and Gilbert Rodman, 191–212. New York: Routledge, 2000.

———. "Thinking the Internet: Cultural Studies versus the Millennium." In *Doing Internet Research*, ed. Steve Jones, 257–87. Thousand Oaks, Calif.: Sage, 1999.

Stone, Allucquere Roseanne. *The War of Desire and Technology at the Close of the Mechanical Age*. Cambridge: MIT Press, 1995.

Strate, Lance. "The Varieties of Cyberspace: Problems in Definition and Delimitation." *Western Journal of Communication* 63, no. 3 (Summer 1999): 382–412.

Town Online. "About Us." www.townonline.com/terms/about.html. [Defunct]

Trippi, Laura. "More Signs of 911's Complex Effects." *Netvironments*. http://www.netvironments.org/blog/archives/2001_09_01_archives1_html.

Trumbo, Jean. "Describing Multimedia: The Use of Spatial Metaphors and Multimedia

Design." *Visual Communication Quarterly* 53, no. 4 (April 1998): 7–10.

Turkle, Sherry. *Life on the Screen*. New York: Simon & Schuster, 1995.

United States. H.R. 2214. *Reduction in Distribution of Spam Act of 2003*. Washington: GPO, 2003. http://frwebgate.access.gpo.gov/cgi-bin/getdoc.cgi?dbname=108_cong_bills&docid=f:h2214ih.txt.pdf.

———. Cong. *Uniting and Strengthening America by Providing Appropriate Tools Required to Intercept and Obstruct Terrorism (USA PATRIOT Act) Act of 2001*. Washington: GPO, 2001. http://frwebgate.access.gpo.gov/cgi-bin/getdoc.cgi?dbname=107_cong_public_laws&docid=f:publ056.107.pdf.

University of Phoenix. "University of Phoenix: Students." http://achieve.phoenix.edu/students.asp. [Defunct—reprinted at: http://www.colleges.com/colleges/phoenix/students.html.]

Unsworth, John. "Living Inside the (Operating) System: Communities in Virtual Reality." http://www.iath.virginia.edu/pmc/Virtual.Community.html.

Varey, Simon. *Space in the Eighteenth Century Novel*. Cambridge: Cambridge University Press, 1990.

Vejnoska, Jill. "What a Difference a Decade Makes." *Atlanta Journal-Constitution*, January 3, 1999: B1.

Virilio, Paul. *The Aesthetics of Disappearance*. Trans. Philip Beitchman. New York: Semiotext(e), 1991.

———. "The Last Vehicle." Trans. David Antal. In *Looking Back on the End of the World*, eds. Dietmar Kamper and Christoph Wulf, 106–19. New York: Semiotext(e), 1989.

———. *The Lost Dimension*. Trans. Daniel Moshenberg. New York: Semiotext(e), 1989.

———. *Open Sky*. Trans. Julie Rose. New York: Verso, 1997.

———. *The Vision Machine*. Trans. Julie Rose. Bloomington: Indiana University Press, 1994.

Virtual Cities Resource Centre. 1997. http://www.casa.ucl.ac.uk/vc/welcome.htm.

"Vote S. 652." *Congressional Record*, June 14, 1995. S8310-S8363. http://thomas.loc.gov/r104/r104.html.

Warner, Michael. *The Letters of the Republic*. Cambridge: Harvard University Press, 1990.

Watt, Ian. *The Rise of the Novel*. Berkeley: University of California Press, 1957.

Web-based Education Commission. *The Power of the Internet for Learning: Moving from Promise to Practice*, Washington, D.C., 2000. http://www.ed.gov/offices/AC/WBEC/FinalReport/WBECReport.pdf.

Wertheim, Margaret. *The Pearly Gates of Cyberspace*. New York: Norton, 1999.

Whittaker, Steve, and Candace Sidner. "Email Overload: Exploring Personal Information Management of Email." In *Culture of the Internet*, ed. Sara Kiesler, 277–95. Mahwah, N.J.: Lawrence Erlbaum, 1997.

Wiener, Norbert. *The Human Use of Human Beings*. Garden City, N.Y.: Anchor, 1954.

Williams, Raymond. *Television*. New York: Schocken, 1975.

Willson, Michele. "Community in the Abstract: A Political and Ethical Dilemma?" In *Virtual Politics*, ed. David Holmes, 145–62. London: Sage, 1997.

Woods, Lebbeus. "The Question of Space." In *Technoscience and Cyberculture*, 279–92. New York: Routledge, 1996.

Wooley, Benjamin. *Virtual Worlds*. Malden, Mass.: Blackwell, 1992.

Yahoo! "Newspapers: By Region." http://dir.yahoo.com/News_and_Media/Newspapers/By_Region/.

The Yankee Group. "The Yankee Group Reports Significant Shift in Online Consumer Population." October 16, 2000. http://www.yankeegroup.com/webfolder/yg21a.nsf/press/D3582D369EFDE9F98525697A0044E01E. [Defunct]

Young, Iris Marion. *Throwing like a Girl and Other Essays in Feminist Philosophy and Social Theory*. Bloomington: Indiana University Press, 1990.

Zook, Matthew. "Geography of Internet Users." 2005. http://www.zooknic.com/Users/index.html.

———. "Growth of Domains in US and the World." http://www.zooknic.com/Domains/us_and_world.html.

———. "Percentage of the World's Domains in the Top Twenty-five Countries, January 2000." http://www.zooknic.com/Domains/Domains_by_country.pdf.

———. "Zooknic Internet Geography Project." http://www.zooknic.com.

MARK NUNES is associate professor and chair in the Department of English, Technical Communication, and Media Arts at Southern Polytechnic State University in Marietta, Georgia. He has written frequently during the past decade on the social and cultural implications of network technology.